INCREDIBLE
FISHING
STORIES

INCREDIBLE
FISHING
STORIES

CLASSIC ANGLING TALES
FROM AROUND THE WORLD

EDITED BY JAY CASSELL

Skyhorse Publishing

Individual stories reprinted here with permission:

"The Evolution of a Fly Fisher" © Joan Salvato Wulff; "Midstream Crisis" © Lamar Underwood. From *Editors in the Stream* (Halo Books, 1992); "Brannigan's Trout" © Nick Lyons. From *Full Creel* (Grove Atlantic, 2001); "Romancing the Falls" © James R. Babb. From *Fish Won't Let Me Sleep* (Skyhorse, 2016); "Sashimi" © Henry Hughes. From *Back Seat with Fish* (Skyhorse, 2016); "Oblivious" © Richard Chiappone. From *Liar's Code* (Skyhorse, 2016); "Eastern Steelhead" © Jerry Hamza. From *Outdoor Chronicles* (Skyhorse, 2015); "Zone of Habitability" © W. D. Wetherell.

Skyhorse Publishing books may be purchased in bulk at special discounts for sales promotion, corporate gifts, fund-raising, or educational purposes. Special editions can also be created to specifications. For details, contact the Special Sales Department, Skyhorse Publishing, 307 West 36th Street, 11th Floor, New York, NY 10018 or info@skyhorsepublishing.com.

Skyhorse® and Skyhorse Publishing® are registered trademarks of Skyhorse Publishing, Inc.®, a Delaware corporation.

Visit our website at www.skyhorsepublishing.com.

10 9 8 7 6 5 4 3 2 1

Library of Congress Cataloging-in-Publication Data is available on file.

Cover design by Tom Lau
Cover photo credit: iStockphoto

Print ISBN: 978-1-5107-1380-2
Ebook ISBN: 978-1-5107-1385-7

Printed in China

TABLE OF CONTENTS

INTRODUCTION

There is a rich and varied tradition of fine literature in the world of angling. Dating back to 1496, when Dame Juliana Berners wrote *The Treatise of Fishing with an Angle*, through Izaak Walton's *The Compleat Angler* in 1653, up to the likes of *The Old Man and the Sea* (Hemingway), *A River Runs Through It* (Maclean), *Trout Bum* (Gierach), and *The Longest Silence* (McGuane); books about fishing run the gamut from entertainment to education, from escapism to guides on where to go fishing, for what and with what. There is no shortage of good books that address every angler's needs and desires. Just listing the titles of them all would take up a full book all by itself.

The esteemed author Roderick Haig-Brown did a wonderful job of summing up his love of fishing in the following passage from *A River Never Sleeps*:

> I still don't know why I fish or why other men fish, except that we like it and it makes us think and feel. But I do know that if it were not for the strong, quick life of rivers, for their sparkle in the sunshine, for the cold grayness of them under rain and the feel of them about my legs as I set my feet hard down on rocks or sand or gravel, I should fish less often. A river is never quite silent, it can never, of its very nature, be quite still; it is never quite the same from one day to the next. It has its own life and its own beauty, and the creatures it nourishes are alive and beautiful also. Perhaps fishing is, for me, only an excuse to be near rivers. If so, I'm glad I thought of it.

In *My Secret Fishing Life*, Nick Lyons extols writing about fly fishing, and how it seems to be improving as the years go by:

> What interests me most about today's best writing about fly fishing is that it is realer and sharper, less idealized, less part of the specialized tradition of fishing writing and closer to just plain good writing. If this is a sign that fly fishing is being thought of more as a part of life than apart from it, I'm delighted; for the best writing about fly fishing—from Walton to Bergman to McGuane—not only says a few things that make us shrewder fly fishers but also a few that make us wiser human beings.

I would add that good writing about fly fishing—any fishing—also transports us to waters we may never have the opportunity to fish in person and lets us live vicariously through the author's experience. It can help you see the world through a different set of eyes, to catch fish you may never fish for in your life, to experience rivers, lakes, or oceans that you may never see.

In putting together *Incredible Fishing Stories*, I tried to find stories that display the variety and depth of angling literature—not only Walton (and Charles Cotton), but Zane Gray, James Henshall, and John James Audubon, but also writers from today: James Babb, W. D. Wetherill, Jerry Hamza, and Richard Chiappone, to name a few. As you read through them, live their experiences with them, see the world as they see it. In the end, you just may be a bit wiser for it.

Jay Cassell
Katonah, New York
Spring 2017

SECTION ONE

EARLY DAYS—
OF IT AND US

CHAPTER 1

THE COMPLEAT ANGLER (SELECTIONS)

BY IZAAK WALTON AND CHARLES COTTON

Now for the art of catching fish, that is to say, how to make a man that was none to be an angler by a book, he that undertakes it shall under-take a harder task than Mr. Hales, a most valiant and excellent fencer, who, in a printed book called "A Private School of Defence" undertook by it to teach that art or science, and was laughed at for his labor. Not but many useful things might be learnt by that book, but he was laughed at because that art was not to be taught by words, but practice: and so must angling. And in this discourse I do not undertake to say all that is known or may be said of it, but I undertake to acquaint the reader with many things that are not usually known to every angler; and I shall leave gleanings and observations enough to be made out of the experience of all that love and practice this recreation, to which I shall encourage them. For angling may be said to be so like the mathematics that it can never be fully learnt; at least not so fully, but that there will still be more new experiments left for the trial of other men that succeed us.

But I think all that love this game may here learn something that may be worth their money, if they be not poor and needy men: and in case they be, I then wish them to forbear to buy it; for I write not to get money, but for pleasure, and this discourse boasts of no more; for I hate to promise much, and deceive the reader.

And however it proves to him, yet I am sure I have found a high content in the search and conference of what is here offered to the reader's view and censure. I wish him as much in the perusal of it. And so I might here take my leave, but will stay a little and tell him that whereas it is said by many that in fly-fishing for a trout, the angler must observe his twelve several flies for the twelve months of the year; I say he that follows that rule shall be sure to catch fish and be as wise as he that makes hay by the fair days in an almanac, and no surer; for those very flies that used to appear about and on the water in one month of the year may the following year come almost a month sooner or later, as the same year proves colder or hotter; and yet in the following discourse I have set down the twelve flies that are in reputation with many anglers, and they may serve to give him some light concerning them. And he may note that there are in Wales and other countries peculiar flies, proper to the particular place or country; and doubtless, unless a man makes a fly to counterfeit that very fly in that place, he is like to lose his labor, or much of it; but for the generality, three or four flies neat and rightly made, and not too big, serve for a trout in most rivers all the summer. And for winter fly-fishing it is as useful as an almanac out of date. And of these (because as no man is born an artist, so no man is born an angler) I thought fit to give thee this notice.

And for you that have heard many grave, serious men pity anglers; let me tell you, Sir, there be many men that are by others taken to be serious and grave men which we condemn and pity. Men that are taken to be grave, because nature hath made them of a sour complexion, money-getting men, men that spend all their time first in getting, and next in anxious care to keep it, men that are condemned to be rich, and then always busy or discontented. For these poor-rich-men, we anglers pity them perfectly, and stand in no need to borrow their thoughts to think ourselves happy. No, no, Sir, we enjoy a contentedness above the reach of such dispositions, and as the learned and ingenuous Montaigne says, like himself freely, "When my cat and I entertain each other with mutual apish tricks, as playing with a garter, who knows but that I make my cat more sport than she makes me? Shall I conclude her to be simple, that has her time to begin or refuse sportiveness as freely as I myself have? Nay, who knows but that it is a defect of my not understanding her language (for doubtless cats talk and reason with one another) that we agree no better? And who knows but that she pities me for being no wiser, and laughs and censures my folly for making sport for her when we two play together?"

Thus freely speaks Montaigne concerning cats, and I hope I may take as great a liberty to blame any man, and laugh at him too, let him be never so serious, that hath not heard what anglers can say in the justification of their art and recreation. Which I may again tell you is so full of pleasure that we need not borrow their thoughts, to think ourselves happy.

PISCATOR. O, sir, doubt not but that angling is an art! Is it not an art to deceive a trout with an artificial fly? a trout! that is more sharp-sighted than any hawk you have named and more watchful and timorous than your high-mettled merlin is bold! And yet I doubt not to catch a brace or two tomorrow, for a friend's breakfast. Doubt not, therefore, Sir, but that angling is an art and an art worth your learning. The question is rather whether you be capable of learning it! for angling is somewhat like poetry, men are to be born so. I mean, with inclinations to it, though both may be heightened by practice and experience; but he that hopes to be a good angler must not only bring an inquiring, searching, observing wit, but he must bring a large measure of hope and patience and a love and propensity to the art itself; but having once got and practiced it, then doubt not but angling will prove to be so pleasant that it will prove to be, like virtue, a reward to itself.

VENATOR. Sir, I am now become so full of expectation, that I long much to have you proceed and in the order that you propose.

PISCATOR. Then first, for the antiquity of angling, of which I shall not say much but only this: some say it is as ancient as Deucalion's Flood; others, that Belus, who was the first inventor of godly and virtuous recreations, was the first inventor of angling; and some others say, for former times have had their disquisitions about the antiquity of it, that Seth, one of the sons of Adam, taught it to his sons, and that by them it was derived to posterity; others say that he left it engraven on those pillars which he erected and trusted to preserve the knowledge of mathematics, music, and the rest of that precious knowledge and those useful arts, which by God's appointment or allowance and his noble industry were thereby preserved from perishing in Noah's Flood.

These, sir, have been the opinions of several men, that have possibly endeavored to make angling more ancient than is needful or may well be warranted; but for my part, I shall content myself in telling you, that angling is much more ancient than the incarnation of our Savior; for in the Prophet Amos mention is made of fish-hooks; and in the Book of Job—which was long before the days of Amos, for that book is said to have been writ by Moses—mention is made also of fish-hooks, which must imply anglers in those times.

But, my worthy friend, as I would rather prove myself a gentleman, by being learned and humble, valiant and inoffensive, virtuous and communicable, than by any fond ostentation of riches, or, wanting those virtues myself, boast that these were in my ancestors—and yet I grant that where a noble and ancient descent and such merit meet in any man it is a double dignification of that person—so if this antiquity of angling—which for my part I have not forced—shall, like an ancient family, be either an honor or an ornament to this virtuous art which I profess to love and practice, I shall be the gladder that I made an accidental mention of the antiquity of it; of which I shall say no more, but proceed to that just commendation which I think it deserves.

And for that I shall tell you that in ancient times a debate hath risen, and it remains yet unresolved—whether the happiness of man in this world doth consist more in contemplation or action.

Concerning which some have endeavored to maintain their opinion of the first, by saying, "that the nearer we mortals come to God by way of imitation the more happy we are." And they say, "that God enjoys himself only by a contemplation of his own infiniteness, eternity, power, and goodness," and the like. And upon this ground many cloisteral men of great learning and devotion prefer contemplation before action. And many of the fathers seem to approve this opinion, as may appear in their commentaries upon the words of our Savior to Martha, Luke 10:41, 42.

And on the contrary there want not men of equal authority and credit that prefer action to be the more excellent, as namely "experiments in physic and the application of it, both for the ease and prolongation of man's life"; by which each man is enabled to act and do good to others, either to serve his country or do good to particular persons; and they say also "that action is doctrinal and teaches both art and virtue and is a maintainer of human society"; and for these and other like reasons to be preferred before contemplation.

Concerning which two opinions I shall forbear to add a third by declaring my own, and rest myself contented in telling you, my very worthy friend, that both these meet together, and do most properly belong to the most honest, ingenuous, quiet, and harmless art of angling.

And first, I shall tell you what some have observed, and I have found to be a real truth, that the very sitting by the river's side, is not only the quietest and fittest place for contemplation but will invite an angler to it. And this seems to be maintained by the learned Pet. du Moulin, who, in his discourse of the Fulfilling of Prophecies, observes that when God intended to reveal any future event or high notions to his prophets, he then carried them either to the deserts or the sea-shore, that having so separated them from amidst the press of people and business and the cares of the world he might settle their mind in a quiet repose, and make them fit for revelation.

And for the lawfulness of fishing, it may very well be maintained by our Savior's bidding St. Peter cast his hook into the water and catch a fish for money to pay tribute to Caesar. And let me tell you that angling is of high esteem and of much use in other nations. He that reads the voyages of Ferdinand Mendez Pinto shall find that there he declares to have found a king and several priests a-fishing.

And he that reads Plutarch shall find that angling was not contemptible in the days of Marc Antony and Cleopatra and that they in the midst of their wonderful glory used angling as a principal recreation. And let me tell you that in the Scripture angling is always taken in the best sense and that though hunting may be sometimes so taken, yet it is but seldom to be so understood. And let me add this more. He that views the ancient ecclesiastical canons shall find hunting to be forbidden to churchmen, as being a toilsome, perplexing recreation; and shall find angling allowed to clergymen, as being a harmless recreation, a recreation that invites them to contemplation and quietness.

My next and last example shall be that undervaluer of money, the late Provost of Eton College, Sir Henry Wotton, a man with whom I have often fished and conversed, a man whose foreign employments in the service of this nation and whose experience, learning, wit, and cheerfulness made his company to be esteemed one of the delights of mankind. This man, whose very approbation of angling were sufficient to convince any modest censurer of it, this man was also a most dear lover and a frequent practice of the art of angling; of which he would say, " 'Twas an employment for his idle time, which was not then idly spent"; for angling was, after tedious study, "a rest to his mind, a cheerer of his spirits, a diverter of sadness, a calmer of unquiet thoughts, a moderator of passions, a procurer of contentedness; and that it begot habits of peace and patience in those that professed and practiced it." Indeed, my friend, you will find angling to be like the virtue of humility, which has a calmness of spirit and a world of other blessings attending upon it.

Sir, this was the saying of that learned man, and I do easily believe, that peace and patience and a calm content did cohabit in the cheerful heart of Sir Henry Wotton, because I know that when he was beyond seventy years of age, he made this description of a part of the present pleasure that possessed him, as he sat quietly in a summer's evening on a bank a-fishing. It is a description of the spring, which, because it glides as soft and sweetly from his pen as that river does at this time, by which it was then made, I shall repeat it unto you:

This day Dame Nature seemed in love;
The lusty sap began to move;
Fresh juice did stir th' embracing vines,
And birds had drawn their valentines. The jealous trout, that low did lie,
Rose at a well-dissembled fly;
There stood my friend with patient skill

Attending of his trembling quill.
Already were the eaves possessed
With the swift pilgrim's daubed nest;
The groves already did rejoice,
In Philomel's triumphing voice,
The showers were short, the weather mild,
The morning fresh, the evening smiled.
Joan takes her neat-rubbed pail, and now
She trips to milk the sand-red cow;

Where, for some sturdy foot-ball swain,
Joan strokes a syllabub or twain;
The fields and gardens were beset
With tulips, crocus, violet;

And now, though late, the modest rose
Did more than half a blush disclose.
Thus all looks gay, and full of cheer,
To welcome the new-liveried year.

These were the thoughts that then possessed the undisturbed mind of Sir Henry Wotton. Will you hear the wish of another angler, and the commendation of his happy life, which he also sings in verse; viz. Jo. Davors, Esq.?

Let me live harmlessly; and near the brink
Of Trent or Avon have a dwelling place,
Where I may see my quill or cork down sink
With eager bite of perch, or bleak, or dace;
And on the world and my Creator think;
Whilst some men strive ill-gotten goods t'embrace;
And others spend their time in base excess
Of wine or worse, in war and wantonness:

Let them that list these pastimes still pursue,
And on such pleasing fancies feed their fill,
So I the fields and meadows green may view,
And daily by fresh rivers walk at will
Among the daisies and the violets blue,
Red hyacinth, and yellow daffodil,
Purple Narcissus like the morning rays,
Pale gander-grass, and azure culver-keys.

I count it higher pleasure to behold
The stately compass of the lofty sky;
And in the midst thereof, like burning gold,
The flaming chariot of the world's great eye;
The watery clouds that in the air up-rolled,
With sundry kinds of painted colors fly;
And fair Aurora, lifting up her head,
Still blushing rise from old Tithonus' bed;

The hills and mountains raisèd from the plains,
The plains extended level with the ground,
The grounds divided into sundry veins,
The veins enclosed with rivers running round;
These rivers making way through nature's chains,
With headlong course into the sea profound;
The raging sea, beneath the valleys low,
Where lakes and rills and rivulets do flow;
The lofty woods, the forests wide and long,
Adorned with leaves, and branches fresh and green,
In whose cool bowers the birds with many a song
Do welcome with their quire the summer's queen;
The meadows fair where Flora's gifts among
Are intermixed with verdant grass between;
The silver-scalèd fish that softly swim
Within the sweet brook's crystal watery stream.

All these, and many more, of his creation
That made the heavens, the angler oft doth see,
Taking therein no little delectation,
To think how strange, how wonderful they be,
Framing thereof an inward contemplation,
To set his heart from other fancies free;

And whilst he looks on these with joyful eye,
His mind is rapt above the starry sky.

PISCATOR. The Trout is a fish highly valued, both in this and foreign nations. He may be justly said, as the old poet said of wine and we English say of venison, to be a generous fish; a fish that is so like the buck, that he also has his seasons; for it is observed that he comes in and goes out of season with the stag and buck. Gesner says his name is of a German offspring, and says he is a fish that feeds clean and purely, in the swiftest streams, and on the hardest gravel, and that he may justly contend with all fresh water fish, as the mullet may with all sea fish, for precedency and daintiness of taste; and that being in right season, the most dainty palates have allowed precedency to him.

And before I go farther in my discourse, let me tell you that you are to observe that as there be some barren does that are good in summer, so there be some barren trouts that are good in winter; but there are not many that are so; for usually they be in their perfection in the month of May and decline with the buck. Now you are to take notice that in several countries, as in Germany and in other parts, compared to ours, fish do differ much in their bigness and shape, and other ways; and so do trouts. It is well known that in the Lake Leman, the Lake of Geneva, there are trouts taken of three cubits long, as is affirmed by Gesner, a writer of good credit, and Mercator says the trouts that are taken in the Lake of Geneva are a great part of the merchandise of that famous city. And you are further to know that there be certain waters that breed trouts remarkable both for their number and smallness. I know a little brook in Kent that breeds them to a number incredible, and you may take them twenty or forty in an hour, but none greater than about the size of a gudgeon. There are also in divers rivers, especially that relate to, or be near to the sea, as Winchester or the Thames about Windsor, a little trout called a samlet or skegger Trout, in both which places I have caught twenty or forty at a standing, that will bite as fast and as freely as minnows; these be by some taken to be young salmons, but in those waters they never grow to be bigger than a herring.

There is also in Kent, near to Canterbury, a trout called there a Fordidge trout, a Trout that bears the name of the town where it is usually caught, that is accounted the rarest of fish, many of them near the bigness of a salmon, but known by their different color, and in their best season they cut very white; and none of these have been known to be caught with an angle, unless it were one that was caught by Sir George Hastings, an excellent angler, and now with God; and he hath told me, he thought that trout bit not for hunger but wantonness; and it is the rather to be believed, because both he then and many others before him have been curious to search into their bellies, what the food was by which they lived; and have found out nothing by which they might satisfy their curiosity.

Concerning which you are to take notice that it is reported by good authors that grasshoppers and some fish have no mouths, but are nourished and take breath by the porousness of their gills, man knows not how; and this may be believed, if we consider that when the raven hath hatched her eggs, she takes no further care, but leaves her young ones to the care of the God of nature, who is said, in the Psalms, "to feed the young ravens that call upon him." And they be kept alive and fed by a dew, or worms that breed in their nests, or some other ways that we mortals know not. And this may be believed of the Fordidge Trout which, as it is said of the stork that he knows his season, so he knows his times, I think almost his day, of coming into that river out of the sea, where he lives, and, it is like, feeds, nine months of the year, and fasts three in the River of Fordidge. And you are to note that those townsmen are very punctual in observing the time of beginning to fish for them; and boast much that their river affords a trout that exceeds all others. And just so does Sussex boast of several fish, as namely a Shelsey cockle, a Chichester lobster, an Arundel mullet, and an Amerly trout.

And now, for some confirmation of the Fordidge trout, you are to know that this Trout is thought to eat nothing in the fresh water; and it may be the better believed because it is well known that swallows, which are not seen to fly in England for six months in the year but about Michelmas leave us for a hotter climate, yet some of them that have been left behind their fellows have been found many thousands at a time in hollow trees, where they have been observed to live and sleep out the whole winter without meat; and so Albertus observes that there is one kind of frog that hath her mouth naturally shut up about the end of August and that she lives so all the winter; and though it be strange to some, yet it is known to too many among us to be doubted.

And so much for these Fordidge trouts, which never afford an angler sport, but either live their time of being in the fresh water by their meat formerly gotten in the sea, not unlike the swallow or frog, or by the virtue of the fresh water only; or as the birds of paradise and the chameleon are said to live, by the sun and the air.

There is also in Northumberland a trout called a bull-trout, of a much greater length and bigness than any in these southern parts; and there is in many rivers that relate to the sea salmon-trouts, as much different from others both in shape and in their spots, as we see sheep in some countries differ one from another in their shape and bigness, and in the fineness of the wool; and, certainly, as some pastures breed larger sheep; so do some rivers by reason of the ground over which they run breed larger trouts.

Now the next thing that I will commend to your consideration is that the trout is of a more sudden growth than other fish. Concerning which you are also to take notice that he lives not so long as the perch and divers other fishes do, as Sir Francis Bacon hath observed in his *History of Life and Death*.

And next you are to take notice that he is not like the crocodile, which if he lives never so long, yet always thrives till his death; but 'tis not so with the trout, for after he is come to his full growth, he declines in his body, and keeps his bigness or thrives only in his head till his death. And you are to know that he will about (especially before), the time of his spawning get almost miraculously through weirs and flood-gates against the stream, even through such high and swift places as is almost incredible. Next, that the trout usually spawns about October or November, but in some rivers a little sooner or later. Which is the more observable because most other fish spawn in the spring or summer when the sun hath warmed both the earth and water and made it fit for generation. And you are to note that he continues many months out of season; for it may be observed of the trout that he is like the buck or the ox that will not be fat in many months, though he go in the very same pastures that horses do which will be fat in one month; and so you may observe that most other fishes recover strength and grow sooner fat and in season than the trout doth.

And next you are to note that till the sun gets to such a height as to warm the earth and the water the trout is sick and lean and lousy and un-wholesome; for you shall in winter find him to have a big head and then to be lank and thin and lean; at which time many of them have sticking on them sugs, or trout-lice, which is a kind of worm in shape like a clove or pin with a big head, and sticks close to him and sucks his moisture; these, I think, the trout breeds himself, and never thrives till he free himself from them, which is till warm weather comes; and then, as he grows stronger, he gets from the dead, still water into the sharp streams and the gravel and there rubs off these worms or lice, and then as he grows stronger, so he gets him into swifter and swifter streams, and there lies at the watch for any fly or minnow that comes near to him; and he especially loves the May-fly, which is bred of the cod-worm or caddis; and these make the trout bold and lusty, and he is usually fatter and better meat at the end of that month than at any time of the year.

Now you are to know that it is observed that usually the best trouts are either red or yellow, though some, as the Fordidge trout, be white and yet good; but that is not usual. And it is a note observable that the female trout hath usually a less head and a deeper body than the male trout, and is usually the better meat. And note that a hog-back and a little head to any fish, either trout, salmon, or other fish, is a sign that that fish is in season.

But yet you are to note that as you see some willows or palm-trees bud and blossom sooner than others do, as some trouts be in some rivers sooner in season; and as some hollies or oaks are longer before they cast their leaves, so are some trouts in some rivers longer before they go out of season.

And you are to note that there are several kinds of trouts. But these several kinds are not considered but by very few men; for they go under the general name of trouts; just as pigeons do in most places, though it is certain there are tame and wild pigeons; and of the tame there be helmits and runts and carriers and croppers, and indeed too many to name. Nay, the Royal Society have found and published lately that there be thirty and three kinds of spiders; and yet all, for aught I know, go under that one general name of spider. And it is so with many kinds of fish, and of trouts especially, which differ in their bigness and shapes and spots and color. The great Kentish hens may be an instance, compared to other hens; and doubtless there is a kind of small trout which will never thrive to be big that breeds very many more than others do that be of a larger size. Which you may rather believe, if you consider that the little wren and titmouse will have twenty young ones at a time, when usually the noble hawk or the musical throstle or blackbird shall exceed not four or five.

And now you shall see me try my skill to catch a trout; and at my next walking, either this evening or tomorrow morning, I will give you directions how you yourself shall fish for him.

VENATOR. Trust me, master, I see now it is a harder matter to catch a trout than a chub; for I have put on patience and followed you these two hours and not seen a fish stir, neither at your minnow nor your worm.

PISCATOR. Well, scholar, you must endure worse luck sometime, or you will never make a good angler. But what say you now? There is a trout now, and a good one too, if I can but hold him; and two or three turns more will tire him. Now you see he lies still, and the sleight is to land him. Reach me that landing-net. So, Sir, now he is mine own. What say you now? is this not worth all my labor and your patience?

VENATOR. On my word, master, this is a gallant trout; what shall we do with him?

PISCATOR. Marry, e'en eat him to supper. We'll go to my hostess from whence we came; she told me, as I was going out of door, that my brother Peter, a good angler and a cheerful companion, had sent word he would lodge there tonight and bring a friend with him. My hostess has two beds, and I know you and I may have the best. We'll rejoice with my brother Peter and his friend, tell tales, or sing ballads, or make a catch, or find some harmless sport to content us, and pass away a little time without offence to God or man.

VENATOR. A match, good master, let's go to that house, for the linen looks white and smells of lavender, and I long to lie in a pair of sheets that smell so. Let's be going, good master, for I am hungry again with fishing.

PISCATOR. Nay, stay a little, good scholar. I caught my last trout with a worm, now I will put on a minnow and try a quarter of an hour about yonder tree for another, and so walk towards our lodging. Look you, scholar, thereabout we shall have a bite presently, or not at all. Have with you, Sir! On my word, I have hold of him. Oh, it is a great logger-headed chub! Come, hang him upon that willow twig, and let's be going.

VENATOR. Well now, good master, as we walk toward the river, give me direction, according to your promise, how I shall fish for a trout.

PISCATOR. My honest scholar, I will take this very convenient opportunity to do it. The trout is usually caught with a worm or a minnow, which some call a penk, or with a fly, viz. either a natural or an artificial fly. Concerning which three I will give you some observations and directions.

And, first, for worms. Of these there be very many sorts, some bred only in the earth, as the earth-worm, others of or amongst plants, as the dug-worm, and others bred either out of excrements or in the bodies of living creatures, as in the horns of sheep or deer, or some of dead flesh, as the maggot or gentle, and others.

Now these be most of them particularly good for particular fishes. But for the trout the dew-worm, which some also call the lob-worm, and the brandling are the chief; and especially the first for a great trout, and the latter for a less. There be also of lob-worms some called squirrel-tails, a worm that has a red head, a streak down the back, and a broad tail, which are noted to be the best because they are the toughest and most lively and live longest in the water; for you are to know that a dead worm is but a dead bait and like to catch nothing, compared to a lively, quick, stirring worm. And for a brandling he is usually found in an old dunghill or some very rotten place near to it, but most usually in cow-dung or hog's-dung, rather than horse-dung, which is somewhat too hot and dry for that worm. But the best of them are to be found in the bark of the tanners which they have cast up in heaps after they have used it about their leather.

There are also divers other kinds of worms which for color and shape alter even as the ground out of which they are got; as the marsh-worm, the tag-tail, the flag-worm, the dock-worm, the oak-worm, the gilt-tail, the twachel or lob-worm, which of all others is the most excellent bait for a salmon, and too many to name, even as many sorts as some think there be of several herbs or shrubs or of several kinds of birds in the air. Of which I shall say no more but tell you that what worms so ever you fish with are the better for being long kept before they are used. And in case you have not been so provident, then the way to cleanse and scour them quickly is to put them all night in water if they be lob-worms, and then put them into your bag with fennel. But you must not put your brandlings above an hour in water and then put them into fennel, for sudden use; but if you have time and purpose to keep them long, then they be best preserved in an earthen pot, with good store of moss, which is to be fresh every three or four days in summer and every week or eight days in winter; or at least the moss taken from them and clean washed and wrung betwixt your hands till it be dry, and then put it to them again. And when your worms, especially the brandling, begins to be sick and lose of his bigness, then you may recover him by putting a little milk or cream, about a spoonful in a day, into them by drops on the moss; and if there be added to the cream an egg beaten and boiled in it, then it will both fatten and preserve them long. And note that when the knot which is near to the middle of the brandling begins to swell, then he is sick; and if he be not well looked to, is near dying. And for moss you are to note that there be divers kinds of it which I could name to you, but I will only tell you that which is likest; a buck's-horn is the best, except it be soft white moss that grows on some heaths and is hard to be found. And note that in a very dry time when you are put to an extremity for worms walnut-tree leaves squeezed into water, or salt in water to make it bitter or salt, and then that water poured on the ground where you shall see worms are used to rise in the night will make them to appear above ground presently.

And now, I shall show you how to bait your hook with a worm so as shall prevent you from much trouble and the loss of many a hook too, when you fish for a trout with a running line, that is to say, when you fish for him by hand at the ground. I will direct you in this as plainly as I can, that you may not mistake.

Suppose it be a big lob-worm. Put your hook into him somewhat above the middle and out again a little below the middle. Having so done, draw your worm above the arming of your hook; but note that at the entering of your hook it must not be at the head-end of the worm but at the tail-end of him, that the point of your hook may come out toward the head-end. And having drawn him above the arming of your hook, then put the point of your hook again into the very head of the worm till it come near to the place where the point of the hook first came out. And then draw back that part of the worm that was above the shank or arming of your hook, and so fish with it. And if you mean to fish with two worms, then put the second on before you turn back the hook's-head of the first worm. You cannot lose above two or three worms before you attain to what I direct you; and having attained it, you will find it very useful, and thank me for it. For you will run on the ground without tangling.

Now for the minnow, or penk, he is not easily found and caught till March, or in April, for then he appears first in the river, nature having taught him to shelter and hide himself in the winter in ditches that be near to the river, and there both to hide and keep himself warm in the mud or in the weeds, which rot not so soon as in a running river, in which place if he were in winter, the distempered floods that are usually in that season would suffer him to take no rest, but carry him headlong to mills and weirs to his confusion. And of these minnows, first, you are to know that the biggest size is not the best; and next, that the middle size and the whitest are the best; and then you are to know that your minnow must be so put on your hook that it must turn round when 'tis drawn against the stream, and, that it may turn nimbly, you must put it on a big-sized hook, as I shall now direct you, which is thus: put your hook in at his mouth, and out at his gill; then, having drawn your hook two or three inches beyond or through his gill, put it again into his mouth, and the point and beard out at his tail; and then tie the hook and his tail about very neatly with a white thread, which will make it the apter to turn quick in the water; that done, pull back that part of your line which was slack when you did put your hook into the minnow the second time; I say, pull that part of it back so that it shall fasten the head so that the body of the minnow shall be almost straight on your hook; this done, try how it will turn, by drawing it across the water or against a stream; and if it do not turn nimbly, then turn the tail a little to the right or left hand, and try again till it turn quick; for if not, you are in danger to catch nothing; for know, that it is impossible that it should turn too quick. And you are yet to know that in case you want a minnow, then a small loach, or a stickleback, or any other small fish will serve as well. And you are yet to know that you may salt them and by that means keep them fit for use three or four days or longer; and that of salt, bay-salt is the best.

And here let me tell you, what many old anglers know right well, that at some times and in some waters a minnow is not to be got; and therefore let me tell you I have (which I will show to you) an artificial minnow that will catch a trout as well as an artificial fly. And it was made by a handsome woman that had a fine hand, and a live minnow lying by her: the mould or body of the minnow was cloth and wrought upon or over it thus with a needle; the back of it with very sad French green silk, and paler green silk towards the belly, shadowed as perfectly as you can imagine, just as you see a minnow; the belly was wrought also with a needle, and it was, a part of it, white silk; and another part of it with silver thread; the tail and fins were of a quill which was shaven thin; the eyes were of two little black beads; and the head was so shadowed and all of it so curiously wrought and so exactly dissembled that it would beguile any sharp-sighted trout in a swift stream. And this minnow I will now show you, and if you like it, lend it you to have two or three made by it; for they be easily carried about an angler, and be of excellent use; for note that a large trout will come as fiercely at a minnow as the highest-mettled hawk doth seize on a partridge, or a grey-hound on a hare. I have been told that one hundred sixty minnows have been found in a trout's belly. Either the Trout had devoured so many, or the miller that gave it a friend of mine had forced them down his throat after he had taken him.

Now for flies, which is the third bait wherewith trouts are usually taken. You are to know that there are so many sorts of flies as there be of fruits. I will name you but some of them: as the dun-fly, the stone-fly, the red-fly, the moor-fly, the tawny-fly, the shell-fly, the cloudy or blackish-fly, the flag-fly, the vine-fly; there be of flies, caterpillars and canker-flies, and bear-flies; and indeed too many either for me to name, or for you to remember. And their breeding is so various and wonderful that I might easily amaze myself and tire you in a relation of them.

And yet I will exercise your promised patience by saying a little of the caterpillar, or the palmer-fly or worm, that by them you may guess what a work it were in a discourse but to run over those very many flies, worms, and little living creatures with which the sun and summer adorn and beautify the river-banks and meadows, both for the recreation and contemplation of us anglers, and which, I think, myself enjoy more than any other man that is not of my profession.

Pliny holds an opinion that many have their birth or being from a dew that in the spring falls upon the leaves of trees, and that some kinds of them are from a dew left upon herbs or flowers; and others from a dew left upon coleworts or cabbages. All which kinds of dews, being thickened and condensed, are by the sun's generative heat most of them hatched and in three days made living creatures; and these of several shapes and colors; some being hard and tough; some smooth and soft; some are horned in their head, some in their tail, some have none; some have hair, some none; some have sixteen feet, some less, and some have none, but (as our Topsel hath with great diligence observed) those which have none move upon the earth or upon broad leaves, their motion being not unlike to the waves of the sea. Some of them he also observes to be bred of the eggs of other caterpillars and that those in their time turn to be butterflies; and again that their eggs turn the following year to be caterpillars. And some affirm that every plant has its particular fly or caterpillar which it breeds and feeds. I have seen, and may therefore affirm it, a green caterpillar, or worm, as big as a small peascod, which had fourteen legs, eight on the belly, four under the neck, and two near the tail. It was found on a hedge of privet, and was taken thence and put into a large box and a little branch or two of privet put to it, on which I saw it feed as sharply as a dog gnaws a bone. It lived thus five or six days and thrived and changed the color two or three times, but by some neglect in the keeper of it, it then died and did not turn to a fly. But if it had lived, it had doubtless turned to one of those flies that some call flies of prey, which those that walk by the rivers may in summer see fasten on smaller flies and I think make them their food. And 'tis observable that as there be these flies of prey which be very large, so there be others, very little, created I think only to feed them, and bred out of I know not what; whose life, they say, nature intended not to exceed an hour, and yet that life is thus made shorter by other flies, or accident.

'Tis endless to tell you what the curious searchers into nature's productions have observed of these worms and flies. But yet I shall tell you what Aldrovandus, our Topsel, and others say of the palmer-worm or caterpillar: that whereas others content themselves to feed on particular herbs or leaves (for most think those very leaves that gave them life and shape give them a particular feeding and nourishment and that upon them they usually abide), yet he observes that this is called a pilgrim or palmer-worm for his very wandering life and various food; not contenting himself, as others do, with any one certain place for his abode nor any certain kind of herb or flower for his feeding, but will boldly and disorderly wander up and down and not endure to be kept to a diet or fixed to a particular place.

Nay, the very colors of caterpillars are, as one has observed, very elegant and beautiful. I shall, for a taste of the rest, describe one of them which I will some time the next month show you feeding on a willow-tree, and you shall find him punctually to answer this very description: his lips and mouth somewhat yellow, his eyes black as jet, his forehead purple, his feet and hinder parts green, his tail two-forked and black, the whole body stained with a kind of red spots which run along the neck and shoulder-blade, not unlike the form of St. Andrew's cross or the letter X made thus crosswise, and a white line drawn down his back to his tail; all which add much beauty to his whole body. And it is to me observable that at a fixed age this caterpillar gives over to eat, and towards winter comes to be covered over with a strange shell or crust called an aurelia, and so lives a kind of dead life without eating all the winter. And as others of several kinds turn to be several kinds of flies and vermin the spring following, so this caterpillar then turns to be a painted butterfly.

VENATOR. Master, I can neither catch with the first nor second angle. I have no fortune.

PISCATOR. Look you, scholar, I have yet another. And now, having caught three brace of trouts, I will tell you a short tale as we walk towards our breakfast: a scholar—a preacher I should say—that was to preach to procure the approbation of a parish that he might be their lecturer had got from his fellow-pupil the copy of a sermon that was first preached with great commendation by him that composed and preached it; and though the borrower of it preached it word for word as it was at first, yet it was utterly disliked as it was preached by the second. Which the sermon-borrower complained of to the lender of it; and was thus answered: "I lent you, indeed, my fiddle, but not my fiddle-stick; for you are to know that everyone cannot make music with my words, which are fitted for my own mouth." And so, my scholar, you are to know that as the ill pronunciation or ill accenting of words in a sermon spoils it, so the ill carriage of your line or not fishing even to a foot in a right place makes you lose your labor. And you are to know that though you have my fiddle, that is, my very rod and tacklings with which you see I catch fish, yet you have not my fiddle-stick, that is, you yet have not skill to know how to carry your hand and line nor how to guide it to a right place. And this must be taught you—for you are to remember I told you angling is an art—either by practice or a long observation or both. But take this for a rule: when you fish for a trout with a worm, let your line have so much and not more lead than will fit the stream in which you fish; that is to say, more in a great troublesome stream than in a smaller that is quieter; as near as may be, so much as will sink the bait to the bottom and keep it still in motion, and not more.

But now, let's say grace, and fall to breakfast. What say you, scholar, to the providence of an old angler? Does not this meat taste well? and was not this place well chosen to eat it? for this sycamore-tree will shade us from the sun's heat.

VENATOR. All excellent good, and my stomach excellent too. And now I remember and find that true which devout Lessius says, "That poor men and those that fast often have much more pleasure in eating than rich men and gluttons, that always feed before their stomachs are empty of their last meat and so rob themselves of that pleasure that hunger brings to poor men." And I do seriously approve of that saying of yours, "That you had rather be a civil, well-grounded, temperate, poor angler than a drunken lord." But I hope there is none such. However, I am certain of this, that I have been at many very costly dinners that have not afforded me half the content that this has done, for which I thank God and you.

And now, good master, proceed to your promised direction for making and ordering my artificial fly.

PISCATOR. My honest scholar, I will do it, for it is a debt due unto you by my promise. And because you shall not think yourself more engaged to me than indeed you really are, I will freely give you such directions as were lately given to me by an ingenious brother of the angle, an honest man, and a most excellent fly-fisher.

You are to note that there are twelve kinds of artificial-made flies to angle with upon the top of the water. Note, by the way, that the fittest season of using these is in a blustering windy day, when the waters are so troubled that the natural fly cannot be seen, or rest upon them. The first is the dun-fly in March; the body is made of dun wool, the wings, of the partridge's feathers. The second is another dun-fly; the body of black wool, and the wings made

Olive Woolly Worm.

of the black drake's feathers and of the feathers under his tail. The third is the stone-fly in April; the body is made of black wool made yellow under the wings and under the tail and so made with wings of the drake. The fourth is the ruddy-fly in the beginning of May; the body made of red wool, wrapt about with black silk, and the feathers are the wings of the drake, with the feathers of a red capon also, which hang dangling on his sides next to the tail. The fifth is the yellow or greenish fly, in May likewise; the body made of yellow wool; and the wings made of the red cock's hackle or tail.

The sixth is the black-fly, in May also; the body made of black wool, and lapt about with the herle of a peacock's tail, the wings are made of the wings of a brown capon, with his blue feathers in his head. The seventh is the sad yellow-fly in June; the body is made of black wool, with a yellow list on either side, or the wings taken off the wings of a buzzard, bound with black braked hemp. The eighth is the moorish-fly; made with the body of duskish wool, and the wings made of the blackish mail of the drake. The ninth is the tawny-fly, good until the middle of June; the body made of tawny wool, the wings made contrary one against the other, made of the whitish mail of the wild drake. The tenth is the wasp-fly in July; the body made of black wool, lapt about with yellow silk, the wings made of the feathers of the drake or of the buzzard. The eleventh is the shell-fly, good in mid-July; the body made of greenish wool, lapt about with the herle of a peacock's tail, and the wings made of the wings of the buzzard. The twelfth is the dark drake-fly, good in August; the body made with black wool, lapt about with black silk, his wings are made with the mail of the black drake, with a black head. Thus have you a jury of flies likely to betray and condemn all the trouts in the river.

I shall next give you some other directions for fly-fishing such as are given by Mr. Thomas Barker, a gentleman that hath spent much time in fishing; but I shall do it with a little variation.

First, let your rod be light, and very gentle. I take the best to be of two pieces. And let not your line exceed, especially for three or four links next to the hook, I say, not exceed three or four hairs at the most, though you may fish a little stronger above, in the upper part of your line. But if you can attain to angle with one hair, you shall have more rises, and catch more fish. Now you must be sure not to cumber yourself with too long a line, as most do. And before you begin to angle, cast to have the wind on your back; and the sun, if it shines, to be before you, and to fish down the stream; and carry the point or top of your rod downward, by which means the shadow of yourself and rod too will be the least offensive to the fish; for the sight of any shade amazes the fish and spoils your sport, of which you must take great care.

In the middle of March—till which time a man should not in honesty catch a trout—or in April, if the weather be dark or a little windy or cloudy, the best fishing is with the palmer-worm, of which I last spoke to you; but of these there be divers kinds, or at least of divers colors. These and the May-fly are the ground of all fly-angling. Which are to be thus made:

First, you must arm your hook with the line in the inside of it; then take your scissors and cut so much of a brown mallard's feather as in your own reason, will make the wings of it, you having withal regard to the bigness or littleness of your hook; then lay the outmost part of your feather next to your hook; then the point of your feather next the shank of your hook; and having so done, whip it three or four times about the hook with the same silk with which your hook was armed; and having made the silk fast, take the hackle of a cock or capon's neck or a plover's top, which is usually better; take off the one side of the feather, and then take the hackle, silk, or crewel, gold or silver thread; make these fast at the bent of the hook, that is to say, below your arming; then you must take the hackle, the silver or gold thread, and work it up to the wings, shifting or still removing your finger as you turn the silk about the hook and still looking at every stop or turn that your gold or what materials soever you make your fly of do lie right and neatly; and if you find they do so, then when you have made the head, make all fast; and then work your hackle up to the head, and make that fast; and then with a needle or pin divide the wing into two; and then with the arming silk whip it about cross-ways betwixt the wings; and then with your thumb you must turn the point of the feather towards the bent of the hook; and then work three or four times about the shank of the hook; and then view the proportion; and if all be neat and to your liking, fasten.

I confess no direction can be given to make a man of a dull capacity able to make a fly well. And yet I know this, with a little practice, will help an ingenious angler in a good degree. But to see a fly made by an artist in that kind is the best teaching to make it. And then an ingenious angler may walk by the river and mark what flies fall on the water that day, and catch one of them, if he sees the trouts leap at a fly of that kind: and then having always hooks ready-hung with him and having a bag always with him with bear's hair or the hair of a brown or sad-colored heifer, hackles of a cock or capon, several colored silk and crewel to make the body of the fly, the feathers of a drake's head, black or brown sheep's wool, or hog's wool, or hair, thread of gold and of silver; silk of several colors, especially sad-colored, to make the fly's head; and there be also other colored feathers, both of little birds and of speckled fowl—I say, having those with him in a bag and trying to make a fly, though he miss at first, yet shall he at last hit it better even to such a perfection as none can well teach him. And if he hit to make his fly right and have the luck to hit also where there is store of trouts, a dark day, and a right wind, he will catch such store of them as will encourage him to grow more and more in love with the art of fly-making.

VENATOR. But, my loving master, if any wind will not serve, then I wish I were in Lapland, to buy a good wind of one of the honest witches that sell so many winds there and so cheap.

PISCATOR. Marry, scholar, but I would not be there, nor indeed from under this tree. For look how it begins to rain, and by the clouds, if I mistake not, we shall presently have a smoking shower, and therefore sit close. This sycamore-tree will shelter us. And I will tell you, as they shall come into my mind, more observations of fly-fishing for a trout.

But first for the wind, you are to take notice that of the winds the south wind is said to be best. One observes that when the wind is south,

It blows your bait into a fish's mouth.

Next to that the west wind is believed to be the best. And having told you that the east wind is the worst, I need not tell you which wind is the best in the third degree. And yet, as Solomon observes, that "he that considers the wind shall never sow"; so he that busies his head too much about them, if the weather be not made extreme cold by an east wind, shall be a little superstitious. For as it is observed by some that "There is no good horse of a bad color"; so I have observed that if it be a cloudy day and not extreme cold, let the wind sit in what corner it will and do its worst. And yet take this for a rule, that I would willingly fish standing on the lee-shore. And you are to take notice that the fish lies or swims nearer the bottom and in deeper water in winter than in summer; and also nearer the bottom in any cold day, and then gets nearest the lee-side of the water.

But I promised to tell you more of the fly-fishing for a trout; which I may have time enough to do, for you see it rains May butter. First for a May-fly, you may make his body with greenish-colored crewel, or willowish color, darkening it in most places with waxed silk, or ribbed with black hair, or some of them ribbed with silver thread, and such wings for the color as you see the fly to have at that season, nay, at that very day on the water. Or you may make the oak-fly, with an orange-tawny and black ground, and the brown of a mallard's feather for the wings. And you are to know that these two are most excellent flies, that is, the May-fly and the oak-fly. And let me again tell you that you keep as far from the water as you can possibly, whether you fish with a fly or worm, and fish down the stream. And when you fish with a fly, if it be possible, let no part of your line touch the water, but your fly only; and be still moving your fly upon the water, or casting it into the water, you yourself being also always moving down the stream. Mr. Barker commends several sorts of the palmer-flies, not only those ribbed with silver and gold, but others that have their bodies all made of black, or some with red, and a red hackle. You may also make the hawthorn-fly, which is all black, and not big, but very small, the smaller the better. Or the oak-fly, the body of which is orange color and black crewel, with a brown wing. Or a fly made with a peacock's feather is excellent in a bright day. You must be sure you want not in your magazine-bag the peacock's feather and grounds of such wool and crewel as will make the grasshopper. And note that usually the smallest flies are the best; and note also that the light fly does usually make most sport in a dark day, and the darkest and least fly in a bright or clear day; and lastly note that you are to repair upon any occasion to your magazine-bag: and upon any occasion vary and make them lighter or sadder according to your fancy or the day.

And now I shall tell you that the fishing with a natural fly is excellent, and affords much pleasure. They may be found thus: the May-fly usually in and about that month near to the river-side, especially against rain; the oak-fly on the butt or body of an oak or ash from the beginning of May to the end of August; it is a brownish fly and easy to be so found, and stands usually with his head downward, that is to say, towards the root of the tree; the small black-fly, or hawthorn-fly, is to be had on any hawthorn bush after the leaves be come forth. With these and a short line, as I showed to angle for a chub, you may dape or dop, and also with a grasshopper, behind a tree or in any deep hole; still making it to move on the top of the water as if it were alive and still keeping yourself out of sight, you shall certainly have sport if there be trouts; yea, in a hot day, but especially in the evening of a hot day.

And now, scholar, my direction for fly-fishing is ended with this shower, for it has done raining. And now look about you, and see how pleasantly that meadow looks; nay, and the earth smells so sweetly too. Come let me tell you what holy Mr. Herbert says of such days and flowers as these, and then we will thank God that we enjoy them, and walk to the river and sit down quietly, and try to catch the other place of trouts.

> Sweet day, so cool, so calm, so bright,
> The bridal of the earth and sky,
> Sweet dews shall weep thy fall tonight,
> For thou must die.

> Sweet rose, whose hue, angry and brave,
> Bids the rash gazer wipe his eye,
> Thy root is ever in its grave,
> And thus must die.

Sweet spring, full of sweet days and roses,
A box where sweets compacted lie;
My music shows you have your closes,
And all must die.

Only a sweet and virtuous soul
Like seasoned timber never gives,
But when the whole world turns to coal,
Then chiefly lives.

VENATOR. I thank you, good master, for your good direction for fly-fishing and for the sweet enjoyment of the pleasant day, which is so far spent without offence to God or man; and I thank you for the sweet close of your discourse with Mr. Herbert's verses, which, I have heard, loved angling; and I do the rather believe it, because he had a spirit suitable to anglers and to those primitive Christians that you love and have so much commended.

No life, my honest scholar, no life so happy and so pleasant as the life of a well-governed angler; for when the lawyer is swallowed up with business and the statesman is preventing or contriving plots, then we sit on cowslip-banks, hear the birds sing, and possess ourselves in as much quietness as these silent silver streams which we now see glide so quietly by us. Indeed, my good scholar, we may say of angling as Dr. Boteler said of strawberries, "Doubtless God could have made a better berry, but doubtless God never did"; and if so I might be judge, God never did make a more calm, quiet, innocent recreation than angling.

CHAPTER 2

TROUT: MEETING THEM ON THE "JUNE RISE"

BY "NESSMUK" [GEORGE WASHINGTON SEARS]

Pine Creek, Berks County, Pennsylvania.

There is a spot where plumy pines
O'erhang the sylvan banks of Otter;
Where wood-ducks build among the vines
That bend above the crystal water.

And there the blue-jay makes her nest
In thickest shade of water beeches;
The fish-hawk, statuesque in rest,
Keeps guard o'er glassy pools and reaches.

'Tis there the deer come down to drink,
From laurel brakes and wooded ridges;
The trout, beneath the sedgy brink,
Are sharp on ship-wrecked flies and midges.

And of the scores of mountain trout-streams that I have fished, the Otter is associated with the most pleasant memories.

It is, or was, a model trout-stream; a thing to dream of. Having its rise within three miles of the village, it meandered southward for ten miles through a mountain valley to its confluence with the second fork of Pine Creek, six miles of the distance being through a forest without settler or clearing.

The stream was swift, stony, and exceptionally free of brush, fallen timber and the usual debris that is so trying to the angler on most wooded streams. Then, it was just the right distance from town. It was so handy to start from the village in the middle of an afternoon in early summer, walk an hour and a half at a leisurely pace, and find one's self on a brawling brook where speckled trout were plenty as a reasonable man could wish.

Fishing only the most promising places for a couple of miles always gave trout enough for supper and breakfast, and brought the angler to the "Trout-House," as a modest cottage of squared logs was called, it being the last house in the clearings and owned by good-natured Charley Davis, who never refused to entertain fishermen with the best his little house afforded.

His accommodations were of the narrowest, but also of the neatest, and few women could fry trout so nicely as Mrs. Davis. True, there was only one spare bed, and, if more than two anglers desired lodgings, they were relegated to the barn, with a supply of buffalo skins and blankets. On a soft bed of sweet hay this was all that could be desired by way of lodgings, with the advantage of being free from mosquitoes and punkies. The best of rich, yellow butter with good bread were always to be had at Charley's, and his charges were 12½ cents for meals, and the same for lodgings.

The two miles of fishing above the "Trout-House" led through clearings, and the banks were much overgrown with willows, making it expedient to use bait, or a single fly. I chose the latter; my favorite bug for such fishing being the red hackle, though I am obliged to confess that the fellow who used a white grub generally beat me.

But the evening episode was only preliminary; it meant a pleasant walk, thirty or forty brook-trout for supper and breakfast, and a quiet night's rest. The real angling commenced the next morning at the bridge, with a six-mile stretch of clear, cold, rushing water to fish. My old-fashioned creel held an honest twelve pounds of dressed trout, and I do not recollect that I ever missed filling it, with time to spare, on that stretch of water. Nor, though I could sometimes fill it in a forenoon, did I ever continue to fish after it was full. Twelve pounds of trout is enough for any but a trout-hog.

But the peculiar phase of trout lore that most interested me, was the "run" of trout that were sure to find their way up stream whenever we had a flood late in May or the first half of June. They were distinct and different from the trout that came up with the early spring freshets. Lighter in color, deeper in body, with smaller heads, and better conditioned altogether. They could be distinguished at a glance; the individuals of any school were as like as peas in color and size, and we never saw them except on a summer flood. The natives called them river trout. They came in schools of one hundred to five times as many, just as the flood was subsiding, and they had a way of halting to rest at the deep pools and spring-holes along their route. Lucky was the angler who could find them at rest in a deep pool, under a scooped out bank, or at the foot of a rushing cascade. At such times they seemed to lose their usual shyness, and would take the fly or worm indifferently, until their numbers were reduced more than one-half. To "meet them on the June rise" was the ardent desire of every angler who fished the streams which they were accustomed to ascend. These streams were not numerous. The First, Second, and Third Forks of Pine Creek, with the Otter, comprised the list so far as I know. And no man could be certain of striking a school at any time; it de-pended somewhat on judgment, but more on luck. Two or three times I tried it on the Otter and missed; while a friend who had the pluck and muscle to make a ten-mile tramp over the mountain to Second Fork took forty pounds of fine trout from a single school. It was a hoggish thing to do; but he was a native and knew no reason for letting up.

At length my white day came around. There was a fierce rain for three days, and the raging waters took mills, fences and lumber downstream in a way to be remembered. Luckily it also took the lumbermen the same way, and left few native anglers at home. When the waters had subsided to a fair volume, and the streams had still a suspicion of milkiness, I started at 3 p.m. of a lovely June afternoon for the Trout-House. An easy two hours walk, an hour of delightful angling, and I reached the little hostelry with three dozen brook trout, averaging about seven inches in length only, but fresh and sweet, all caught on a single red hackle, which will probably remain my favorite bug until I go over the last carry (though I notice it has gone well out of fashion with modern anglers).

A supper of trout; an evening such as must be seen and felt to be appreciated; trout again for breakfast, with a dozen packed for lunch, and I struck in at the bridge before sunrise for an all day bout, "to meet 'em on the June rise." I didn't do it. I took the entire day to whip that six miles of bright, dashing water. I filled a twelve-pound creel with trout, putting back everything under eight inches. I put back more than I kept. I had one of the most enjoyable days of my life; I came out at the lower bridge after sundown—and I had not seen or caught one fresh-run river trout. They were all the slender, large-mouthed, dark-mottled fish of the gloomy forest, with crimson spots like fresh drops of blood. But I was not discouraged. Had the trout been there I should have met them. I walked half a mile to the little inn at Babb's, selected a dozen of my best fish for supper and breakfast, gave away the rest, and, tired as a hound, slept the sleep of the just man.

At 4 o'clock the next morning I was on the stream again, feeling my way carefully down, catching a trout at every cast, and putting them mostly back with care, that they might live; but for an hour no sign of a fresh-run river trout.

Below the bridge there is a meadow, the oldest clearing on the creek; there are trees scattered about this meadow that are models of arboreal beauty, black walnut, elm, ash, birch, hickory, maple, etc. Most of them grand, spreading trees. One of them, a large, umbrageous yellow-birch, stood on the left bank of the stream, and was already in danger of a fall by

"The swifter current that mined its roots."

It was here that I met them on the June rise.

I dropped my cast of two flies just above the roots of the birch, and on the instant, two fresh-run, silver-sided, red-spotted trout immolated themselves, with a generous self-abnegation that I shall never forget.

Standing there on that glorious June morning, I made cast after cast, taking, usually, two at each cast. I made no boyish "show" of playing them. They were lifted out as soon as struck. To have fooled with them would have tangled me, and very likely have scattered the school.

It was old-time angling; I shall not see it again.

My cast was a red hackle for tail-fly, with something like the brown hen for hand-fly. I only used two, with four-foot leader; and I was about the only angler who used a fly at all in those days, on these waters.

I fished about one hour. I caught sixty-four trout, weighing thirteen and three quarter pounds. I caught too many. I was obliged to string some of them, as the creel would not hold them all. But my head was moderately level. When I had caught as many as I thought right I held up; and I said, if any of these natives get on to this school, they will take the last trout, if it be a hundred pounds. And they will salt them down. So when I was done, and the fishing was as good as the start, I cut a long "staddle," with a bush at the top, and I just went for that school of trout. I chevied, harried and scattered them, upstream and down, until I could not see a fish. Then I packed my duffle and went to the little inn for breakfast. Of course every male biped was anxious to know "where I met 'em." I told them truly; and they started, man and boy, for the "Big Birch," with beech rods, stiff linen lines, and a full stock of white grubs.

I was credibly informed afterwards, that these backwoods cherubs did not succeed in "Meeting 'em on the June rise." I have a word to add, which is not important though it may be novel.

There is a roaring, impetuous brook emptying into Second Fork, called "Rock Run." It heads in a level swamp, near the summit of the mountain. The swamp contains about forty acres, and is simply a level bed of loose stones, completely overgrown with bright green moss.

"Rock Run" heads in a strong, ice-cold spring, but is soon sunken and lost among the loose stones of the swamp. Just where the immense hemlocks, that make the swamp a sunless gloom, get their foothold, is one of the things I shall never find out. But, all the same, they are there.

And "Rock Run" finds its way underground for 80 rods with never a ray of sunlight to illuminate its course. Not once in its swamp course does it break out to daylight. You may follow it by its heavy gurgling, going by ear; but you cannot see the water. Now remove the heavy coating of moss here and there, and you may see glimpses of dark, cold water, three or four feet beneath the surface. Drop a hook, baited with angle-worm down these dark watery holes, and it will be instantly taken by a dark, crimson-spotted specimen of simon pure *Salmo fontinalis*. They are small, four to six inches in length, hard, sweet; the beau ideal of mountain trout. Follow this subterranean brook for eighty rods, and you find it gushing over the mountain's brink in a cascade that no fish could or would attempt to ascend. Follow the roaring brook down to its confluence with Second Fork, and you will not find one trout in the course of a mile. The stream is simply a succession of falls, cascades, and rapids, up which no fish can beat its way for one hundred yards. And yet at the head of this stream is a subterranean brook stocked with the finest specimens of *Salmo fontinalis*. They did not breed on the mountain top. They cannot ascend the stream. Where did they originate? When, and how did they manage to get there? I leave the questions to savants and naturalists. As for myself, I state the fact—still demonstrable—for the trout are yet there. But I take it to be one of the conundrums "no fellah can ever find out."

P.S.—A word as to bugs, lures, flies, etc. Now I have no criticism to offer as regards flies or lures. I saw a Gotham banker in 1880, making a cast on Third lake, with a leader that carried twelve flies. Why not? He enjoyed it; and he caught some trout. Even the guides laughed at him. I did not: he rode his hobby, and he rode it well. Fishing beside him, with a five-dollar rod, I caught two to his one. What did he care? He came out to enjoy himself after his own fashion, and he did it. Like myself, he only cared for the sport—the recreation and enough trout for supper. (I cannot cast twelve flies.)

Now my favorite lures—with forty years' experience—stand about thus. Tail fly, red hackle; second, brown hen; third, Romeyn. Or, tail fly, red ibis; second, brown hackle; third, queen of the waters. Or, red hackle, queen, royal coachman. Sometimes trout will not rise to the fly. I respect their tastes. I use then—tail fly, an angle worm, with a bit of clear pork for the head, and a white miller for second. If this fails I go to camp and sleep. I am not above worms and grubs, but prefer the fly. And I take but what I need for present use. Can all brother anglers say the same?

CHAPTER 3

TROUTING ALONG THE CATASAUQUA

BY "FRANK FORESTER" [HENRY WILLIAM HERBERT]

Brook Trout, North America. Salmo fontinali by Henry William Herbert, 1851. The University of Washington.

"And this 'clattering creek,' what sort of water is it?" asked Frank; "that I may learn at once the whole lay of the land."

"A real mountain burn."

"I'm thinking of trying it myself tomorrow," said Robins. "Mr. Langdale tells me it can only be fished with bait, and that's what I'm best at. Besides, there are bigger fish in it."

"But fewer," answered Langdale. "No, Robins, I'd advise you to stick to the 'Stony,' unless you'll try a cast of the fly with us over the pool and down the Catasauqua."

"No, no," replied St. Clair, half indignantly, "none of your flies for me, and no canoe-work. But why do you advise me against it? You said there were no trees, bait-fishing and big fish. What is there against it?"

"The toughest crag-climbing and the most difficult fishing you ever tried."

"What like fishing is it, Lancelot?" asked Frank.

"Exactly what that capital sportsman, Colquhoon of Luss, describes in his excellent book, the 'Moor and Loch,' under the title of 'Moorburn'."

"I remember," replied Frank. "Is it as bad as that?"

"Worse; but the fish much larger. I have caught them up to two pounds."

"I should like to hear about that. Can't you read it to me?" asked the Wallstreet man, eager for information.

"I've no objection," said Langdale, "if Frank has not. He has read it fifty times already."

"I'm convenient," answered Frank, laying down his knife and fork, the last duck having disappeared.

"Well, then, here goes. Now, Scipio, look alive and clear away the table; bring us our pipes and our coffee; and then we'll to bed, for we must be afoot by day-break."

And with the word he rose, and, after turning over a few volumes on his crowded shelves, brought down the volume in question, with its pages underlined, and interlined, and filled with marginal notes and references. This done, he ensconced himself in the chimney corner, threw on a fresh log, and read as follows:

"'In most of the small Highland burns, there is a succession of cataracts and pools, with a parapet of rock rising perpendicularly on each side, and often scarcely footing enough for a dog to pass. The greater proportion of picturesque-looking brethren of the angle would almost start at the idea of continuing their pastime under such disadvantages. They therefore make a circuit, and come down again upon the burn, where it is more easy to fish, and the ground less rugged. The trout in these places are thus left until many of them grow large, and each taking possession of a favorite nook, drives all the smaller fry away. The difficulty of reaching these places is, I admit, often great, the angler having sometimes to scramble up on his hands and knees, covered with wet moss or gravel, and then drag his fishing-rod after him. These lyns should always be fished up-stream, otherwise the moment you appear at the top of the waterfall or rock, the trout are very like to see you, and slink into their hiding-place. The burn, however, must always be low, as at no other time can you distinguish the snug retreat of these little tyrants, which, indeed, they often leave, during the slightest flood, in search of prey. By fishing up the stream, your head will be on a level with the different eddies and pools, as they successively present themselves, and the rest of your person out of sight. Hold the baited hook with the left hand, jerking out the rod, underhanded, with your right, so as to make the bait fall softly at the lower end of the pool. The trout always take their station either there or at the top where the water flows in, ready to pounce on worms, snails, slugs, etc., as they enter or leave the pool. Should a trout seize the bait, a little time may be given to allow it to gorge, which it will most likely do without much ceremony. If large, care must be taken to prevent it from getting to the top of the lyn, which may probably harbor another expectant. The best plan is, if possible, to persuade it to descend into the pool below. Having deposited the half-pounder in your creel, you will now crawl upon hands and knees, just so near the top of the lyn as will enable you to drop the bait immediately below the bubbling foam, nearly as favorite a station for an overgrown, monopolizing trout as the other. Except in such situations, the burn trout seldom exceeds a quarter of a pound, and may be pulled out with single gut, without much risk of breaking it. In these lyns, however, I have occasionally taken them upward of a pound, which is easily accounted for. As soon as the trout grows to a sufficient size to intimidate his pigmy neighbors, he falls back into the best pool for feeding, not occupied by a greater giant than himself, and as these lyns are almost always in precipices very difficult of access, he remains undisturbed and alone, or with a single companion, driving all others away, until he may at last attain to a pound weight.'

"Now, I fear, brother angler, that you are in some respects what the indefatigable Gael would call a 'picturesque angler'; so I advise you in good faith, stick to the 'Stony Brook'; fish it from the long fall carefully down. Scipio shall attend you with the landing-net and plenty of worms and minnows; the last, hooked through the lip and back fin, will do you yeoman service in the lower pools; and Frank and I will join you in the afternoon."

"Agreed," said Mr. Robins; "I'll take your advice, I believe; and now I guess I'll turn in. Good night."

"Time, too," said Frank, laughing. "He was beginning to get a little white about the gills. Could that be his old Otard; he did not drink so much of it."

"Lord help you, no! he'd drink a gallon of it and no hurt. No! But he will persist in smoking Cavendish tobacco and kinnikinnic, because he has seen me do it, and, I believe, imagines that it confers some special powers of trout-catching. But come, suppose we turn in, too; you'll be tired after your journey, and a good night's rest will give a steady hand and clear eye tomorrow."

"*Volontiers.*"

So they incontinently joined the Wall Street man, who declared, half asleep, that the bed was not so very bad, after all; while Frank, once ensconced in the fragrant sheets, swore, by the great god Pan, patron of hunters, that never had bed so sweet, so soft, so warm, in every way so excellent, received the limbs of weary hunter. And so, indeed, it proved; for, until Scipio made his entree, with his announcement that breakfast was ready, no one stirred or spoke during the livelong night.

Thereon they all turned, like the Iron Duke, not over, but out. Their sporting toilets were soon made; but Frank and Lancelot, in their old shepherd's plaid jackets and trews and hob-nailed fishing shoes, could not but exchange glances and smiles at the elaborate rig of their friend, which some Broadway artist had, it was evident, elaborated from a Parisian fashion-plate, the high boots of exquisitely enameled leather, the fine doeskin trousers, the many-pocketed, pearl-buttoned shooting jacket of fawn-colored silk plush, the batiste neckerchief and waistcoat, point device, with green and silver fishes embroidered on a blue ground, and, to complete the whole, a cavalier hat, in which, but that it lacked the king's black feather, Rupert might well have charged at Marston Moor or Naseby. He seemed, however, so happy, that it would have been as useless as ill-natured to indoctrinate him; for evidently, as an angler, the man was hopelessly incurable, though, as Frank observed, for Wall-street, he was wonderfully decent.

His weapon was a right good Conroy's general-fishing rod, but without reel, and having its line, an unusually stout silk one, with a superb salmon-gut bottom, which, in good hands, would have held a twenty-pounder, made carefully fast to the top funnel; eschewing all use of the ring and destroying all chance of the rod's regularly bending to its work. But again, to counsel would have been to offend; so our friends held their peace.

The smoked venison ham, broiled troutlings, dry toast and black tea, which furnished their morning meal, were soon finished; and forth they went into the delicious, breezy air of the quiet summer morning, not a sound disturbing the solitude, except the plash and rippling of the rapid waters, the low voices of the never-silent pine-tops, and the twittering of the swallows, as they skimmed the limpid pool.

Up the gorge of the Stony Brook, followed by Scipio, with bait of all kinds enough to have kept the kraten fat for one day at least, a large creel at his back, and gaff and landing-net in hand, away went St. Clair Robins, gay and joyous and confident; and then, but not till then quoth Forester—

"And whither we?"

"To the other side of the pool. You may see the big fish rising under the alders, there, in the shadow of the big hill, from this distance. That shadow will hang there until noon, while all this side of the basin will be in blazing sunshine. Not a fish will bite here, I warrant me, until three o'clock, while we'll fill our basket there with good ones, certain. The best fish in the pool lies under that round-headed stone, just in the tail of the strong eddy, where the 'Clattering Creek' comes in, in the broken water. I rate him a six-pounder, and have saved him for you all the spring. As soon as the sun turns westward, and the hemlocks' shadows cross the white water, you shall kill him, and then we'll away to the Wall Street man"; and therewith the larger birch canoe was manned, paddled gently over to the shady side of the pool and moored in about twenty-foot water, and then, the rods being put together, the reels secured, and the lines carried duly through the rings, the following colloquy followed:

"What flies do you most affect here, Lancelot?" asked Frank.

"Any, at times, and almost all," answered Langdale. "In some weather I have killed well with middle-sized gaudy lake flies; but my favorites, on the whole, are all the red, brown, orange, and yellow hackles, and the blue and yellow duns. And yours?"

"My favorite of all is a snipe feather and mouse body; next to that the black and the furnace hackles."

"And will you use them today?"

"I will; the snipe wing for my stretcher. I mean to kill the big chap with him this evening."

"Be it so! to work."

And to work they went; but, though most glorious the sport to enjoy, or even to see performed gnostically, to read of it described, is as little interesting as to describe it is difficult. Suffice it to say, that before the sun had begun to turn westward, sixteen brace and a half were fairly brought to basket by our anglers, one a three-pound-and-a-halfer, three two-pounders, there or there about; not a fish under a pound, all smaller were thrown back unscathed, and very few so small as that, all beautifully fed fish, big-bellied, small-headed, high in color, prime in condition. At one o'clock, they paddled leisurely back to the cabin, lunched frugally on a crust of bread and a glass of sherry, and awaited the hour when the hemlock's shadow should be on the white water.

At the moment they were there; and lo! the big trout was feeding fiercely on the natural fly.

"Be ready, Frank, and when next he rises drop your fly right in the middle of his bell." "Be easy, I mean it." His line, as he spoke, was describing an easy circle around his head; the fish rose not. The second revolution succeeded; the great trout rose, missed his object, disappeared; and, on the instant, right in the centre of the bell, ere the inmost circle had subsided, the snipe feather fell and fluttered. With an arrowy rush, the monster rose, and as his broad tail showed above the surface, the merry music of the resonant click-reel told that Frank had him. Well struck, he was better played, killed unexceptionably; in thirteen minutes he lay fluttering on the greensward, lacking four ounces of a six-pounder. The snipe feather and mouse body won the day in a canter. So off they started up the Stony Brook, to admire the feats of P. St. Clair Robins. It was not long ere they found him; he had reached the lower waters of the brook, full of beautiful scours, eddies, whirlpools and basins, and was fishing quietly down it, wading about knee deep with his bait, he was roving with a minnow, some ten yards down the stream, playing naturally enough in the clear, swirling waters. Some trees on the bank hung thickly over his head; a few yards behind him was a pretty rocky cascade, and above that an open upland glade, lighted up by a gleam of the westering sun; and, altogether, with his gay garb, he presented quite a picturesque, if not a very sportsmanly appearance.

"After all," said Frank, as unseen themselves, they stood observing him, "he does not do it so very badly as one might have expected."

But before the words had passed his lips, a good fish, at least a pounder, threw itself clear out of the water and seized his minnow. In a second, in the twinkling of an eye, by a movement never before seen or contemplated by

A large brown trout, finning in a pool.

mortal angler, he ran his right hand up to the top of the third joint of his rod, which he held perpendicularly aloft, and with his left grasped his line, mid length, and essayed to drag the trout by main force out of his element. The tackle was stout, the stream strong, the bottom slippery, the fish active, and, before anyone could see how it was done, hand and foot both slipped, the line parted, the rod crashed in the middle, the fish went over the next fall with a joyous flirt of his tail, and the fisherman, hapless fisherman, measured his own length in the deepest pool of the Stony Brook.

He was soon fished out, equipped in dry rigging, comforted with a hot glass of his favorite cognac; but he would not be consoled. He was off at daylight the following morning, and, for aught that I have heard, Cotton's Cabin beheld him nevermore.

SECTION TWO
THE WARM WATER MIX

CHAPTER 4

BLACK BASS AS A GAME FISH

BY JAMES A. HENSHALL

"He is a fish that lurks close all winter; but is very pleasant and jolly after mid-April, and in May, and in the hot months."

—Izaak Walton

A good-sized smallmouth bass, taken from the Susquehanna River in Pennsylvania. Photo Credit: Jay Cassell.

Those who have tasted the lotus of salmon or trout fishing, in that Utopian clime of far away—while reveling in its aesthetic atmosphere, and surrounded by a misty halo of spray from the waterfall, or enveloped by the filmy gauze and iridescent tomes, sung idylls, chanted paeans, and poured out libations in honor and praise of the silver-spangled salmon, or the ruby-studded trout, while it is left to the vulgar horde of black bass anglers to stand upon the mountain of their own doubt and presumption, and, with uplifted hands, in admiration and awe, gaze with dazed eyes from afar upon that forbidden land—that terra incognita—and then, having lived in vain, die and leave no sign.

It is, then, with a spirit of rank heresy in my heart; with smoked glass spectacles on my nose, to dim the glare and glamour of the transcendent shore; with the scales of justice across my shoulder—*M. salmoides* in one scoop and *M. dolomieu* in the other—I pass the barriers and confines of the enchanted land, and toss them into a stream that has been depopulated of even fingerlings, by the dilettanti of salmon and trout fishers; for I would not, even here, put black bass in a stream inhabited by salmon or brook trout.

While watching the plebeian interlopers sporting in an eddy, their bristling spines and emerald sides gleaming in the sunshine, I hear an awful voice from the adjacent rocks exclaiming: "Fools rush in where angels fear to tread!" Shade of Izaak Walton defend us! While appealing to Father Izaak for protection, I quote his words: "Of which, if thou be a severe, sour complexioned man, then I here disallow thee to be a competent judge."

Seriously, from Izaak Walton to the present day, the salmon and trout of Great Britain have been sung in song and story as game-fishes, and it is sufficient to say that they deserve all the praise bestowed upon them. And as our ideas of fish and fishing have derived mostly from English authors, it follows that many American writers and anglers have been obsessed by their teaching, even down to the present day, as in dry fly-fishing.

Now, while we have in America the same salmon as in Great Britain, and several species of trout equally as good or better than the brown trout, we also have many other game-fishes equally worthy, and among them the black bass.

I feel free to assert, that, were the black bass a native of Great Britain, it would rank fully as high in the estimation of British anglers as either the trout or the salmon. I am borne out in this by the opinions of British sportsmen whose statements have been received without question.

W. H. Herbert (Frank Forester) writing of the black bass, says:

This is one of the finest of the American fresh-water fishes: it is surpassed by none in boldness of biting, in fierce and violent resistance when hooked, and by a very few only in excellence upon the board. (*Fish and Fishing*, 1850)

Parker Gillmore ("Ubique") says:

I fear it will be almost deemed heresy to place this fish (black bass) on a par with the trout; at least, some such idea I had when I first heard the two compared; but I am bold, and will go further. I consider he is the superior of the two, for he is equally good as an article of food, and much stronger, and untiring in his efforts to escape when hooked. (*Prairie and Forest*, 1874)

In regard to the comparative gameness of the black bass and the brook trout the following opinions of American anglers are added. Seth Green, one of the fathers of fish-culture and a lifelong angler for trout, among other fishes, has this to say:

This is among the finest sporting as well as food fish in America. Bites fiercely at fly or trolling spoon; makes a vigorous fight for life, liberty and happiness, showing a perfect willingness 'to fight it out on that line if it takes all summer,' and at last when subdued and brought to the table does honor to the cook who prepares it, and pleasure to the palate that enjoys it. (*Fish Hatching and Fish Catching*, 1879)

Robert B. Roosevelt, who, with Seth Green, was a Fish Commissioner of New York, and co-author of *Fish Hatching, and Fish Catching*, and a notable angler for salmon and trout, says of the black bass:

A fish that is inferior only to the salmon and trout, if even to the latter; that requires the best of tackle and skill in its inveiglement, and exhibits courage and game qualities of the highest order. (*Superior Fishing*, 1865)

E. E. Millard, a veteran fly-fisher for trout for fifty years, who has camped many summers on the famous Nipigon, and who is a true and faithful lover of the brook trout, has this to say in comparing the trout and the black bass as game-fishes:

When the acrobatic bass approaches with every spine bristling it signifies fight, and he dies battling face to the foe—not that the trout tamely submits at the first prick of the steel; far from it. He is a fighter, though not a scientific one, having no appreciation of the finer and more artistic points of the game. He looks the fighter, having the neck and shoulders of the pugilist, but is rather too beautiful, which, however, does not always follow, and there is lacking a little of the Irish in his composition, though when put to the crowning test, he hangs on with bulldog tenacity, lacking only the resourcefulness of the smallmouth bass, the generally recognized champion of finny warriors, and of whom I can well believe that, inch for inch and pound for pound, he is the gamest fish that swims. (*Days on the Nipigon*, 1917)

Now, while salmon fishing is, unquestionably, the highest branch of piscatorial sport; and while trout fishing in Canada, Maine, and the Lake Superior region justifies all the extravagant praise bestowed upon it, I am inclined to doubt the judgment and good taste of those anglers who snap their fingers in contempt of black bass fishing, while they will wade in a stream with brush and logs, catch a few trout weighing six or eight to the pound, and call it the only artistic angling in the world! While they are certainly welcome to their opinion, I think their zeal is worthy of a better cause.

The black bass is eminently an American fish, and is truly representative in his characteristics. He has the faculty of asserting himself and making himself completely at home wherever placed. He is plucky, game, brave, and unyielding to the last when hooked. He has the arrowy rush and vigor of the trout, the untiring strength and bold leap of the salmon, while he has a system of fighting tactics peculiarly his own.

Among anglers, the question is often raised as to what constitutes a game-fish, and what particular species are to be considered best among game-fishes. In coordinating the essential attributes of game-fishes, each inherent trait and quality must be duly and impartially considered. Their habits and habitat; their aptitude to rise to the artificial fly; their manner of resistance and struggle for freedom when hooked; their finesse and intelligence; and their excellence as food must all be taken into account and duly weighed.

The black bass is more advanced in the scheme of evolution, and exhibits traits of a higher organization than either the salmon or trout. It is worthy of note that the highest development of fishes is shown in those with spiny-rayed fins as in the black bass, striped bass, channel bass, etc., while those of a lower development have soft-rayed fins as in the salmon, trout, whitefish, pike, etc.

In the animal creation the highest intelligence is exemplified by the parental instinct or care of the young. This is shown in the highest degree among mammals, next among birds, in but few reptiles, and scarcely at all among fishes. In the two hundred, or more, families of fishes, those that evince any parental instinct or manifest any care of their young can be counted on the fingers of one hand. The black bass stands pre-eminent in this respect, and is a bright and shining example to all the finny tribe in its habit of watching and guarding its nest and caring for its young brood when hatched.

Most fishes in fresh and salt water abandon their eggs as soon as emitted and fertilized. The salmon and trouts deposit their eggs in the shallowest water and leave them to the tender mercies of predatory fish, birds, and reptiles during an incubation of two or three months.

The black bass will rise to the artificial fly as readily as the salmon or the brook trout, under the same conditions; and will take the live minnow, or other live bait, under any and all circumstances favorable to the taking of any other fish. I consider him, inch for inch and pound for pound, the gamest fish that swims. The royal salmon and the lordly trout must yield the palm to a black bass of equal weight.

That he will eventually become the leading game-fish of America is my oft-expressed opinion and firm belief. This result, I think, is inevitable; if for no other reasons, from a force of circumstances occasioned by climatic conditions and the operation of immutable natural laws, such as the gradual drying up and dwindling away of the small trout streams, and the consequent decrease in brook trout, both in quality and quantity; and by the introduction of predatory fish in waters where the trout still exists.

Another prominent cause of the decline and fall of the brook trout, is the erection of dams, saw-mills, and factories upon trout streams, which, though to be deplored, cannot be prevented; the march of empire and the progress of civilization cannot be stayed by the honest, though powerless, protests of anglers.

But, while the ultimate fate of the brook trout is sealed beyond peradventure, in open, public waters, we have the satisfaction of knowing that in the black bass we have a fish equally worthy, both as to game and edible qualities, and which at the same time is able to withstand and defy many of the causes that will, in the end, effect the annihilation and extinction of the brook trout.

As to a comparison of game qualities as between the small-mouth bass and the large-mouth bass, I hold that, other things being equal, and where the two species inhabit the same waters, there is no difference in game qualities; for, while the small-mouth is probably more active in its movements, the large-mouth bass is more powerful; and no angler can tell from its manner of resistance whether he is fast to one or the other.

Both species of black bass rise equally well to the artificial fly; though, if there be any difference in this respect, I think the large-mouth bass has the advantage. In a letter Count Von dem Borne, of Germany (who was very successful in introducing and propagating the black bass in that country), wrote me that the large-mouth black bass rose better to the artificial fly than the small-mouth bass. My own experience rather favors this view, and it has likewise been brought to my notice by anglers in various parts of the country.

The current but erroneous opinion that the small-mouth bass exceeds the large-mouth bass in game qualities, has been very widespread, and has been much enhanced by the endorsement of several of our best ichthyologists, who unfortunately, however, are not, and do not pretend to be, anglers, but who imbibed this opinion second-hand from prejudiced anglers who ought to have known better. But as the black bass is becoming better known, and fly fishing for the species is being more commonly practiced, this unfair and unmerited comparison is fast dying out.

Fish inhabiting swiftly-running streams are always more vigorous and gamy than those in still waters, and it is probable that where the large-mouth bass exists alone in very shallow and sluggish waters, of high temperature and thickly grown with algae, it will exhibit less combative qualities, consequent on the enervating influences of its environment; but where both species inhabit the same waters, and are subject to the same conditions, I am convinced that no angler can tell whether he has hooked a large-mouth or a small-mouth bass, from their resistance and mode of fighting, provided they are of equal weight, until he has the ocular evidence.

I use the expression "equal weight" advisedly, for most anglers must have remarked that the largest bass of either species are not necessarily the hardest fighters; on the contrary, a bass of two or two and a half pounds' weight will usually make a more gallant fight than one of twice the size, and this fact, I think, will account in a great measure for the popular idea that the small-mouth bass is the "gamest" species for this reason:

Where the two species co-exist in the same stream or lake, the large-mouth bass always grows to a larger size than the other species, and an angler having just landed a two-pound small-mouth bass after a long struggle, next hooks a large-mouth bass weighing four or five pounds, and is surprised, probably, that it "fights" no harder or perhaps not so hard as the smaller fish—in fact, seems "logy"; he, therefore, reiterates the cry that the small-mouth bass is the gamest fish.

But, now, if he next succeeds in hooking a large-mouth bass of the same size as the first one caught, he is certain that he is playing a small-mouth bass until it is landed, when to his astonishment it proves to be a large-mouth bass; he merely says, "he fought well for one of his kind," still basing his opinion of the fighting qualities of the two species upon the first two caught.

Perhaps his next catch may be a small-mouth bass of four pounds, and which, though twice the weight of the large-mouth bass just landed, does not offer any greater resistance, and he sets it down in his mind as a large-mouth bass. Imagine the angler's surprise, then, upon taking it into the landing net, to find it a small-mouth bass, and one which, from its large size and the angler's preconceived opinion of the species should have fought like a Trojan.

Now, one would think that the angler would be somewhat staggered in his former belief; but no, he is equal to the occasion, and in compliance with the popular idea, he merely suggests that "it was out of condition, somehow," or "was hooked so as to drown it in the struggle"; and so, as his largest fish will necessarily be big-mouth bass, and because they do not fight in proportion to their size, they are set down as lacking in game qualities—of course, leaving the largest small-mouth bass out of the calculation.

Gentle reader, this is not a case of special pleading, nor is the angler a creation of the imagination lugged in as an apologist for the large-mouth bass; he is a veritable creature of fish and blood, of earth earthy, and with the self-conceit, weaknesses and shortcomings characteristic of the genus *Homo*. I have met him and heard his arguments and sage expressions scores of times, and if the reader will reflect a moment I am sure he will recognize him.

Many years ago I was at Gogebic Lake, Wisconsin, where, among a number of prominent anglers, were Dr. F., and Dr. T., both of New York City. Dr. F. had a very extensive angling experience in all parts of the country, and Dr. T. was well known as a participant in the fly- and bait-catching contests in the tournaments of the National Rod and Reel Association of that day.

Dr. T. was a firm believer in the superior game qualities of the small-mouth bass, and declared that he could invariably tell what species of black bass he had hooked, from its manner of "fighting." Dr. F. was confident he could not do so. The matter was finally put to a practical test, when Dr. T. was forced to acknowledge himself vanquished, and that he nor any other angler could make the distinction, for one fish was as "gamy" as the other. I might add that this result will be obtained wherever the two species exist in the same waters.

Mr. S. C. Clarke, a veteran angler of sixty years' experience, and whose opinion is titled to great weight, says: "I will say that, from an acquaintance with both species for more than forty years, from Minnesota to Florida, I have found little or no difference between them. I have taken them with fly, spoon, and bait, as many as fifty in a day (in early times), and up to six and a half pounds' weight."

A few years before his death, Fred Mather wrote as follows:

A bad name, given to the big-mouth bass when black bass first began to attract the attention of anglers, has stuck. It may interest a younger generation of anglers to know that forty years ago these gamy fishes were hardly known to anglers, and as soon as they began to attract attention some persons, to show their exquisite discrimination, began to praise one to the detriment of the other. Dr. Henshall and I have had the courage to fight this, and to say that in game qualities there is little difference, and that what there is depends on the weight of the fish, two pounds being its fighting weight. Further than to say that the big-mouth is not so capricious about taking the fly as his brother—i.e., will usually take it more freely—I have not room to go into this subject here. I have written all this before and intend to keep at it until justice is done to a noble game-fish.

Mr. Henry Talbott, an angler of wide experience, and who has written so entertainingly and instructively on black bass angling in the Potomac, says: "There are some anglers who consider there is but one black bass, the small-mouth, and that the other is useless for food, lacking in gamy qualities and only fished for by the misguided. In this they are mistaken, and it is a theory they will abandon and resent when their experience is wider.

"It is possible that in the Florida lakes they may be tame sport, and there seems to be a general agreement that in some of the swamps of Ohio the big-mouth is an inferior fish, but there is yet to be found his superior where he has a fair chance.

"Taking the two fish at their best, there is no man living can tell the difference in their taking the fly, in their fight to the boat, or on the platter, by any other sign than that one has a more capacious smile than the other; and by the same token he is just a little the better jumper and will leave the water oftener after being hooked, and is as long in coming to the net as his cousin."

Owing to my admiration for the black bass as a game-fish, and my championship of its cause for many years, and my efforts to place it in the front rank of game-fishes, and my desire to have it placed in new waters, I am sometimes, thoughtlessly and unjustly, accused of being opposed to the brook trout, and of advising the stocking of trout streams with my "favorite" fish. Nothing can be further from the truth.

I am utterly opposed to the introduction of black bass into waters in which there is the remotest chance for the brook trout or rainbow trout to thrive. I yield to no one in love and admiration of the brook trout. I was perfectly familiar with it before I ever saw a black bass; but I am not so blinded by prejudice but that I can share that love with the black bass, which for several reasons is destined to become the favorite game-fish of America. "My offending hath this extent, no more."

Let us look this thing squarely in the face. I do not wish to disturb any-one's preference, but I do want to disabuse the minds of anglers of all preju-dice in the matter. The brook trout must go. It has already gone from many streams, and is fast disappearing from others. It is sad to contemplate the ex-tinction of the "angler's pride" in public waters, but the stern fact remains that in this utilitarian age its days are numbered and its fate irrevocably sealed. As the red man disappears before the tread of the white man, the "living arrow" of the mountain streams goes with him.

The trout is essentially a creature of the pine forests. Its natural home is in waters shaded by pine, balsam, spruce, and hemlock, where the cold mountain brooks retain their low temperature, and the air is redolent of bal-samic fragrance; where the natural food of the trout is produced in the great-est abundance, and where its breeding grounds are undisturbed.

But the iron has entered its soul. As the buffalo disappears before the iron horse, the brook trout vanishes before the axe of the lumberman. As the giants of the forest are laid low, and the rank and file decimated and the wooden walls of the streams battered down, the hot, fiery sun leaps through the breaches, disclosing the most secret recesses of forest and stream to the bright glare of midday. The moisture of the earth is dissipated, the mosses and ferns become shriveled and dry, the wintergreen and partridge-berry, the ground pine and trailing arbutus struggle feebly for existence; the waters de-crease in size and increase in temperature, the conditions of the food supply and of the breeding grounds of the brook trout are changed; it deteriorates in size and numbers and vitality, until finally, in accordance with the im-mutable laws of nature and the great principle of the "survival of the fittest" (not the fittest from the angler's point of view, but the fittest to survive the changes and mutations consequent on the march of civilization), it disap-pears altogether.

Much has been said about the "trout hog" in connection with the de-crease of the trout. But while he deserves all the odium and contempt heaped upon him by the honest angler, the result would be the same were the trout allowed undisturbed and peaceable possession of the streams, so far as the fish-hook is concerned, while the axe of the lumberman continues to ring its death knell.

Let us, then, cherish and foster and protect the crimson-spotted favorite of our youthful days as long as possible in public waters, and introduce the rainbow trout, the Dolly Varden, the steelhead, the red-throat trout, or the English brown trout, when he has disappeared; and when all these succumb, then, and not till then, introduce the black bass. But let us give these cousins of the brook trout a fair trial first, and without prejudice. There are plenty of lakes, ponds, and large streams in the eastern states into which the black bass can be introduced without interfering with trout waters.

For many years to come brook trout will be artificially cultivated, and the supply thus kept up in preserved waters by wealthy angling clubs; but by the alteration of the natural conditions of their existence they will gradually decrease in size and quality, until finally they will either cease to be or degenerate to such a degree as to forfeit even this praiseworthy protection.

I must dissent from the statement sometimes made that the black bass is the bluefish of freshwaters. The black bass is voracious—so are all game-fishes—but not more so than the brook trout. The character of a fish's teeth determines the nature of its food and the manner of its feeding. The bluefish has the most formidable array of teeth of any fish of its size—compressed, lancet-shaped, covered with enamel, and exceedingly strong and sharp, in fact, miniature shark teeth—while the black bass has soft, small, brush-like teeth, incapable of wounding, and intended only for holding its prey, which is swallowed whole. The brook trout has longer, stronger and sharper teeth than the bass, and a large, long mouth, capable of swallowing a bigger fish than a black bass of equal weight. The mouth of the bass is very wide, for the purpose of taking in crawfish with their long and aggressive claws, and not, as supposed by some, for the swallowing of large fishes. The black bass gets the best of other game-fishes, not by devouring the fishes themselves, but by devouring their food. For this reason, more than any other, they should not be introduced into the same waters with brook trout. The pike or pickerel is the bluefish of fresh waters, and in dental capacity and destructive possibilities is not far behind it.

The brook trout, I think, is the most beautiful of all fishes, as a fresh-run salmon is the handsomest and most perfect in form. The salmon is a king, the brook trout a courtier, but the black bass, in his virescent cuirass and spiny crest, is a doughty warrior whose prowess none can gainsay.

I have fished for brook trout in the wilds of Canada, where a dozen would rise at every cast of the fly, and it would be a scramble as to which should get it—great lusty trout, from a half-pound to two pounds in weight—but the black fly made life a burden by day, and the mosquito by night. The glory and beauty of the madly rushing stream breaking wildly over the great black rocks, and the quiet, glassy pools below reflecting the green spires of spruce and fir, availed nothing to swollen eyelids and smarting brow.

I have cast from early morn till dewy eve, on a good salmon stream in New Brunswick, for three days in succession without a single rise. I have cast standing in a birch-bark canoe until both arms and legs were weary with the strain, and then rested by casting while sitting—but all in vain. The swift-flowing, crystal stream reflected back the fierce glare of the northern sun and flowed on in silence toward the sea. The fir-clad hills rose boldly on either side, and stood in silent, solemn grandeur—for neither note of bird or hum of bee disturbed the painful silence of the Canadian woods.

At such times would flash on memory's mirror many a fair scene of limpid lake or rushing river, shadowed by cool, umbrageous trees, and vocal with myriads of voices—where the black bass rose responsive to the swish of the rod and dropping of the fly. Or, should the bass be coy and shy, or loth to leave his lair beneath some root or shelving rock—the melody of the birds, the tinkle of a cow-bell, the chirp of a cricket, the scudding of a squirrel, filled up the void and made full compensation.

The true angler can find real pleasure in catching little sunfish, or silver-sides, if the stream and birds, and bees and butterflies do their part by him; while the killing of large or many fish, even salmon or trout, in silence and solitude, may fail to fully satisfy him.

I can find something beautiful or interesting in every fish that swims. I have an abiding affection for everyone, from the lowly, naked bull-head, the humble scavenger of the waters, to the silver-spangled king who will not deign to soil his dainty lips with food during his sojourn in crystal streams, and I love the brook trout best of all. But, as an angler, I can find more true enjoyment, more blessed peace, in wading some rushing, rocky stream, flecked by the shadows of over-hanging elm and sycamore, while tossing the silken gage to the knight in Lincoln-green, my ears conscious of the rippling laughter of the merry stream, the joyous matin of the woodland thrush, the purring undertone of the quivering leaves—my eyes catching glimpses of hill and meadow, wren and robin, bee and bittern, fern and flower, and my breath inhaling the sweet fragrance of upland clover and elder-blossom—I say I can find more true enjoyment in this— than paying court to the lordly salmon in his drear and silent demesne, or in wooing the lovely trout with anointed face, gloved hands, and head swathed in gauze.

If this be treason, my brother, make the most of it. I am content. It is my honest conviction. After killing every species of game-fish east of the Rocky

Bass are often found in picturesque lakes. This one is in New York's Adirondack Mountains. Photo Credit: Jay Cassell.

Mountains, from Canada to Florida, and some in foreign lands, I find the knightly bass and his tourney-field all sufficient.

The Capture of the Bass
My brother of the angle, go with me
This perfect morning in the leafy June,
To yonder pool below the rapid's foot.
Approach with caution; let your tread be soft;
Beware the bending bushes on the brink.
Disturb no branch, nor twig, nor leaf, my friend,
The finny tribe is wary.

Rest we here.
Behold the lovely scene!
The rippling stream,
Now dancing, sparkling, in the morning sun;
The blue-eyed violet nodding at your feet;
The red-bird, all ablaze, with swelling throat,
The dreamy, droning hum of insect wings
Is mingled ever with the rustling leaves.
Sleek, well-fed cattle there contented stand,
On gravelly shoal beneath the spreading beech.
Across the narrow stream a sycamore,
A weather-beaten giant, old and gray,
With scarr'd arms stretching o'er the silent pool,
With gnarl'd and twisted roots bathed in the flood
For, lo, these hundred years.

Beneath those roots
With watchful eye—proud monarch of the pool—
A cunning bass doth lie, on balanced fin,
In waiting for his prey.

And now with rod,
With faithful reel, and taper'd line of silk,
With mist-like leader and two fairly flies—
Dark, bush hackles, both—I make a cast.

With lengthen'd line I quickly cast again,
And just beneath the tree the twin-like lures
As gently drop as falling autumn leaves;
And half-submerged, like things of life they seem,
Responsive to the rod and line.
But look!
Saw you that gleam beneath the flood?
A flash—
A shadow—then a swirl upon the pool?
My hand, responsive to the sudden thrill,
Strikes in the steel—the wary bass is hooked!
And now with lightning speed he darts away
To reach his lair—his refuge 'neath the roots.
The singing reel proclaims him almost there—
I "give the butt"—the ever-faithful rod
In horse-shoe curve checks his headlong flight.
Right lustily he tugs and pulls, Egad!
But still the barb is fast.

The hissing line—
The rod now bending like a slender reed
Resists the tight'ning strain. He turns his course—
In curving reaches, back and forth, he darts,
Describing arcs and segments in the pool.
Ha! nobly done! as with a mighty rush
He cleaves the crystal stream, and at one bound,
Full half a fathom in the realm above

He nimbly takes an atmospheric flight—
His fins extended, stiff with bristling points—
His armor brightly flashing in the sun—
His wide-extended jaws he shakes in rage
To rid him of the hook.

And now I lower
The pliant rod in court'sy to the brave.
The line relieved, somewhat, of steady strain,
Outwits the wily bass—the hook holds fast!
Now back again he falls with angry splash
To seek the aid of snag, or root of tree;

For thus, my friend, he oft escapes, I trow,
By fouling line or hook—
He never sulks!
Not he; while life remains, or strength holds good,
His efforts never cease.
Now up the stream—
Now down again—I have him well in hand.
Now reeling in, or erstwhile giving line;
He swims now fast or slow—now high or low.
The steady strain is still maintained, you see!
The good rod swaying like a wind-blown rush—
He surges thro' the flood.

Another leap!
Ye Gods! How like an angry beast he shakes
His brisling mane, and dives below again!
And did you mark, my friend, his shrewd intent,
As when he fell upon the slacken'd line?
If then he'd found it stretched and taut, I ween,

He would have made his safe and sure escape.
But haply then the tip was slightly lowered—
And so, with yielding line, the hook held fast.
Now truly, friend, he makes a gallant fight!
In air or water—all the same to him—
His spiny crest erect; he struggles still.
No sulking here! but like a mettl'd steed
He champs the bit, and ever speeds the best
With firm-held, tighten'd rein.

He's off again!
Now down the stream he flashes like a shaft
From long-bow swiftly sped—his last bold spurt—
The effort cost him dear—his worsted strength
Is ebbing fast. And now in lessening curves
He feebly swims, and labors with the tide.
And as I reel the line he slowly yields,
And now turns up his breast-plate, snowy white—
A vanquished, conquered knight.

And now my friend
The landing-net.
With firm and cautious hand
Beneath the surface hold it.
Take him in.
Now lift him out and gently lay him down.
How bright his tunic, bronze and glossy green!
A fitting rival to the velvet sward.
And see the ragged rent the hook hath made!
You marvel how it held him safe and fast!
'Twas by the equal and continual strain
Of supple rod and ever-faithful reel.

'Twas work well done.

Oh valiant, noble bass!
Fit dweller of the merry, brawling stream.
Thy once-loved pool beneath thy giant tree,
Thy fancied stronghold 'neath its tangled roots,
Shall know thee never more. Thy race is run!

Now in thy creel,
My doubting friend, we'll gently lay him down
Upon a bed of cool and graceful ferns,
Yet sparkling with the early morning dew—
A warrior in repose!

Life-Size Black Bass by Winslow Homer, 1904. Art Institute of Chicago.

CHAPTER 5

CARP FISHING

BY "FRANK FORESTER" [HENRY WILLIAM HERBERT]

A rendering of a carp.

This, I confess, I regard as very miserable sport; for though the fish is shy and wary, the difficulty in taking him arises only from his timidity and unwillingness to bite, and he is as lazy when hooked as he is slow to bite.

His proper haunts are deep, stagnant, slow-flowing streams, or ponds with muddy bottoms; and he lies under weeds, and among the stems and flat leaves of water-lilies, flags, and marsh-grasses.

Not indigenous to this country, he has been naturalized in the waters of the Hudson, where he is, for the present, protected by severe legislative enactments. He will doubtless, ere long, become very plentiful; and as he is a rich fish when cooked *secundum artem*, and by many esteemed a great delicacy, he is likely enough to become a favorite with the angler.

Hofland thus describes the method of baiting the ground and fishing for Carp in England, and his directions are the best I have seen; they may be followed with implicit confidence:

"In rivers, the Carp prefer those parts where the current is not too strong, and where the bottom is marly, or muddy; and in lakes or ponds are to be found near beds of water-lilies, and other aquatic plants. Old Carp are very crafty and wary, and will not easily be taken by the angler; but young ones, when a pond is well stocked, may be easily taken in great quantities.

"Notwithstanding these instances of familiarity, it is by no means easy to make a large Carp familiar with your bait: to do this, the greatest nicety and caution must be observed; but if the young angler, who has been often foiled in his attempts, will patiently and implicitly follow my instructions, he will become a match for this cunning fish.

"Use a strong rod with running-tackle, and have a bottom of three yards of fineish gut, and a hook No. 9 or 10; use a very light quill-float, that will carry two small shot, and bait with a well-scoured red worm.

"Now plumb the depth with the greatest nicety, and let your bait just touch, or all but touch, the bottom; but you are not yet prepared; for a forked stick must be fixed into the bank, on which you must let your rod rest, so that the float will fall over the exact spot you have plumbed. Now throw in a sufficient quantity of ground-bait, of bread and bran worked into a paste, and made into little balls; or, in want of these, throw in the garbage of chickens or ducks; and all this is to be done on the evening of the day before you intend to fish.

"The next morning, if in summer, be at the pond-side where you have baited and plumbed your depth, by four o'clock at least, and, taking your rod and line, which is already fixed to the exact depth, bait with a small, bright, red, worm; then approach the water cautiously, keeping out of sight as much as possible, and drop your bait exactly over the spot you plumbed over night; then rest part of your rod on the forked stick, and the bottom of it on the ground.

"You must now retire a few paces, keeping entirely out of sight, but still near enough to observe your float; when you perceive a bite, give a little time;

indeed, it is better to wait till you see the float begin to move off, before you strike, which you may then do smartly; and, as the Carp is a leather-mouthed fish, if you manage him well, there is no fear of losing him, unless the pond is very weedy. Be careful to have your line free, that, if a large fish, he may run out some of your line before you attempt to turn him; as he is a very strong fish, and your tackle rather light, you must give him careful play before you land him.

"The extreme shyness of the large Carp makes all this somewhat tedious process necessary to insure success; but I can safely assert, that I scarcely ever took this trouble in vain. Various baits are recommended for Carp, such as green peas parboiled, pastes of all descriptions, gentles, caterpillars, &c.; but I have found the red worm the best, and next to this, the gentle and plain bread-paste. Those who prefer a sweet paste may dip the bread in honey. Paste and gentle will answer better in autumn than spring. April and May are, in my opinion, the best months for Carp fishing; and very early in the morning, or late in the evening, is the best time for pursuing your sport."

The above mode of baiting bottom-grounds, and of fishing with the worm, in all its particulars, may be pursued with perfect success in all ponds and slow-running streams, for all the many species of the Carp family, which are, for the most part, the least carnivorous of fishes, and consequently the most difficult to allure, as the Bream, Roach, Dace, Chub, and Shiner, as they are provincially termed, though by no means identical with the European fishes of the same names. The Suckers (Catastomi), a sub-genus of the same family, will hardly take any bait whatsoever.

While fishing, as above described, both small river Perch and Eels of all sizes are likely to be hooked, as the baited bottom-ground allures all those species which seek their food at the bottom to its vicinity.

CHAPTER 6

A BIG MUSKELLUNGE

BY W. N. HULL

A muskellunge, often called the "wolf of the waters."

The summer days began to drag. The brick walls of the city glimmered in the hot sunshine. Offices were like bake-ovens.

"Let's escape to the country," said Bob, fanning himself vigorously and mopping the perspiration from his jolly fat face.

"I know what's on your mind, Bob; you want another dog-fish."

"Let's go this time for muskellunge."

It was scarcely necessary for him to make the suggestion; I was ready to do anything to escape the terrible heat.

Next evening found us on board one of the boats of the Goodrich Line, steaming slowly out of the Chicago River and cutting a passage through the black veil of night which hung like a pall over the lake.

After a more refreshing sleep upon the cool waters of the lake than the summer had so far granted us, we landed next morning at Grand Haven. We transferred to a smaller steamer, and in two hours more we found ourselves fanned by the cool air of the upper lakes, and we turned into the Muskegon River and ran up to the city of Muskegon.

How delightful it is on a hot summer day to sit forward upon the upper deck of a lake steamer and be fanned by the rushing air as the boat speeds along!

We hire an electric launch to take us over to the other side of the bay, and there engage a man with a rowboat to row us up the bay while we take turns trolling for the muskellunge.

Our line is at least three hundred feet long and a good strong one. On the end is a monster spoon-hook, gaily ornamented with gaudy feathers. We want a large fish or none.

Bob now has the line on the stern seat, Charley is at the oars, and I am the gentleman at the bow. The gaff-hook lies near me, and I may have one stroke of skillful work to do. We are about fifty feet from the shore. Bob plays out two hundred feet of line, and Charley is rowing so slowly that there is scarcely a move of the water. The wind has risen slightly and raises a ripple upon the lake. This is favorable for a good catch.

An hour passes, and we have not had a strike. Charley says the fish are here, and we must be patient and keep a sharp lookout. We talk in low voices, and the fish are not frightened by anything uncommon among them this beautiful summer morning.

We started in at nine o'clock, and it is now ten. The movement and work are lazy and monotonous, and day-dreaming is creeping over the rower and the gentleman in the bow.

But Bob is alert. He has the business end of the expedition. He is an old fisherman and a true lover of the sport. He draws upon the line, causing the spoon to revolve more swiftly, and again lets it out, giving the spoon a slower movement. Memory goes wool-gathering and roams across the continent. Again I am at Pacific Cottage on the Atlantic shore and the delightful days pass all too quickly; but my dreams are almost broken and we are almost upset by Bob, who springs to his feet shouting, "A strike! A strike!"

Sure enough, the line is playing out fast, and the "whale," as Charley calls him, is taking—we were about to say a bee-line, but probably it would be more correct to call it a fish-line—for his haunts in deep water. Bob holds him with a firm and skillful hand.

"He's well hooked," says Charley. "There's plenty of sport ahead for you city chaps. Ten to one you don't land him."

"I take you," says Bob, but does not take his eye off the line, nor his hands from the push and pull.

Now the fish changes his mind and shoots for the shore, but finding himself in shallow water, he turns again. In the shallow water we have caught glimpses that lead us to believe he is a rare fish.

"How much will he weigh, Charley?" I ask.

"With his own scales?" says Charley interrogatively, with a cunning look. "Any way," I answer, and feel I have silenced Charley with my witty gun, but his reply takes a more practical turn:

"Don't count your chickens before they are hatched, nor weigh your fish till he is caught," and he slowly turns the boat as he sees the fish make a break up the lake.

"The line is all out, and he is actually pulling us along." It does seem so, and naturally we wonder if the line will stand the strain.

"Turn again, Charley; he's running down the lake," and Bob reaches rapidly hand over hand upon the slacking line.

The muskellunge is called the "wolf of the waters" and is the hardest fighter ever hooked. Bob's fish thrashes the waters like a mad bull. He jumps and he turns. He strikes with his tail, and whirls with a sudden wrench upon the line that tests its strength and his own jaws. But every effort and every swift run weakens him. He cares less and less for escape, and comes nearer the boat.

I have the gaff-hook ready.

"Pull him a little nearer, Bob," I shout.

"I can't do it," says Bob, "let him go again."

But he does not turn very far. Again Bob pulls him toward the boat, in and out, in and out for at least an hour and a half.

In the meantime Charley is telling how, away up in the mountain streams, two men in a canoe, with pole and reel, have great sport catching these big fellows that have crept up, like the salmon of the Pacific, as far as possible, to spawn.

"Strike him! Yank him in!" shouts Bob.

I am standing in the boat, keeping it as steady as I can, as I watch my chance.

A wrong blow may break the hook or line and the fish will be lost. "Next time, sure," I reply.

Now he comes so near that his whole body is seen, and he seems to be pausing to take breath. I take a careful blow with the gaff-hook and a sudden pull toward the boat. The fish comes in.

"Jump on him! Where's the hatchet?" shouts Bob. "He's the wolf of the waters, and will fight to the bitter end."

The hatchet lies at Charley's feet. He seizes it and with one blow with the sharp edge he splits the captive's head almost open, and the fish is surely ours; he quivers a little, and gives up his life.

"How much will he weigh now, Charley?"

"Thirty pounds," says Charley.

Later the scales reveal the fact that Charley was excited eight pounds, for the fish actually weighs but twenty-two pounds.

Bob's face is flushed with excitement. He chuckles and laughs, still keeping his eye upon the fish and stroking him occasionally all the way down to dinner.

"Isn't he a beauty?"

"Looks much like a pickerel."

"He is broader and more chunky."

"Tell you how we'll have him cooked. We'll have him stuffed, covered with slices of salt pork, and baked."

"If we had him down at the office we could bake him without an oven."

"Now, don't say office here; it sickens me to think of it."

But when we did return to the office, of all the stories Bob told to the calling friends, this is the one that he lingered longest over and made the most of. He always affirms that this was one of the best sporting events of his life.

CHAPTER 7

FISHING IN THE OHIO

BY JOHN JAMES AUDUBON

The Black River, Elyria, Ohio.

It is with mingled feelings of pleasure and regret that recall to my mind the many pleasant days I have spent on the shores of the Ohio. The visions of former years crowd on my view, as I picture to myself the fertile soil and genial atmosphere of our great western garden, Kentucky, and view the placid waters of the fair stream that flows along its western boundary. Methinks I am now on the banks of the noble river. Twenty years of my life have returned to me; my sinews are strong, and the "bowstring of my spirit is not slack"; bright visions of the future float before me, as I sit on a grassy bank, gazing on the glittering waters. Around me are dense forests of lofty trees and thickly tangled undergrowth, amid which are heard the songs of feathered choristers, and from whose boughs hang clusters of glowing fruits and beautiful flowers. Reader, I am very happy. But now the dream has vanished, and here I am in the British Athens, penning an episode for my *Ornithological Biography*, and having before me sundry well-thumbed and weather-beaten folios, from which I expect to be able to extract some interesting particulars respecting the methods employed in those days in catching Cat-fish.

But, before entering on my subject, I will present you with a brief description of the place of my residence on the banks of the Ohio. When I first landed at Henderson in Kentucky, my family, like the village, was quite small. The latter consisted of six or eight houses; the former of my wife, myself, and a young child. Few as the houses were, we fortunately found one empty. It was a log-cabin, not a log-house; but as better could not be had, we were pleased. Well, then, we were located. The country around was thinly peopled, and all purchasable provisions rather scarce; but our neighbors were friendly, and we had brought with us flour and bacon-hams. Our pleasures were those of young people not long married, and full of life and merriment; a single smile from our infant was, I assure you, more valued by us than all the treasures of a modern Croesus would have been. The woods were amply stocked with game, the river with fish; and now and then the hoarded sweets of the industrious bees were brought from some hollow tree to our little table. Our child's cradle was our richest piece of furniture, our guns and fishing-lines our most serviceable implements, for although we began to cultivate a garden, the rankness of the soil kept the seeds we planted far beneath the tall weeds that sprung up the first year. I had then a partner, a "man of business," and there was also with me a Kentucky youth, who much preferred the sports of the forest and river to either day-book or ledger. He was naturally, as I may say, a good woodsman, hunter, and angler, and, like me, thought chiefly of procuring supplies of fish and fowl. To the task accordingly we directed all our energies.

Quantity as well as quality was an object with us, and although we well know that three species of Cat-fish existed in the Ohio, and that all were sufficiently good, we were not sure as to the best method of securing them. We determined, however, to work on a large scale, and immediately commenced making a famous "trot-line." Now, reader, as you may probably know nothing about this engine, I shall describe it to you.

A trot-line is one of considerable length and thickness, both qualities, however, varying according to the extent of water, and the size of the fish you expect to catch. As the Ohio, at Henderson, is rather more than half a mile in breadth, and as its fishes weigh from one to a hundred pounds, we manufactured a line which measured about two hundred yards in length, as thick as the little finger of some fair one yet in her teens, and as white as the damsel's finger well could be, for it was wholly of Kentucky cotton, just, let me tell you, because that substance stands the water better than either hemp or flax. The main line finished, we made a hundred smaller ones, about five feet in length, to each of which we fastened a capital hook of Kirby and Co.'s manufacture. Now for the bait!

It was the month of May. Nature had brought abroad myriads of living beings: they covered the earth, glided through the water, and swarmed in the air. The Cat-fish is a voracious creature, not at all nice in feeding, but one who, like the vulture, contents himself with carrion when nothing better can be had. A few experiments proved to us that, of the dainties with which we tried to allure them to our hooks, they gave a decided preference, at that season, to live toads. These animals were very abundant about Henderson. They ramble or feed, whether by instinct or reason, during early or late twi-light more than at any other time, especially after a shower, and are unable to bear the heat of the sun's rays for several hours before and after noon. We have a good number of these crawling things in America, particularly in the western and southern parts of the Union, and are very well supplied with frogs, snakes, lizards, and even crocodiles, which we call alligators; but there is enough of food for them all, and we generally suffer them to creep about, to leap or to flounder as they please, or in accordance with the habits which have been given them by the great Conductor of all.

During the month of May, and indeed until autumn, we found an abun-dant supply of toads. Many "fine ladies," no doubt, would have swooned, or

A catfish.

at least screamed and gone into hysterics, had they seen one of our baskets filled with these animals, all alive and plump. Fortunately we had no trage-dy queen or sentimental spinster at Henderson. Our Kentucky ladies mind their own affairs, and seldom meddle with those of others farther than to do all they can for their comfort. The toads, collected one by one, and brought home in baskets, were deposited in a barrel for use. And now that night is over, and as is the first trial we are going to give our trot-line, just watch our movements from that high bank beside the stream. There sit down under the large cotton-wood tree. You are in no danger of catching cold at this season.

My assistant follows me with a gaff hook, while I carry the paddle of our canoe; a boy bears on his back a hundred toads as good as ever hopped. Our line—oh, I forgot to inform you that we had set it last night, but without the small ones you now see on my arm. Fastening one end to yon sycamore, we paddled our canoe, with the rest nicely coiled in the stern, and soon reached its extremity, when I threw over the side the heavy stone fastened to it as a sinker. All this was done that it might be thoroughly soaked, and without kinks or snarls in the morning. Now, you observe, we launch our light bark, the toads in the basket are placed next to my feet in the bow; I have the small lines across my knees already looped at the end. Nat, with the paddle, and assisted by the current, keeps the stern of our boat directly downstream; and David fixes, by the skin of the back and hind parts, the living bait to the hook. I hold the main line all the while, and now, having fixed one linelet to it, over goes the latter. Can you see the poor toad kicking and flouncing in the water? "No"—well, I do. You observe at length that all the lines, one after another, have been fixed, baited, and dropped. We now return swiftly to the shore.

"What a delightful thing is fishing!" have I more than once heard some knowing angler exclaim, who, "with the patience of Job," stands or slowly moves along some rivulet twenty feet wide, and three or four feet deep, with a sham fly to allure a trout, which, when at length caught, weighs half a pound. Reader, I never had such patience. Although I have waited ten years, and yet seen only three-fourths of the Birds of America engraved, although some of the drawings of that work were patiently made so long ago as 1805, and although I have to wait with patience two years more before I see the end of it, I never could hold a line or a rod for many minutes, unless I had—not a "nibble," but a hearty bite, and could throw the fish at once over my head on the ground. No, no—if I fish for trout, I must soon give up, or catch, as I have done in Pennsylvania's Lehigh, or the streams of Maine, fifty or more in a couple of hours. But the trot-line is in the river, and there it may patiently wait, until I visit it toward night. Now I take up my gun and note-book, and, accompanied by my dog, intend to ramble through the woods until breakfast. Who knows but I may shoot a turkey or a deer? It is barely four o'clock; and see what delightful mornings we have at this season in Kentucky!

Evening has returned. The heavens have already opened their twinkling eyes, although the orb of day has yet scarcely withdrawn itself from our view. How calm is the air! The nocturnal insects and quadrupeds are abroad; the bear is moving through the dark cane-brake, the land crows are flying towards their roosts, their aquatic brethren towards the interior of the forests, the squirrel is barking his adieu, and the Barred Owl glides silently and swiftly from his retreat, to seize upon the gay and noisy animal. The boat is pushed off from the shore; the mainline is in my hands; now it shakes; surely some fish have been hooked. Hand over hand I proceed to the first hook. Nothing there! But now I feel several jerks stronger and more frequent than before. Several hooks I pass; but see, what a fine Cat-fish is twisting around and round the little line to which he is fast! Nat, look to your gaff—hook him close to the tail. Keep it up, my dear fellow!—there now, we have him. More are on, and we proceed. When we have reached the end many goodly fishes are lying in the bottom of our skiff. New bait has been put on, and, as we return, I congratulate myself and my companions on the success of our efforts; for there lies fish enough for ourselves and our neighbors.

A trot-line at this period was perfectly safe at Henderson, should I have allowed it to remain for weeks at a time. The navigation was mostly performed by flat-bottomed boats, which during calm nights floated in the middle current of the river, so that the people on board could not observe the fish that had been hooked. Not a single steamer had as yet ever gone down the Ohio; now and then, it is true, a barge or a keel-boat was propelled by poles and oars; but the nature of the river is such at that place, that these boats when ascending were obliged to keep near the Indian shore until above the landing of the village (below which I always fixed my lines), when they pulled across the stream.

Several species or varieties of Cat-fish are found in the Ohio, namely the Blue, the White, and the Mud Cats, which differ considerably in their form and color, as well as in their habits. The Mud Cat is the best, although it seldom attains so great a size as the rest. The Blue Cat is the coarsest, but when not exceeding from four to six pounds, it affords tolerable eating. The White Cat is preferable to the last, but not so common; and the Yellow Mud Cat is the best and rarest. Of the blue kind some have been caught that weighed a hundred pounds. Such fishes, however, are looked upon as monsters.

The form in all the varieties inclines to the conical, the head being disproportionately large, while the body tapers away to the root of the tail. The eyes, which are small, are placed far apart, and situated as it were on the top of the forehead, but laterally. Their mouth is wide, and armed with numerous small and very sharp teeth, while it is defended by single-sided spines, which when the fish is in the agonies of death, stand out at right angles, and are so firmly fixed as sometimes to break before you can loosen them. The Cat-fish has also feelers of proportionate length, apparently intended to guide its motions over the bottom, whilst its eyes are watching the objects passing above.

Trot-lines cannot be used with much success unless during the middle stages of the water. When very low, it is too clear, and the fish, although extremely voracious, will rarely risk its life for a toad. When the waters are rising rapidly, your trot-lines are likely to be carried away by one of the numerous trees that float in the stream. A "happy medium" is therefore best.

When the waters are rising fast and have become muddy, a single line is used for catching Cat-fish. It is fastened to the elastic branch of some willow several feet above the water, and must be twenty or thirty feet in length. The entrails of a Wild Turkey, or a piece of fresh venison, furnish good bait; and if,

A white perch.

when you visit your line the next morning after you have set it, the water has not risen too much, the swinging of the willow indicates that a fish has been hooked, and you have only to haul the prize ashore.

One evening I saw that the river was rising at a great rate, although it was still within its banks. I knew that the White Perch were running, that is, ascending the river from the sea, and anxious to have a tasting of that fine fish, I baited a line with a crayfish, and fastened it to the bough of a tree. Next morning as I pulled in the line, it felt as if fast at the bottom, yet on drawing it slowly I found that it came. Presently I felt a strong pull, the line slipped through my fingers, and next instant a large Cat-fish leaped out of the water. I played it for a while, until it became exhausted, when I drew it ashore. It had swallowed the hook, and I cut off the line close to its head. Then passing a stick through one of the gills, I and a servant tugged the fish home. On cutting it open, we, to our surprise, found in its stomach a fine White Perch, dead, but not in the least injured.

The Perch had been lightly hooked, and the Cat-fish, after swallowing it, had been hooked in the stomach, so that, although the instrument was small, the torture caused by it no doubt tended to disable the Cat-fish. The Perch we ate, and the cat, which was fine, we divided into four parts, and distributed among our neighbors. My most worthy friend and relative, Nicholas Berthoud, Esq., who formerly resided at Shippingport in Kentucky, but now in New York, a better fisher than whom I never knew, once placed a trot-line in "the basin" below "Tarascon's Mills," at the foot of the Rapids of the Ohio, I cannot recollect the bait which was used; but on taking up the line we obtained a remarkably fine Cat-fish, in which was found the greater part of a suckling pig!

SECTION III
A TOUCH OF SALT

CHAPTER 8

THE TARPON OF TURNER'S RIVER

BY A. W. DIMOCK

A Florida tarpon.

Marco is the name of a post office, but the place is called Collier's. Ask any child on the West Coast of Florida about Marco and he will shake his head, but mention Collier and the infant will brighten up and say: "Dat's Tap'n Bill!" Island, bay, hotel, houses, boat-building plant, and even the atmosphere are, and always have been, Collier's. When Ponce de Leon was cavorting about the peninsula pestering the inhabitants with his inquiries about a spring, he stopped at Collier's. Everybody who goes down the coast stops there. The only way to avoid a long detour around the Cape Romano Shoals is to go through Collier's Bay to Coon Key, and one cannot pass through Collier's Bay without calling at the store.

Summer is the time to visit Collier. When the little mail boat lands me with my family at the dock Captain Bill meets me with:

"Well, how are you? The hotel isn't open, you know."

"Glad of it. That's why I am here. Where's that baggage truck?"

Then I wheel our baggage to the hotel, we select the choice rooms, and spread our belongings all over the place as if we owned the whole business. When the dinner bell rings we sit down with the family and occasional tramps like ourselves who stop in on their way down the coast. Instead of the colorless crowd of tourists who occupy the tables when the hotel is open, we meet itinerant preachers and teachers, lighthouse keepers and land seekers, scientists and Seminoles.

We take possession of the island, and wandering forth with big baskets return laden with a score of varieties of fruits from avocado, pears, bananas, and cocoanuts down through the alphabet to sapadilloes and tamarinds.

As evening approaches we sit on the sheltered piazza that overlooks the bay, and, if the tide favors, watch the porpoises at play, and, more rarely, we witness the dizzy leaps of a dozen or a score of tarpon each minute.

From Collier's Bay to Coon Key the channel twists and turns among sand flats and oyster reefs, between wooded banks and around tiny keys without blaze or buoy, stake, or sign to point out the path. After years of observation and practice I can take a boat over the course, if the day is clear, without running on a bank more than once in three trips.

Yet a boy to the manner born has piloted me through the maze on a night so dark that I could scarcely see his face as I sat beside him. He chatted with me throughout the trip with his hand resting carelessly on the wheel which he idly swung to and fro without apparent thought or purpose. His every act was so casual that I had just figured out that we were hopelessly lost somewhere in the Ten Thousand Islands when he leaned past me to shut off the gasoline from the motor. A minute later the boat rubbed gently against some object that I couldn't see.

"Where are we?" I asked.

"At your own dock," was the amazing reply.

My captain carried us over the same course in the same mysterious manner and I was only sure we had passed Coon Key through the broader sweep of the wind and the gentle rise and fall of the boat on the slight swell from the Gulf. Going down the coast I got my bearings and felt rather than saw its familiar features. I was conscious of the nearness of Horse and Panther Keys, and off Gomez Point I had a mental picture of the old man for whom it was named as I last saw him at his home. He was then well along in his second century, and year by year his recollection of the first Napoleon, under whom he served, became clearer and of the details of their intimacy more distinct. Sand-fly Pass, leading to Chokoloskee Bay, was our goal for the night, and nothing but a nose was needed to find it even in Cimmerian darkness. Its mouth was guarded by a pelican key, from which a rookery of the birds sent forth lines of stench as a Fresnal lens radiates light.

In the morning we entered Chokoloskee Bay, and crossing it anchored within the mouth of Allen's River, near the Storter store.

Chokoloskee Bay, Florida.

For nearly two miles Allen's River is a considerable stream. Beyond that distance it divides and spreads over flats until it is only navigable to a light draft skiff. Near the mouth of the river we caught and released a few tarpon of good size, but when a mile up the stream I struck a ten-pound fish I returned to the Irene and rigged up an eight-ounce fly rod. The fish rose best to a tiny strip of mullet, cast and skittered along the surface, or trolled. They preferred light flies to those of more brilliant coloring. Yet their tastes changed as often as the colors of a chameleon, and they turned up their noses to-day at the lure that best pleased them yesterday.

The light fly rod is too flexible to fasten the hook in the hard mouth of the tarpon with any approach to certainty. In the beginning the fly fisherman will fail, nine times out of ten, to fasten the hook in the mouth of the striking tarpon. Then he will learn to thrust the butt of his rod away from the fish when it seizes the bait, and clutching the line or reel bring a strong, straight pull to bear on the hook in the mouth of the fish.

My first fish on the fly rod in Allen River weighed about four pounds, but it took longer to land than its predecessor of twenty times that weight. It led me into a narrow creek where an out-thrusting branch from the bank forced me to step out of the canoe in water waist deep. I followed the fish up the shallowing stream, walking on the bank when the bushes permitted and wading in the channel when trees came to the water's edge.

When the tarpon had had fun enough with me in shallow water it led me back to the deeper river. I nearly capsized the canoe as I got aboard while playing the fish, which cavorted up and down and across the stream, leaping several feet in the air every minute or two for a quarter of an hour before yielding.

In two days I had a score of strikes and landed half that number of tarpon after an average contest of an hour with each. The largest one was four feet long and weighed therefore about thirty-two pounds, but it was an exceptionally active fish and wore itself out in half an hour. By a series of frantic leaps, one of which took it over the bow of the canoe within reach of my hand.

During the two days' fishing there was seldom an interval of ten minutes between the landing of one tarpon and the strike of its successor. On the third day the tarpon were as abundant as ever and jumped all around the canoe, but not a strike could I get. If Solomon had ever fished for tarpon he would have added the way of a tarpon in the water to that of an eagle in the air, a serpent on a rock, and the other things that were beyond his comprehension.

We sailed to the south end of Chokoloskee Bay, where Turner's River connects it with the network of waterways through which tidal water flows in all directions around the big and little keys of the Ten Thousand Islands which extend from Cape Romano to Sable. Channels navigable to tarpon of the greatest draft connect Turner's River with the Gulf of Mexico, while from scores of tiny streams and shallow watercourses it collects the output of many tarpon nurseries.

I began business on Turner's River with an eight-ounce fly rod, and soon was fast to a ten-pound tarpon which thirty minutes later was captured and freed half a mile up the stream. Scarcely had a fresh lure been thrown out when there was a tug on my line and, as I believe, the largest tarpon that was ever caught on a fly rod shot a dozen feet in the air. Three times in quick succession it leaped violently, shaking its head to dislodge the hook.

Down the river the tarpon dashed till only a few feet of line was left on my little reel. The slight strain I could put on the line wouldn't have feazed a fish one tenth the size of the one to which I was fast. I needed more yards than I had feet of line to offer a chance of tiring this creature whose length exceeded mine by a foot. One more stroke of that propeller tail and my goose would be cooked.

I yelled to the captain to paddle for his life, regardless of the fact that he was already putting in licks that endangered it. Soon he was gaining faster than I could take in line and I shouted to him to slow up, changing the next instant to a cry to go ahead. When the trouble was over I asked the captain if I had screamed at him very often.

"Most all the time, but I didn't mind. I knew you was excited and didn't rightly know what you said," was his reply.

The line never again ran so low as in that first dash of the tarpon. Yet a hundred times the end of our hopes seemed near, but always the fish swam slower, or the captain paddled faster. The wild leaps of the creature were startling but welcome, for they tired the tarpon without carrying away line. We had followed the fish up, down, and across the river, and after an hour's struggle were well out in the bay, yet at all times we had kept within two hundred feet of our quarry.

Always we feared the tarpon's getting too far away. Sometimes the danger was of its coming too near, and more than once it sprang at us with wide-open jaws, falling short of the canoe by inches only, and once it sprang fairly against the captain, nearly capsizing the craft.

The sport of fishing is in inverse ratio to the size of the tackle compared with the activity, strength, and weight of the fish. Linus Yale, as skillful with trout as he was ingenious with locks, used to hitch his horse to a tree by a mountain brook near his New England home and forget for the day the anxieties of the inventor and the burdens of the manufacturer.

All trouble was left behind as he constructed a line from hairs in his horse's tail, attached a hook of his own forging, tinier than was ever made before, with an almost microscopic fly, and with a reed like rod, made on the ground, captured the wariest trout in the brook. When with this flimsy tackle he landed a trout of large size he rejoiced more than when picking the Hobbs lock gave him world-wide fame.

As I followed my big fish the game increased in interest. It was more like chess than fishing. Strength availed little, for the utmost strain I could put on the line through the light rod was no restraint on the powerful tarpon. The creature must be made to tire itself out and do the chief work in its own capture and at the same time be kept within the narrow limits that the shortness of my line established.

When the reel was nearly empty the line was held lightly, while the captain paddled strongly. As we neared the quarry a quick twitch of the line usually sent the tarpon high in the air and off on another dash. As the reel buzzed the captain invited apoplexy by his efforts, while I encouraged him to increase them.

At times the fish seemed to be on to our game and refused to jump when called on. It even became immune to the splash of the paddle and made an ingenious move that threatened checkmate. The tarpon was beside us and the line short when it dived beneath the canoe and swam swiftly away on the other side. There is only one move to meet that attack, and it usually ends in a broken rod and a lost fish. I dropped the rod flat on the water, thrusting it beneath the surface elbow deep, while my finger kept a light pressure on the line. Happily the tip swung to the tarpon without breaking and the fish was played from a rod under water until the captain had turned the canoe around.

The strain of a single pound on a fly rod is more exhausting to the fisherman than ten or even twenty times that pull on a tarpon rod, and I was glad when the camera man said he had used his last plate and offered to change places with me. Usually when plates were out we got rid of the fish as soon as we could, but this was an unusual fish, destined to hold long the record for an eight-ounce rod capture, if once we could slide it over the side of the little canoe. The craft might be swamped the next minute, but the record would be safe.

The tarpon noticed the new hand at the bellows and went over his repertoire brilliantly. He traveled a mile up the river in search of a place to hide from the human gadfly that worried him and sulked under a bank for some minutes before allowing himself to be coaxed out. He pranced down the stream to the hay, with occasional leaps by the way, and the captain struggled mightily every foot of the course to keep within the limits of the line. In the bay a new terror possessed him and he dashed about as if crazy.

He saw his fate in the thing that he couldn't shake off, as the creature of the forest knows when the wolf is on his track, and he exhausted himself in his panic. Then he rolled over and lay quietly on his back with gasping gills in apparent surrender while the canoe was paddled beside him.

"I'm afraid we'll capsize if I take it aboard," said the captain.

"Get it in the canoe first and capsize afterwards all you want, only don't move till I measure it," replied the camera man.

After the tarpon had been found to measure six feet six inches, the captain got a grip on the corner of its mouth, and lifting its head over the side of the canoe was about to slide it inside when a powerful stroke of the fish's tail sent the head outboard and the captain was given his choice between swamping the canoe or releasing the fish. He let the tarpon go, for which I abused him at the time, but forgave him later when I saw that the hook was still fast in the creature's mouth. It was many minutes before the captain got another chance at the fish, but when he had renewed his hold and was ready to haul it aboard he sang out to me:

"I'll hang on to him this time if he lands me in—Halifax, so look out for the pieces of your canoe!"

But the tarpon slid into the canoe without a flutter, and slipping under the thwarts lay flat in the bottom. The trouble came later when, the rod having been laid aside, camera man and captain worked together to get the slippery thing out from under the thwarts and overboard. They would probably have swamped the canoe anyhow, but the tarpon made the thing sure and secured his revenge by a flap of his tail that landed him in the bay with his tormentors. It was a fitting end to the adventure, for, after the final scrimmage, canoe and canoe men sadly needed the scrubbing they got in the nearby shallow water to which they swam.

We hit the top of the tarpon season at Turner's River, on the West Coast of Florida, and for three days the fish stood in line, waiting their turn like metropolitans seeking good seats at the opera or holding their places in the bread line. No sooner had we turned loose an exhausted tarpon than a fresh one presented itself for the vacant chair. Twenty tarpon a day was our score, of fish that ran from ten to thirty pounds each. Most of them were taken on the fly rod, for which they were too large, as their weight was light for a heavy rod in such blasé hands as ours were becoming by that time.

Much of the action of a fly rod is wasted with a fish of the tarpon type weighing over five pounds, and much time lost from the camera standpoint, since it is hard to hold the fish near the canoe. A stiff, single-action, tournament style of fly rod fits the agile baby tarpon down to the ground, while a withy, double-action article couldn't follow for a minute the fish's changes of mind.

"These fish are too little for the big rod, too big for the little rod, and we have nothing between," I observed to the camera man just after landing on a tarpon rod a ten-pound fish in as many minutes.

"Let's go down the coast," was the reply. "There are big fish in the big rivers and babies in the creeks at the head of Harney."

I agreed to this as I threw out a freshly baited hook and trolled for another ten pounder. But it was a tarpon of ten stone or more that struck before twenty feet of line had run out, and as the creature shot up toward the sky I shouted:

"There's a seven-footer for you, the biggest tarp of the trip!"

It may have been the biggest, but I shall never know for sure. I threw myself back on the rod with a force that would have slung a little fish to the horizon and my guaranteed rod snapped like glass. I hung on to the broken rod and the tarpon played me for a few minutes, after which he sailed away with half of my line as a trophy.

Before running down the coast we went back to the Storter store in search of a substitute for the broken rod. The captain said he could make a better rod than the old one out of anything, from a wagon tongue to a flag pole. We bought a heavy hickory hoe handle which looked unbreakable, and furnished it with extra fittings which I had on hand. As we sailed down the coast I mended the broken rod and we entered on the new campaign with three heavy tarpon rods in commission.

We were cruising in the land of the crustacean. There were reefs of oysters along the coast. Oyster bars guarded the mouths of the rivers and great bunches of the bivalves clung like fruit to the branches of the trees. Beneath us was one vast clam bed, and dropping our anchor we drove poles in the mud down which we climbed and to which we clung with one hand while digging clams out of the mud with the other. We gathered a hundred or more, as many as the most sanguine of us believed we could eat. They ranged in size from that of the little neck of New York to giant quahaugs, of which single specimens weighed over five pounds.

Our anchorage that night was beside the little pelican key that separates the mouths of Broad and Rodger's rivers, and we roasted clams on the beach beside the latter. It was the toss of a copper which stream we should fish in the morning. Their sources and mouths were the same in each caw and a creek united their middles like the band of the Siamese twins. We chose Rodger's River because of its beauty, the great palms that adorned it, and the legends connected with its abandoned plantation, rotting house, and overgrown graves.

Big herons rose sluggishly from flooded banks before us and with hoarse cries flew up the river, dangling their preposterous legs. Fly-up-the-creeks flitted silently away, while lunatic snake birds, made crazy by worms in their brains, watched us from branches that overhung the stream, and when we were almost beneath them dropped into the water as awkwardly as if they had been shot.

We admired beautiful trees, great vines, fragrant flowers, and blossoming orchids as the tarpon bait was trolled from the trailing canoe, and from the mouth of the river to the cut-off no tarpon disturbed our meditations. Hurrying sharks showed huge fins above the surface, slowly rolling porpoises turned teen eyes upon us as they passed, otters lifted their little round heads, and a great manatee, frightened by a sudden glimpse of our outfit, left a long wake of swirls like those of an outgoing liner.

Crossing to Broad River by the crooked cut-off, we traveled a mile and a half to gain a third of that distance. Projecting roots held us back, overhanging branches brushed us harshly, while with bare faces we swept away scores of great spider habitations, suspended from bridges which their occupants had engineered across the stream. Yet I had little cause of complaint, since the only spiders that ran down my neck were the few that escaped the camera man, whose position in the bow of the leading craft gave him the first chance at the arachnids, or vice versa.

As there wasn't a tarpon in Rodger's River, we looked upon trolling down its companion stream as a mere formality, yet no sooner had I put out my line after turning down Broad River than the bait was seized by a splendid specimen of the silver king. The camera man missed the early leaps, for he had been slow in getting out his artillery, but after it had been brought into action he was kept busy. We were carried up into Broad River Bay, where the channels were so overhung with manatee grass that at every turn my line was loaded almost to the breaking point.

When the motor boat, maneuvering for position, got out of the middle of the channel, the propeller twisted a wad of the grass about the shaft and the motor stopped. Then Joe leaned over the stern of the boat, with head and arms under water as he tore at the clinging mass, while the camera man relieved his mind by energetic exhortation.

The tarpon led us through Broad River Bay to a series of deep channels which we had long known as the home of the manatee, several specimens of which we had captured there. The surrender of our quarry came after we had entered the broad, shallow, island-dotted bay that stretches from the heads of Broad, Rodger's, and Lossman's rivers across to the narrow strip of swamp prairie and forest that separates it from the Everglades.

After releasing the tarpon I fished no more till we were back in Broad River, when, again, on putting out my line, the bait was seized by a tarpon whose length we estimated at five feet since we never had a chance to measure it. The fish attended strictly to business, and after a few brilliant preliminary jumps, made straight for the cut-off, where, after turning a few corners and tying the

When hooked, tarpon will fight vigorously, often jumping time and again.

line around some snags, it leaped joyously high in air, free of all bonds and in full possession of a valuable tarpon hook and a goodly section of costly line.

We traveled a mile down the river before throwing out another lure, and found ourselves in a tarpon town meeting. There were scores of them, leaping and cavorting, dashing hither and yon, and behaving as if at a big banquet, but it was a Barmecide feast, for not a food fish could be seen.

"Hang to 'em, if you can," called out the camera man as I baited my hook, "for I've had bad luck with the fish so far to-day."

"The next tarpon stays with me, or I go with him," was my reply, and the next minute one of the family was over my head, fiercely shaking his wide-open jaws to get rid of the hook. But the hook was fast and I hung to the line through the tarpon's first run, though the canoe was nearly capsized before the captain could head it for the flying fish. The thwarted creature, after three wild leaps, headed straight for the canoe, and diving under it brought the strain of his weight on the tip of the rod, which broke in two parts. I clung to the butt, and as the fish was of medium size soon brought it to the captain's hand, despite the broken tip.

We had now no rod nearer than the Irene, which was five miles distant, but the fish were in biting humor and the opportunity was not to be lost. There was a hand line in the motor boat, and I handed it to the captain, for my muscles were aching, and I thought to rest them with the paddle. The broken rod was left with the camera man, for both the hand line and the captain were strong, mix-ups with big tarpon certain, and a swim in the river the probable outcome.

One tarpon turned back so quickly, after towing us steadily for a quarter of a mile or so, that I couldn't change the course of the canoe till the fish had torn a dozen yards of line from the captain's hands and was that far behind us. The captain pulled fiercely, and the creature turned again and seemed to leap at me with wide-open jaws. Its weight fell on my arm and the side of the canoe, which would have capsized but for some quick balancing by my companion. Thereafter that afternoon the captain played the fish a bit less savagely, for which I was not sorry.

I had no dread of being swamped by a tarpon. It had happened before and would happen again, probably that very day, but I wanted it over, and expecting it every minute for hours got on my nerves.

It was late when the crisis came and we were near the mouth of the river, for each fish we struck had carried us down the stream with the ebbing tide. It was a tarpon of the largest size that turned away from an approaching hammerhead shark, and swimming beside the canoe shot high in the air directly above it.

I held my paddle without moving, waiting, waiting for the canoe to sink under me as it had done before. The captain rose to his feet as the tarpon turned in the air, and by a seeming act of volition threw himself clear of the craft.

"Glad I didn't wait for the spill," said the camera man as he turned the plate holder in his camera, "but I don't see how he missed you. What's become of the fish? Can't you get him to do it again?"

The tarpon had escaped. He had given the line a turnabout the canoe, and of course it had broken.

The Irene was in sight of the mouth of the river as I tied a new hook on the broken line and told the captain I would troll until we reached the boat. But a tarpon lay in wait for me among the oyster reefs, and after he was fast, started back up the river. He was a hard fighter and so erratic in his dashes as he tacked up the stream that every few minutes I had to give him line to keep from capsizing.

"Can't you get that fish nearer the canoe?" shouted the camera man. "How can I photograph him when you're a mile apart?"

"I'll take him inside the canoe, if you want," I replied, though I had no notion of doing it.

I hauled on the line till the fish was twice his length from me and was trying to hold him there when the creature dived till the line ran straight down. Then it loosened, and like an arrow from a bow something shot up from the depths, dashing gallons of water in my face as it passed. I couldn't look up, but I wondered what would happen. Just as I concluded that this tarpon, like the last, had cleared the canoe in his fall, the craft gave a twist, a roll, and plunged me, shoulder first, beneath the surface!

It was a few yards' swim to an oyster reef, where the captain and I re-embarked and were soon paddling for the Irene. It isn't worthwhile to change the few garments one wears when fishing for tarpon just because one has been over-board, so we sat on the deck as we were and ate clams on the half shell while Joe made clam stew for a second course and gave us our choice of stewed smoked turtle or clams for the next one.

CHAPTER 9

BYME-BY-TARPON

BY ZANE GREY

A tarpon jumping out of water, Central America.

To capture the fish is not all of the fishing. Yet there are circumstances which make this philosophy hard to accept. I have in mind an incident of angling tribulation which rivals the most poignant instant of my boyhood, when a great trout flopped for one sharp moment on a mossy stone and then was gone like a golden flash into the depths of the pool.

Some years ago I followed Attalano, my guide, down the narrow Mexican street of Tampico to the bank of the broad Panuco. Under the rosy dawn the river quivered like a restless opal. The air, sweet with the song of black-bird and meadowlark, was full of cheer; the rising sun shone in splendor on the water and the long line of graceful palms lining the opposite bank, and the tropical forest beyond, with its luxuriant foliage festooned by gray moss. Here was a day to warm the heart of any fisherman; here was the beautiful river, celebrated in many a story; here was the famous guide, skilled with oar and gaff, rich in experience. What sport I would have; what treasure of keen sensation would I store; what flavor of life would I taste this day! Hope burns always in the heart of a fisherman.

Attalano was in harmony with the day and the scene. He had cheering figure, lithe and erect, with a springy stride, bespeaking the Montezuma blood said to flow in his Indian veins. Clad in a colored cotton shirt, blue jeans, and Spanish girdle, and treading the path with brown feet never deformed by shoes, he would have stopped an artist. Soon he bent his muscular shoulders to the oars, and the ripples circling from each stroke hardly disturbed the calm Panuco. Down the stream glided long Indian canoes, hewn from trees and laden with oranges and bananas. In the stern stood a dark native wielding an enormous paddle with ease. Wild-fowl dotted the glassy expanse; white cranes and pink flamingoes graced the reedy bars; red-breasted kingfishers flew over with friendly screech. The salt breeze kissed my cheek; the sun shone with the comfortable warmth Northerners welcome in spring; from over the white sand-dunes far below came the faint boom of the ever-restless Gulf.

We trolled up the river and down, across from one rush-lined lily-padded shore to the other, for miles and miles with never a strike. But I was content, for over me had been cast the dreamy, care-dispelling languor of the South.

When the first long, low sell of the changing tide rolled in, a stronger breeze raised little dimpling waves and chased along the water in dark, quick-moving frowns. All at once the tarpon began to show, to splash, to play, to roll. It was as though they had been awakened by the stir and murmur of the miniature breakers. Broad bars of silver flashed in the sunlight, green backs cleft the little billows, wide tails slapped lazily on the water. Every yard of river seemed to hold a rolling fish. This sport increased until the long stretch of water, which had been as calm as St. Regis Lake at twilight, resembled the quick current of a Canadian stream. It was a fascinating, wonderful sight. But it was also peculiarly exasperating, because when the fish roll in this sportive, lazy way they will not bite. For an hour I trolled through this whirlpool of flying spray and twisting tarpon, with many a salty drop on my face, hearing all around me the whipping crash of breaking water.

"Byme-by-tarpon," presently remarked Attalano, favoring me with the first specimen of his English.

The rolling of the tarpon diminished, and finally ceased as noon advanced. No more did I cast longing eyes upon those huge bars of silver. They were buried treasure. The breeze quickened as the flowing tide gathered strength, and together they drove the waves higher. Attalano rowed across the

The Pánuco River, Mexico.

river into the outlet of one of the lagoons. This narrow stream was unruffled by wind; its current was sluggish and its muddy waters were clarifying under the influence of the now fast-rising tide.

By a sunken log near shore we rested for lunch. I found the shade of the trees on the bank rather pleasant, and became interested in a blue heron, a russet-colored duck, and a brown-and-black snipe, all sitting on the sunken log. Nearby stood a tall crane watching us solemnly, and above in the treetop a parrot vociferously proclaimed his knowledge of our presence. I was wondering if he objected to our invasion, at the same time taking a most welcome bite for lunch, when directly in front of me the water flew up as if propelled by some submarine power. Framed in a shower of spray I saw an immense tarpon, with mouth agape and fins stuff, close in pursuit of frantically leaping little fish.

The fact that Attalano dropped his sandwich attested to the large size and close proximity of the tarpon. He uttered a grunt of satisfaction and pushed out the boat. A school of feeding tarpon closed the mouth of the lagoon. Thousands of mullet had been cut off from their river haunts and were now leaping, flying, darting in wild haste to elude the great white monsters. In the foamy swirls I saw streaks of blood.

"Byme-by-tarpon!" called Attalano, warningly.

Shrewd guide! I had forgotten that I held a rod. When the realization dawned on me that sooner or later I would feel the strike of one of these silver tigers a keen, tingling thrill of excitement quivered over me. The primitive man asserted himself; the instinctive lust to conquer and to kill seized me, and I leaned forward, tense and strained with suspended breath and swelling throat.

Suddenly the strike came, so tremendous in its energy that it almost pulled me from my seat; so quick, fierce, bewildering that I could think of nothing but to hold on. Then the water split with a hissing sound to let out a great tarpon, long as a door, seemingly as wide, who shot up and up into the air. He wagged his head and shook it like a struggling wolf. When he fell back with a heavy splash, a rainbow, exquisitely beautiful and delicate, stood out of the spray, glowed, paled, and faded.

Five times he sprang toward the blue sky, and as many he plunged down with a thunderous crash. The reel screamed. The line sang. The rod, which I had thought stiff as a tree, bent like a willow wand. The silver king came up far astern and sheered to the right in a long, wide curve, leaving behind a white wake. Then he sounded, while I watched the line with troubled eyes. But not long did he sulk. He began a series of magnificent tactics new in my experience. He stood on his tail, then on his head; he sailed like a bird; he shook himself so violently as to make a convulsive, shuffling sound; he dove, to come up covered with mud, marring his bright sides; he closed his huge gills with a slap and, most remarkable of all, he rose in the shape of a crescent, to straighten out with such marvelous power that he seemed to actually crack like a whip.

After this performance, which left me in a condition of mental aberration, he sounded again, to begin a persistent, dragging pull which was the most disheartening of all his maneuvers; for he took yard after yard of line until he was far away from me, out in the Panuco. We followed him, and for an hour crossed to and fro, up and down, humoring him, responding to his every caprice, as if he verily were a king. At last, with a strange inconsistency more human than fishlike, he returned to the scene of his fatal error, and here in the mouth of the smaller stream he leaped once more. But it was only a ghost of his former efforts—a slow, weary rise, showing he was tired. I could see it in the weakening wag of his head. He no longer made the line whistle.

I began to recover the long line. I pumped and reeled him closer. Reluctantly he came, not yet broken in spirit, though his strength had sped. He rolled at times with a shade of the old vigor, with a pathetic manifestation of the temper that became a hero. I could see the long, slender tip of his dorsal fin, then his broad tail and finally the gleam of his silver side. Closer he came and slowly circled around the boat, eying me with great, accusing eyes. I measured him with a fisherman's glance. What a great fish! Seven feet, I calculated, at the very least.

At this triumphant moment I made a horrible discovery. About six feet from the leader the strands of the line had frayed, leaving only one thread intact. My blood ran cold and the clammy sweat broke out on my brow. My empire was not won; my first tarpon was as if he had never been. But true to my fishing instincts, I held on morosely; tenderly I handled him; with brooding care I riveted my eye on the frail place in my line, and gently, ever so gently, I began to lead the silver king shoreward. Every smallest move of his tail meant disaster to me, so when he moved it I let go of the reel. Then I would have to coax him to swim back again.

The boat touched the bank. I stood up and carefully headed my fish toward the shore, and slid his head and shoulders out on the lily-pads. One moment he lay there, glowing like mother-of-pearl, a rare fish, fresh from the sea. Then, as Attalano warily reached for the leader, he gave a gasp, a flop that deluged us with muddy water, and a lunge that spelled freedom.

I watched him swim slowly away with my bright leader dragging beside him. Is it not the loss of things which makes life bitter? What we have gained is ours; what is lost is gone, whether fish, or use, or love, or name, or fame.

I tried to put on a cheerful aspect for my guide. But it was too soon. Attalano, wise old fellow, understood my case. A smile, warm and living, flashed across his dark face as he spoke:

"Byme-by-tarpon."

Which defined his optimism and revived the failing spark within my breast.

It was, too, in the nature of a prophecy.

SECTION IV

TROUT AND THE
LURE OF FEATHERS

CHAPTER 10

THE EVOLUTION OF A FLY FISHER

BY JOAN SALVATO WULFF

Trout fishing can take you to some of the most beautiful places in the world—in this case, New Zealand. It's not all about catching as many fish as you can. Credit Jay Cassell.

I came into fishing as an innocent: my predatory skills, if I had any, were undeveloped. Loving woods and waters I caught calico bass and perch in the nearby Oldham Pond but, in trout streams, not knowing how to "read" water, nor the comfort, food, and safety needs of trout, I saw only the interesting patterns on the water's surface as if they were art.

If trout were rising I could be effective, but if they were not I became painfully aware of this lack of fishing instinct, especially in the company of anglers whom I think of as "natural born predators." In addition to understanding the hydraulics of the stream, to a man they had exceptional vision, as it related to water, seeing trout under the surface when I could not. A boyfriend, the late Johnny Dieckman, was the first of these and later in life Lee Wulff and Ed Van Put are the two who jump into my mind as always surprising me with their ability to catch fish.

With nothing to start with, I had to substitute my ability to fly cast to unlock the secrets of the stream, covering the water and learning inch by inch.

From this beginning, over the ensuing 70 years, I've been lucky enough to fish for most of the fresh and saltwater species that can be enticed to take a fly. Fishing, and especially fly fishing, has been the constant thread in my life. It's been a wonderful journey and, in the last several years, I have come to realize how differently I see the sport from when I began. It's an evolution I believe I share with others who have a passion for fly fishing.

The early stages of fishing are familiar to most anglers: the focus is on 1) The number. How many did you get? 2) The biggest fish. How big? Show me a photo. And then the most difficult: the wise old brown trout instead of the eternally innocent brookies; permit instead of bonefish. Feeling as if you've learned something.

These three stages play to our competitive nature; measuring ourselves against others whenever there is something to count. And they may stay with us forever in terms of particular species: most, biggest, most difficult. I, for instance, in the latter category, still feel the "need" to catch a 15–20 permit.

After Stage 3 the scope broadens; we enter the stages that are about more than catching fish.

It was Lee who raised my consciousness to Stage 4: giving something back to the resource; looking at the sport from the point of view of the fish. It's about preserving their gene pools as well as their habitat. Lee's wisdom, as early as 1939, that "a good game fish is too valuable to be caught only once" has been the concept that has let growing numbers of anglers enjoy the sport with, perhaps, the same number of fish.

The national conservation organizations are there to lead the way: the Federation of Fly Fishers, Trout Unlimited, the Atlantic Salmon Federation, the International Game Fish Association. I am a member of all of them and find that each group's efforts are distinct and necessary to keep our sport healthy.

In addition to making the sport more meaningful, there is another benefit to "belonging": gatherings of fishing experts willing to share their expertise at conclaves, symposiums, and club programs. It's a win/win situation for anglers of all levels. As involvement grows, your coterie of acquaintances expands and I can easily say that the best people I have ever met have been in this stage of my evolution.

If the first 3 stages are the "youth" of our fishing lives, "giving back" could be considered to be our "middle years," because there is more!

The golden years: Stage 5. Just being there. When people ask me to name my favorite place to fish, I can only say "wherever I am." And my answer to the question, "which is your favorite fish?" is "whatever I'm fishing for."

Evasive answers? Perhaps. It's just that, as my experience has broadened and I've learned the character of different waters and species of fish, I have come to love and admire them all. It's like partaking of good food. Think of how many different dishes you really love and appreciate each time you have them. Different, but equally wonderful. Remember, I'm talking about a lifetime.

In these years, catching fish has become less important; I can be fishless and still have had a good day. I can now fish "through" a companion and be as happy about their catch as they are because I know the challenges, and feelings of joy and satisfaction, that commemorate success.

These years are also a time when I can handicap myself if the fishing is too easy. Lee introduced the idea: "If you catch 3 fish on the same fly, change the fly. See what else they will take."

"Reduce your tippet strength." "Use a smaller hook." Lee was an inspiration through the "pureness" of his approach. He always gave the advantage to the fish, through his simple tackle.

He used no drag; just a click to keep the reel from overrunning, even with Atlantic salmon and tarpon. And with this tackle, he established a standard: one minute per pound to land the fish. The fish then had to swim away without the need to be revived. Lee's skills in playing fish were legendary.

I love this stage; the pressure is off! Challenge yourself! The competition is now with the fish—not other anglers.

I have one more stage to include in these golden years: #6. Replace yourself. This is about bringing young people into our sport. Unless we do this, our sport will be diminished; first in numbers of anglers and then, with fewer anglers working to preserve the habitat, in quality. Grandkids are the obvious and I am particularly blessed in this regard. I introduced Alex and Andrew to fly fishing when each became 5 and a half years old with two hands on the rod and a roll cast. They have both caught trout, and Alex has caught Atlantic salmon, on Royal Wulffs. Because I don't tie flies, I gave them fly tying lessons with a professional when they were 7. When I am long gone, they will be fly fishing together.

My cup runneth over.

Old age is approaching but I don't want to limit my enjoyment of the sport by defining it. In these past two years I have caught the largest tarpon of my life (approximately 125 pounds) and enjoyed sailfishing in Guatemala. This summer I was able to fish for steelhead on the Dean River in British Columbia, after hoping to for 40 plus years.

My most memorable fish are those I didn't land: a monster Atlantic salmon on Norway's Alta River, which played me for a few minutes, and another huge salmon on New Brunswick's Restigouche. The latter was on my last, "last cast."

It was nearly dark and, having covered the water from 20 feet on out, the cast was the longest I could make. The fish struck and dashed upriver, partly out of the water, which is how we knew he was a big one. Then he turned and raced downriver, into my backing. The guide thought the river was too high to follow the fish in the dark and headed back to shore, in spite of my protests. I found myself unhappily positioned 90 degrees from where the salmon was heading. The end was predictable: the fish never stopped—and nearly emptied my reel before the hook pulled out.

However, the reason I continue to think of this particular fish is not because I lost it, but because of the wonder of it all: how magical it was to reach out into that enormous river with a tiny artificial offering, when it was dark enough to keep me from seeing the fly land, and actually connect to a wild creature of such a size.

And magical it is. Starting as an innocent, this very ordinary woman has had an extraordinary life through the magic of fly fishing. And I plan to continue. So it's not over till it's over, and this very ordinary woman, having had an extraordinary life through the magic of sport fishing, plans to continue.

Fishing a high-mountain lake in Nevada. As we get older, most of us tend to become more reflective, more appreciative of the beauty that surrounds us. Photo Credit: Jay Cassell.

CHAPTER 11

THE VALUE OF OBSERVATION

BY GEORGE M. L. LABRANCHE

A Quiet Pool on a Sunny Day by Winslow Homer, 1889.

S everal years ago I was looking on at a tennis match between the champion of America and one of the best men England ever sent to this country, and as I watched their play I could not help but marvel at the accuracy with which the players placed their shots. Their drives were wonderful for direction and speed. On nearly every return the ball barely cleared the net and was seldom more than a few inches above the top as it passed over. A friend who knew many of the experts told me how they attained to their remarkable precision. It was the custom of many of them, he said, when preparing for the big matches, to practice for accuracy by driving the ball against a wall. He said this was particularly true of the American champion, and that it was not unusual for him to use up a dozen or more balls in a day's practice. The wall had painted across its face a line of contrasting color at a height from the ground equivalent to that of the top of a regulation tennis net, and upon the line were painted a number of disks about ten inches in diameter. Standing at a distance from the wall equivalent to the distance of the base-line of a regulation tennis-court from the net, the player would return the ball on its rebound from the wall, striving each time to so place it that it would strike just above the line. The accomplishment of a satisfactory score after a succession of drives would convince the player that he had good control of his stroke, and he would then turn his attention to the disks, against each of which he would drive twenty or more shots, taking them in turn and keeping a record of hits in each case. The accuracy developed by such practice was truly remarkable, and I hesitate to mention the number of times in succession one expert made clean hits—it seemed an incredible number.

I have seen golfers practicing the weak places in their game for hours with as much zeal and earnestness as if they were playing a match, and a polo player of my acquaintance practices his strikes upon a field at his home, riding his ponies as daringly and recklessly as though a championship depended upon his efforts. The devotees of these and similar active sports are keenly alive to the necessity of constant practice, that spirit of competition which is so much a part of them making any endeavor that will aid toward high efficiency or improve game or form, seem worthwhile. And in all sports, particularly those in which the competition is individual, whenever and wherever opportunity presents itself there will be found hundreds of enthusiasts following every ply of the expert, keenly studying his method, observing his form, and absorbing and storing the knowledge so gained for their own practice later on court or field. So, too, even though competition has no place in fly fishing, and should have none, the angler ought to strive always to "play a good game." He should practice the tactics of his art with the same zeal as do the followers of competitive sports if he hopes ever to become an expert fly fisherman in the highest sense of that misused term.

The casual angler who looks upon fishing as merely incidental to his periods of recreation, during which his chief concern is the recuperation of tired brain and unstrung nerves, may feel that he is making a business of his pleasure by devoting much time to the study of his angling. In a measure this is true, and it would be asking much, indeed, of him who thinks of fly fishing only as a pastime. But to he who realizes that it is a sport—a sport that is also an art—there is no incident, complex or simple, that is unworthy of his attention and consideration. No sport affords a greater field for observation and study than fly fishing, and it is the close attention paid to the minor happenings upon the stream that marks the finished angler. The careless angler frequently overlooks incidents, or looks upon them as merely trivial, from which he might learn much if he would but realize their meaning at the time.

Of greatest importance to the dry fly angler is that mastery of the rod and line that enables him to place his fly lightly and accurately upon the water. I venture to assert that one who has had the advantage of expert instruction in handling a rod, and is thereby qualified to deliver a fly properly, will raise more trout upon his first attempt at fishing a stream than another who, though he knows thoroughly the haunts and habits of the fish, casts indifferently. The contrast between the instructed novice and the uninstructed veteran would be particularly noticeable were they to cast together over the same water in which fish were rising freely. Whether or not the novice would take more fish than the veteran is another question. Lacking experience, the novice would probably hook few fish and land fewer. But he would be starting right, and the necessity of overcoming later on that bad form likely to be acquired by all who begin without competent knowledge of the veteran who would come to him in time.

The beginner should watch the expert and should study particularly the action of the rod. He should note that the power which impels the line forward starts from the butt, travels the entire length of the rod, is applied by a slight forward push rather than by a long sweep, and ends in a distinct snap. He will soon learn that the wrist must do the real work, and no better scheme for teaching this has ever been devised than the time-honored one of holding a fly book or a stone between the casting arm and the body. The proper action of the rod will be best learned if he fastens that part of the butt below the reel to the forearm with a piece of string, a strap of leather, or a stout rubber band, the effect of which device will be to stop the rod in an almost perpendicular position when the line is retrieved. The pull of the line as it straightens out behind him will be distinctly felt, will give him a good idea of the power and action of his rod, and serve as a signal for the forward cast. He should practice casting as often as his spare time will allow—over water when possible, but over grass if necessary. He should not wait until the stream is reached and actual fishing problems begin to press upon his notice for solution. His mind will then be occupied with many other things; hence, the knack of handling the rod should have been already acquired.

After the beginner is satisfied that he can properly place and deliver his fly, he should turn his attention to study of the fish and the currents of the stream. If he has been a wet fly angler his experience will stand him in good stead, as it will qualify him to locate the likely haunts of the fish. Long and varied though his experience may have been, however, the use of the dry fly will open avenues of observation and knowledge that were hidden from him while he practiced the old method. My own experience is responsible for this rather broad statement, but not until after I had become an ardent advocate of the dry fly, and had abandoned the wet fly for good and all, did I realize the truth of it. In the beginning I was ever on the alert for rising fish, and, instead of boldly assailing promising water, wasted much time, on many occasions, scrutinizing the water for some indication that a fish was feeding. In this way I frequently discovered non-feeding fish lying in places where I had not expected to find them. Such fish were then the more easily approached because I was able to assume a position myself that would not disclose my presence.

Just as frequently, too, I have seen fine fish cruising about, and have taken many that might have been driven away by the slightest movement on my part. In many cases I have been compelled to remain absolutely motionless for ten or fifteen minutes before a fish would come to rest long enough to make worthwhile an attempt to get a fly to it. Nearly every time, too, that a fish has been hooked I have seen it actually take the fly—an action always in-structive, because fish vary greatly in their manner of taking, and interesting, because in it lies one of the real charms of fly fishing.

The continued use of a floating fly upon water where the angler sees no indication of feeding fish, but where experience tells him that they may lie, seems to develop in him a remarkable keenness of vision. This is a direct result, perhaps, of the attention he gives to his fly. My own experience is that while I am watching my fly float down-stream some stone of irregular forma-tion, peculiar color, or difference in size from others about it, lying upon the bottom, arrests my eye, with the effect of making the water appear shallower or clearer than it really is.

My fly appears to be the center of a small area upon the surface of the water through which everything is seen as clearly as though through water-glass, the shadow of the fly itself upon the bottom often being plainly discernible. Anglers who fish the dry fly learn to identify the living shadow that appears suddenly under the fly as a trout ready to take it on its next drift down-stream, and to recognize a fish as it sidles out from the bank or swings uncertainly toward the fly just as it passes the boulder that shelters him. In either way an interesting opportunity is afforded, particularly for exercising a very necessary attribute—self-control.

It may be that many happenings I now see upon the stream passed un-noticed when I used the wet fly because of some lack of concentration and observation. If this be so, I have the newer method to thank for the de-velopment of those faculties. I have learned not to overlook a single minor happening. Perhaps my keenness to ascribe some meaning to the slightest incident has resulted in the building of many fine structures of theory and dogma upon poor foundations. This may be true, but I am certain that their weaknesses have always become apparent to me in time; and, on the other hand, I am just as certain that I have been greatly benefited by my habit of close attention to the little things that happen on the stream. For instance, I cherished the belief for many years that one advantage of up-stream fishing lay in the fact that when the fly was taken the hook was driven into the fish's mouth instead of being pulled away, as in down-stream fishing. I thought this to be one of the strongest arguments in favor of up-stream fishing, and, theoretically, it is. But I know now that many fish that take a floating do so when they are headed down-stream. While there are still many reasons why up-stream fishing is the better method, this particular argument no longer has weight with me.

As I remember it, the strongest admonition of my early schooling on the stream was never to remain long in one place. I was taught to believe that if a rise was not effected on the first few casts subsequent effort on that water was wasted—that the trout would take the fly at once or not at all. I clung to this belief for years, until one day I saw a fine fish lying in shallow water and took him after casting a dozen or more times. Since then I have taken fish after upwards of fifty casts, and I rarely abandon an attempt for one that I can see if I feel certain that it has not discovered me. Even when I have not actually seen a fish, but have known or believed one to be lying nearby, the practice has proven effective. Thus I have had the satisfaction of accomplishing a thing once believed to be impossible; but I have gained more than that: I have learned to be persevering and, what is still more important, deliberate. The man who hurries through a trout stream defeats himself. Not only does he take few fish but he has no time for observation, and his experience is likely to be of little value to him.

The beginner must learn to look with eyes that see. Occurrences of apparently little importance at the moment may, after consideration, assume proportions of great value. The taking of an insect, for instance, may mean nothing more than a rising trout; but the position occupied by this fish may indicate the position taken by others in similar water. The flash of a trout, changing his position preparatory to investigating the angler's fly, will frequently disclose the spot occupied by him before he changed his position; and, later on, when the fish are not in the keenest mood for feeding, a fly presented there accurately may bring a rise. The quick dart up-stream of a small trout from the tail of a pool is a pretty fair indication that a large fish occupies the deeper water above; it indicates just as certainly, however, that the angler has little chance of taking him, the excitement of the smaller fish having probably been communicated to his big relative.

The backwater formed by a swift current on the up-stream side of a boulder is a favorite lurking-place of brown trout. I was fishing such places one day, and found the trout occupying them in rather a taking mood. In approaching a boulder which looked particularly inviting, and while preparing to deliver my fly, I was amazed to see the tail and half the body of a fine trout out of the water at the side of the rock. For a moment I could not believe that I had seen a fish—the movement was so deliberate and I came to the conclusion that it was fancy or that a water-snake, gliding across the stream, had shown itself. Almost immediately, however, I saw the flash of a trout as he left the backwater and dashed pell-mell into the swift water at the side of the boulder.

Down-stream he came until he was eight or ten feet below the rock, when, turning sharply and rising to the surface, he took from it some insect that I could not see. Up-stream again he went, and shortly resumed his position in the dead water, showing half his body as he stemmed the current at the side of the rock. Once more this performance was repeated, and I knew I had stumbled upon an interesting experience. Hastily measuring the distance, hoping to get my fly to him before some natural insect might excite him to give another exhibition of gymnastic feeding, I dropped it about three feet above him, and, contrary to my usual method of retrieving it as it floated past the up-stream side of the boulder, I permitted it to come down riding the top of the wave, when the same flash came as the trout dashed after it. The fish could be plainly seen almost directly under the fly. As it reached the rapidly flattening water below the rock, he turned and took it viciously, immediately darting up-stream again. He was soundly hooked, however, and I netted a fine fish lacking one ounce of being a pound and a half. My experience heretofore had been that if a fly were placed a yard or so above this point and allowed to float down to the rock a feeding fish would rush forward—often as much as two feet—and take it, immediately turning or backing into his position again. I had assumed from this observation when the fly passed the rock or backwater without a rise it should be retrieved and another try made. This fish satisfied me, however, that when really feeding, or when inclined to feed, trout may be lured comparatively long distances by inviting-looking morsels. Either he did not decide to take the fly until just as it was passing him or else he liked the exercise of the chase. In any event, he was not peculiar in his habit, because four more fish were taken in the same manner the same day.

In most cases when the fly is cast above a boulder lying in swift water (which I consider, under certain conditions, one of the best places to look for brown trout) it will be taken as it approaches the rock, the trout darting out and retiring immediately to avoid being caught in the swifter water on either side of his stronghold. But if it is not taken, and is permitted to float down with the current, it may bring a response.

It was a somewhat similar observation which prompted the practice and, I must say, rather dubious development of what some of my friends are pleased to call the "fluttering" or "bounce" cast. This cast is supposed to represent the action of the fluttering insect, the fly merely alighting upon the water, rising, alighting again, repeating the movement three or four times at most; finally coming to rest and being allowed to float downstream. It rarely comes off, but when it does it is deadly; and, for the good of the sport, I am glad that it is difficult, though sorry, too, for the pleasure of accomplishing it successfully is really greater than that of taking fish with it. The cast is made with a very short line—never over twenty-five feet—and the fly alone touches the water. The action of the fly is very similar to that produced by the method known as "dapping," but instead of being merely dangled from the rod, as is the case when "dapping," the fly is actually cast. It should be permitted to float as far as it will after its fluttering or skipping has ceased. The beginner practicing the cast will do well to cast at right angles to the current, and he should choose rather fast water for his experimenting. The speed of the water will cause the fly to jump, and the action it should have will be the more readily simulated than if the first attempts are made on slow water.

I had made a flying trip to the Brodhead, and, with that strange fatality which seems so often to attend the unfortunate angler rushing off for a weekend in the early season, found the stream abnormally high and horrible weather prevailing. After many attempts to get into the stream, with results equally disastrous to my clothing and temper, I abandoned all idea of wading and walked and crawled along the bank, casting my fly wherever I could but rarely finding good water that could be reached, and rising but a few small fish. As there was a gale blowing in my face directly down-stream, it was practically impossible to place a fly where I wished with any delicacy, and I decided to abandon the sport after trying a pool just above me that I knew contained big fish. My first cast on this water, made during a lull, fell lightly, but brought no response, and after a further half dozen fruitless attempts I began to think of the fine log fire at the house. I made one more cast, however, this time in the teeth of the wind. Using but twenty-five feet of line and a short leader, I was able to straighten both in the air. The wind kept all suspended for an instant, the fly, accompanied by a small part of the leader, finally falling upon the water, where I remained but a fraction of a second, the wind whisking it off and laying it down a foot away. This happened five or six times as the fly came down-stream, and during the time it was traveling a distance of not over eight or ten feet five trout, each apparently over a pound in weight, rose to it, but missed because it was plucked away by the wind just in time to save them. I did not get one of them, and, as it was practically impossible to continue casting under the prevailing conditions, I left the stream. It was brought home solidly to me that day, however, that it was the action of the fly alone that moved the fish—and my day was not badly spent. I cannot say as much of the many other days since then that I have spent in what I feel were rather foolish attempts to imitate the effect produced by the wind on that day.

The study of the positions taken by big fish when they are feeding, and those which they occupy when they are not, is an important part in the education of the fly fisher. Each time the angler takes a good fish or sees one feeding, if he will note in his diary its position, the condition of the water, temperature, atmosphere, time of day, and the insect being taken, he will soon have an accumulation of data from which he may learn how to plan a campaign against particular fish at other times. Extremely interesting in itself, the study of insects is of great value to the angler in his attempts at imitation, and the information gleaned from autopsy might not be acquired in any other manner.

It may be said to be an axiom of the fly fisher that where a small trout is seen feeding rarely need a large one be looked for. But the actions of a small fish in sight may sometimes indicate the presence of a larger one unseen. The taking of a fine trout on a certain stream in Sullivan County, on August 27, 1906, after one of those long periods of drought so common in recent years, convinced me of this. I had been waiting for even a slight fall of rain, and, quite a heavy shower having come up the evening before, I started for this stream. Upon my arrival there I was surprised to learn that not a drop of rain had fallen in weeks, and that the shower which had been heavy twenty miles away had not reached the vicinity. While driving from the station to the house at which I was to stop, along a road that paralleled the stream, the many glimpses I had of the latter filled me with misgivings. At one point the stream and road are very near each other, and, stopping my driver, I got out looking at a famous pool below a dam which had long outlived its usefulness. It was a sizzling-hot day, and at that time—eleven o'clock—the sun was almost directly overhead; yet in the crystalclear water of this pool, with not a particle of shade to cover him, lay a native trout fourteen inches in length which afterward proved to weigh one pound three ounces. Too fine a fish, I thought, as I clambered back into the carriage, to be occupying such a place in broad daylight, and I promised myself to try for him later in the afternoon.

Returning about six o'clock, I found him in the same position, and during the full twenty minutes I watched him, while he appeared to be nervously alert, he never moved. Notwithstanding the fact that everything was against me, and knowing that the chances were more than even that the fish would see me, my rod, or my line, I made plans for approaching him; yet, busy as I was, I could not rid my mind of this ever-recurring thought: with all the known aversion of his kind to heat, and their love of dark nooks, why was this fish out on such a day? Why did he not find a place under the cool shade of the dam? With the instinct strong within him to protect him by hiding, the impulse must have been much stronger that forced him to take so conspicuous a stand—a mark to the animals which prey upon his kind. As there were absolutely no insects upon the water, and scarcely enough current to bring food of other sort to him, he could not have been feeding. The only reason, then, to account for his being there—the thought struck me forcibly enough—was his fear of a bigger fish. The logical conclusion was that if a fish of his inches (no mean adversary) exposed himself the one that bullied him must be quite solid. I tested this fellow's appetite with a small, pinkish-bodied fly of my own invention, and, standing about forty feet below and considerably to the left, dropped it three or four feet above him; but, although it was certain he could see the fly, he made no attempt to go forward and take it. As it neared him, however, he rushed excitedly to the right and then to the left, taking the fly as it came directly over him, and, before I could realize what had happened, came down-stream toward me at a great rate. As he was securely hooked, I kept him coming, and netted him quietly at the lip of the pool.

That this fish did not take the fly the instant it fell meant to me that he was afraid to go forward into the deeper water which harbored his larger fellow; and his action as the fly appeared over him meant that, while he wanted it badly enough, he would not risk an altercation with the other, which might also have seen it. When he did finally decide that the coast was clear, he took it quickly and rushed down toward the shallower water where he might be secure against sudden attack.

If some of the theories developed in those few moments appear fanciful, it must be remembered that my mind was occupied with the thought that the pool contained a larger fish, and the conclusions based upon the subsequent actions of this smaller one only tended to strengthen this belief. Fanciful or not, I was rewarded a few minutes later by the sight of a monster tail breaking the surface just under the water that trickled over the apron of the dam.

A brown trout.

Having prepared a gossamer leader, preferring to risk a smash to not getting a rise, I dropped a small Silver Sedge—which I used because it could be more plainly kept in sight—almost immediately in the swirl and was at once fast in a lusty fish. After many abortive attempts to lead him into the diminutive net I had with me, I flung the thing, in disgust, into the woods. I finally beached the fish and lifted him out in my hand. He was a fine brown trout, eighteen and three quarter inches in length, and weighed, the next morning, two pounds nine ounces.

While I was engaged with this fish another rose in practically the same spot under the apron of the dam. Hurriedly replacing the bedraggled fly with a new one, I waited for the trout to show himself, which he did presently, and again I was fast—this time in one of the best fish I have ever seen in these waters. It seemed an interminable length of time, though probably not over ten minutes, that I was engaged with this one, and it was impossible to move him; he kept alternately boring in toward the dam and sulking. In one of the latter fits I urged him toward me somewhat too strongly, and he was off. Immediately I was afforded a sight of what I had lost as he leaped clear of the water in an evident endeavor to dislodge the thing that had fastened to his jaw. The smash made as he struck the water still resounds in my ear, and when I say that this fish would have been close to five pounds I but exercise the right to that license accorded all anglers to attempt to describe the size of the big ones that get away. Having one good fish in my creel, however, I really had some basis for my calculation—at any rate, he was one of the best fish I have ever risen. Examining my leader, I found it had not broken, but the telltale curl at the end proved that, in the fast gathering gloom, I had been careless in knotting on the fly.

SECTION V

ANGLERS ALL—
AND MATTERS
PHILOSOPHIC

CHAPTER 12

THE ANGLER

BY WASHINGTON IRVING

Fly fishing in Utah. Photo Credit: Jay Cassell.

It is said that many an unlucky urchin is induced to run away from his family, and betake himself to a seafaring life, from reading the history of Robinson Crusoe; and I suspect that, in like manner, many of those worthy gentlemen who are given to haunt the sides of pastoral streams with angle rods in hand, may trace the origin of their passion to the seductive pages of honest Izaak Walton. I recollect studying his *Compleat Angler* several years since, in company with a knot of friends in America, and moreover that we were all completely bitten with the angling mania. It was early in the year; but as soon as the weather was auspicious, and the spring began to melt into the verge of summer, we took rod in hand and sallied into the country, as stark mad as was ever Don Quixote from reading books of chivalry.

One of our party had equaled the Don in the fullness of his equipments: being attired cap-à-pie for the enterprise. He wore a broad-skirted fustian coat, perplexed with half a hundred pockets; a pair of stout shoes, and leathern gaiters; a basket slung on one side for fish; a patent rod, a landing net, and a score of other inconveniences, only to be found in the true angler's armory. Thus harnessed for the field, he was as great a matter of stare and wonderment among the country folk, who had never seen a regular angler, as was the steel-clad hero of La Mancha among the goatherds of the Sierra Morena.

Our first essay was along a mountain brook, among the highlands of the Hudson; a most unfortunate place for the execution of those piscatory tactics which had been invented along the velvet margins of quiet English rivulets. It was one of those wild streams that lavish, among our romantic solitudes, unheeded beauties, enough to fill the sketch-book of a hunter of the picturesque. Sometimes it would leap down rocky shelves, making small cascades, over which the trees threw their broad balancing sprays, and long nameless weeds hung in fringes from the impending banks, dripping with diamond drops. Sometimes it would brawl and fret along a ravine in the matted shade of a forest, filling it with murmurs; and, after this termagant career, would steal forth into open day with the most placid demure face imaginable; as I have seen some pestilent shrew of a housewife, after filling her home with uproar and ill-humor, come dimpling out of doors, swimming and curtseying, and smiling upon all the world.

How smoothly would this vagrant brook glide, at such times, through some bosom of green meadow-land among the mountains: where the quiet was only interrupted by the occasional tinkling of a bell from the lazy cattle among the clover, or the sound of a woodcutter's axe from the neighboring forest.

For my part, I was always a bungler at all kinds of sport that required either patience or adroitness, and had not angled above half an hour before I had completely "satisfied the sentiment," and convinced myself of the truth of Izaak Walton's opinion, that angling is something like poetry—a man must be born to it. I hooked myself instead of the fish; tangled my line in every tree; lost my bait; broke my rod; until I gave up the attempt in despair, and passed the day under the trees, reading old Izaak; satisfied that it was his fascinating vein of honest simplicity and rural feeling that had bewitched me, and not the passion for angling. My companions, however, were more persevering in their delusion. I have them at this moment before my eyes, stealing along the border of the brook, where it lay open to the day, or was merely fringed by shrubs and bushes. I see the bittern rising with hollow scream as they break in upon his rarely-invaded haunt; the kingfisher watching them suspiciously from his dry tree that overhangs the deep black mill-pond, in the gorge of the hills; the tortoise letting himself slip sideways from off the stone or log on which he is sunning himself; and the panic-struck frog plumping in headlong as they approach, and spreading an alarm throughout the watery world around.

I recollect also, that, after toiling and watching and creeping about for the greater part of a day, with scarcely any success, in spite of all our admirable apparatus, a lubberly country urchin came down from the hills with a rod made from a branch of a tree, a few yards of twine, and, as Heaven shall help me! I believe, a crooked pin for a hook, baited with a vile earthworm—and in half an hour caught more fish than we had nibbles throughout the day!

But, above all, I recollect, the "good, honest, wholesome, hungry" repast, which we made under a beech-tree, just by a spring of pure sweet water that stole out of the side of a hill; and how, when it was over, one of the party read old Izaak Walton's scene with the milkmaid, while I lay on the grass and built castles in a bright pile of clouds, until I fell asleep. All this may appear like mere egotism; yet I cannot refrain from uttering these recollections, which are passing like a strain of music over my mind, and have been called up by an agreeable scene which I witnessed not long since.

In a morning's stroll along the banks of the Alun, a beautiful little stream which flows down from the Welsh hills and throws itself into the Dee, my attention was attracted to a group seated on the margin. On approaching, I found it to consist of a veteran angler and two rustic disciples. The former was an old fellow with a wooden leg, with clothes very much but very carefully patched, betokening poverty, honestly come by, and decently maintained. His face bore the marks of former storms, but present fair weather; its furrows had been worn into a habitual smile; his iron-gray locks hung about his ears, and he had altogether the good-humored air of a constitutional philosopher who was disposed to take the world as it went. One of his companions was a ragged wight, with the skulking look of an errant poacher, and I'll warrant could find his way to any gentleman's fish-pond in the neighborhood in the darkest night. The other was a tall, awkward, country lad, with a lounging gait, and apparently somewhat of a rustic beau. The old man was busy in examining the maw of a trout which he had just killed, to discover by its contents what insects were seasonable for bait; and was lecturing on the subject to his companions, who appeared to listen with infinite deference. I have a kind feeling towards all "brothers of the angle," ever since I read Izaak Walton. They are men, he affirms, of a "mild, sweet, and peaceable spirit;" and my esteem for them has been increased since I met with an old *Tretyse of Fishing with the Angle*, in which are set forth many of the maxims of their inoffensive fraternity. "Take good hede," sayeth this honest little tretyse, "that in going about your disportes ye open no man's gates but that ye shet them again. Also ye shall not use this forsayd crafti disport for no covetousness to the encreasing and sparing of your money only, but principally for your solace, and to cause the helth of your body and specyally of your soule."

I thought that I could perceive in the veteran angler before me an exemplification of what I had read; and there was a cheerful contentedness in his looks that quite drew me towards him. I could not but remark the gallant manner in which he stumped from one part of the brook to another; waving his rod in the air, to keep the line from dragging on the ground, or catching among the bushes; and the adroitness with which he would throw his fly to any particular place; sometimes skimming it lightly along a little rapid; sometimes casting it into one of those dark holes made by a twisted root or overhanging bank, in which the large trout are apt to lurk. In the meanwhile he was giving instructions to his two disciples; showing them the manner in which they should handle their rods, fix their flies, and play them along the surface of the stream. The scene brought to my mind the instructions of the sage Piscator to his scholar. The country around was of that pastoral kind which Walton is fond of describing. It was a part of the great plain of Cheshire, close by the beautiful vale of Gessford, and just where the inferior Welsh hills begin to swell up from among fresh-smelling meadows. The day, too, like that recorded in his work, was mild and sunshiny, with now and then a soft-dropping shower, that sowed the whole earth with diamonds.

I soon fell into conversation with the old angler, and was so much entertained that, under pretext of receiving instructions in his art, I kept company with him almost the whole day; wandering along the banks of the stream, and listening to his talk. He was very communicative, having all the easy garrulity of cheerful old age; and I fancy was a little flattered by having an opportunity of displaying his piscatory lore; for who does not like now and then to play the sage?

He had been much of a rambler in his day, and had passed some years of his youth in America, particularly in Savannah, where he had entered into trade, and had been ruined by the indiscretion of a partner. He had afterwards experienced many ups and downs in life, until he got into the navy, where his leg was carried away by a cannon ball, at the battle of Camperdown. This was the only stroke of real good fortune he had ever experienced, for it got him a pension, which, together with some small paternal property, brought him in a revenue of nearly forty pounds. On this he retired to his native village, where he lived quietly and independently; and devoted the remainder of his life to the "noble art of angling."

I found that he had read Izaak Walton attentively, and he seemed to have imbibed all his simple frankness and prevalent good-humor. Though he had been sorely buffeted about the world, he was satisfied that the world, in itself, was good and beautiful. Though he had been as roughly used in different countries as a poor sheep that is fleeced by every hedge and thicket, yet he spoke of every nation with candor and kindness, appearing to look only on the good side of things: and, above all, he was almost the only man I had ever met with who had been an unfortunate adventurer in America, and had honesty and magnanimity enough to take the fault to his own door, and not to curse the country. The lad that was receiving his instructions, I learnt, was the son and heir apparent of a fat old widow who kept the village inn, and of course a youth of some expectation, and much courted by the idle gentlemanlike personages of the place. In taking him under his care, therefore, the old man had probably an eye to a privileged corner in the tap-room, and an occasional cup of cheerful ale free of expense.

There is certainly something in angling, if we could forget, which anglers are apt to do, the cruelties and tortures inflicted on worms and insects, that tends to produce a gentleness of spirit, and a pure serenity of mind. As the English are methodical even in their recreations, and are the most scientific of sportsmen, it has been reduced among them to perfect rule and system. Indeed it is an amusement peculiarly adapted to the mild and highly-cultivated scenery of England, where every roughness has been softened away from the landscape. It is delightful to saunter along those limpid streams which wander, like veins of silver, through the bosom of this beautiful country; leading one through a diversity of small home scenery; sometimes winding through ornamented grounds; sometimes brimming along through rich pasturage, where the fresh green is mingled with sweet-smelling flowers; sometimes venturing in sight of villages and hamlets, and then running capriciously away into shady retirements. The sweetness and serenity of nature, and the quiet watchfulness of the sport, gradually bring on pleasant fits of musing; which are now and then agreeably interrupted by the song of a bird, the distant whistle of the peasant, or perhaps the vagary of some fish, leaping out of the still water, and skimming transiently about its glassy surface. "When I would beget content," says Izaak Walton, "and increase confidence in the power and wisdom and providence of Almighty God, I will walk the meadows by some gliding stream, and there contemplate the lilies that take no care, and those very many other little living creatures that are not only created, but fed (man knows not how) by the goodness of the God of nature, and therefore trust in him."

I cannot forbear to give another quotation from one of those ancient champions of angling, which breathes the same innocent and happy spirit:

> Let me live harmlessly, and near the brink
> Of Trent or Avon have a dwelling-place,
> Where I may see my quill, or cork, down sink,
> With eager bite of pike, or bleak, or dace;
> And on the world and my Creator think:
> Whilst some men strive ill-gotten goods t' embrace;
> And others spend their time in base excess
> Of wine, or worse, in war, or wantonness.
> Let them that will, these pastimes still pursue,
> And on such pleasing fancies feed their fill;
> So I the fields and meadows green may view,
> And daily by fresh rivers walk at will,
> Among the daisies and the violets blue,
> Red hyacinth and yellow daffodil.

On parting with the old angler I inquired after his place of abode, and happening to be in the neighborhood of the village a few evenings afterwards, I had the curiosity to seek him out. I found him living in a small cottage, containing only one room, but a perfect curiosity in its method and arrangement. It was on the skirts of the village, on a green bank, a little back from the road, with a small garden in front, stocked with kitchen herbs, and adorned with a few flowers. The whole front of the cottage was overrun with a honeysuckle. On the top was a ship for a weather-cock. The interior was fitted up in a truly nautical style, his ideas of comfort and convenience having been acquired on the berth-deck of a man-of-war. A hammock was slung from the ceiling, which, in the daytime, was lashed up so as to take but little room. From the centre of the chamber hung a model of a ship, of his own workmanship. Two or three chairs, a table, and a large sea-chest, formed the principal movables. About the wall were stuck up naval ballads, such as "Admiral Hosier's Ghost,"

"All in the Downs," and "Tom Bowline," intermingled with pictures of sea-fights, among which the battle of Camperdown held a distinguished place. The mantel-piece was decorated with sea-shells; over which hung a quadrant, flanked by two wood-cuts of most bitter-looking naval commanders. His implements for angling were carefully disposed on nails and hooks about the room. On a shelf was arranged his library, containing a work on angling, much worn, a Bible covered with canvas, an odd volume or two of voyages, a nautical almanac, and a book of songs.

His family consisted of a large black cat with one eye, and a parrot which he had caught and tamed, and educated himself, in the course of one of his voyages; and which uttered a variety of sea phrases with the hoarse brattling tone of a veteran boatswain. The establishment reminded me of that of the renowned Robinson Crusoe; it was kept in neat order, everything being "stowed away" with the regularity of a ship of war; and he informed me that he "scoured the deck every morning, and swept it between meals."

I found him seated on a bench before the door, smoking his pipe in the soft evening sunshine. His cat was purring soberly on the threshold, and his parrot describing some strange evolutions in an iron ring that swung in the centre of his cage. He had been angling all day, and gave me a history of his sport with as much minuteness as a general would talk over a campaign; being particularly animated in relating the manner in which he had taken a large trout, which had completely tasked all his skill and wariness, and which he had sent as a trophy to mine hostess of the inn.

How comforting it is to see a cheerful and contented old age; and to behold a poor fellow, like this, after being tempest-tost through life, safely moored in a snug and quiet harbor in the evening of his days! His happiness, however, sprung from within himself, and was independent of external circumstances; for he had that inexhaustible good-nature, which is the most precious gift of Heaven; spreading itself like oil over the troubled sea of thought, and keeping the mind smooth and equable in the roughest weather.

On inquiring further about him, I learned that he was a universal favorite in the village, and the oracle of the taproom; where he delighted the rustics with his songs, and, like Sinbad, astonished them with his stories of strange lands, and shipwrecks, and sea-fights. He was much noticed too by gentlemen sportsmen of the neighborhood; had taught several of them the art of angling; and was a privileged visitor to their kitchens. The whole tenor of his life was quiet and inoffensive, being principally passed about the neighboring streams, when the weather and season were favorable; and at other times he employed himself at home, preparing his fishing tackle for the next campaign, or manufacturing rods, nets, and flies, for his patrons and pupils among the gentry.

He was a regular attendant at church on Sundays, though he generally fell asleep during the sermon. He had made it his particular request that when he died he should be buried in a green spot, which he could see from his seat in church, and which he had marked out ever since he was a boy, and had thought of when far from home on the raging sea, in danger of being food for the fishes—it was the spot where his father and mother had been buried.

I have done, for I fear that my reader is growing weary; but I could not refrain from drawing the picture of this worthy "brother of the angle"; who has made me more than ever in love with the theory, though I fear I shall never be adroit in the practice of his art; and I will conclude this rambling sketch in the words of honest Izaak Walton, by craving the blessing of St. Peter's master upon my reader, "and upon all that are true lovers of virtue; and dare trust in his providence; and be quiet; and go a angling."

CHAPTER 13

WHAT AND WHO IS AN ANGLER?

BY THADDEUS NORRIS

The Blue Boat by Winslow Homer, 1892. Museum of Fine Arts, Boston.

I t is not my intention to offer any remarks on the antiquity of angling, or say much in its defense. Dame Juliana Berners, Izaak Walton, and more recent authors, have discoursed learnedly on its origin, and defended it wisely and valiantly from the aspersions and ridicule of those who cannot appreciate its quiet toys, and who know not the solace and peace it brings to the harassed mind, or how it begets and fosters contentment and a love of nature.

I ask any caviller to read Dr. Bethune's *Bibliographical Preface* to his edition Walton; and then Father Izaak's address to the readers of his discourse, "but especially to the honest angler," and accompany him in spirit, as Bethune by the quiet Lea, or Cotton by the bright rippling Dove; and if he be not convinced of the blessed influences of the "gentle art," or if his heart is not warmed, or no recollections of his boyish days come back to him, I give him up without a harsh word, but with a feeling of regret, that a lifetime should be spent without attaining so much of quiet happiness that might have been so easily possessed, and quoting a few sad words from Whittier's Maud Muller, only say "it might have been."

Many anglers, such as Sir Humphrey Davy and Sir Joshua Reynolds, besides some of my own acquaintance, have sought its cheering influences in advanced life. I know of one whose early manhood and maturer years were spent on the boisterous deep, and who, though now past eighty, is still an ardent, but quiet angler; and when no better spot can be found, he will even fish through the ice in winter for roach. No doubt his days have been lengthened out, and the burden of life lightened, by his love of angling.

But how sweetly memories of the past come to one who has appreciated and enjoyed it from his boyhood, whose almost first penny, after he wore jacket and trousers, bought his first fish hook; whose first fishing line was twisted by mother or sister; whose float was the cork of a physic vial, and whose sinkers were cut from the sheet lead of an old tea chest! Thus rigged, with what glad anticipations of sport, many a boy has started on some bright Saturday morning, his gourd, or old cow's horn of red worms in one pocket, and a jackknife in the other, to cut his alder pole with, and wandered "free and far" by still pool and swift waters, dinnerless—except perhaps a slight meal at a cherry tree, or a handful of berries that grew along his path—and come home at night weary and footsore, but exulting in his string of chubs, minnows, and sunnies, the largest as broad as his three fingers! He almost falls asleep under his Saturday night scrubbing, but in the morning, does ample justice to his "catch," which is turned out of the pan, crisp and brown, and matted together like a pancake.

In my school days, a boy might have been envied, but not loved for proficiency in his studies; but he was most courted, who knew the best fishing holes; who had plenty of powder and shot; the best squirrel dog, and the use of his father's long flintlock gun. And I confess, as I write these lines with my spectacles on, that I have still a strong drawing toward this type of a boy, whether I meet him in my lonely rambles, or whether he dwells only in my memory.

Sometimes the recollection of our boyish sports comes back to us after manhood, and one who has been "addicted" to fishing relapses into his old "ailment"; then angling becomes a pleasant kind of disease, and one's friends are apt to become inoculated with the virus, for it is contagious. Or men are informally introduced to each other on the stream, by a good-humored salutation, or an inquiry of "What luck?" or a display of the catch, or the offer of a cigar, or the flask, or a new fly; and with such introduction have become fast friends, from that affinity which draws all true anglers together.

But let me ask what is an angler, and who is a true angler? One who fishes with nets is not, neither is he who spears, snares, or dastardly uses the crazy bait to get fish, or who catches them on set lines; nor is he who is boisterous, noisy, or quarrelsome; nor are those who profess to practice the higher branches of the art, and affect contempt for their more humble brethren, who have not attained to their proficiency, imbued with the feeling that should possess the true angler.

Nor is he who brings his ice chest from town, and fishes all day with worm or fly, that he may return to the city and boastingly distribute his soaked and tasteless trout among his friends and brag of the numbers he has basketed, from fingerlings upwards.

Anglers may be divided into almost as many genera and species as the fish they catch, and engage in the sport from as many impulses. Let me give, "en passant," a sketch of a few of the many I have met with.

There is the Fussy Angler, a great bore; of course you will shun him. The Snob Angler, who speaks confidently and knowingly on a slight capital of skill or experience. The Greedy, Pushing Angler, who rushes ahead and half fishes the water, leaving those who follow in doubt as to whether he has fished a pool or rift carefully, or slurred it over in his haste to reach some well-known place down the stream before his companions. The company of these, the quiet, careful angler will avoid.

We also meet sometimes with the Spick-and-Span Angler, who has a highly varnished rod, and a superabundance of useless tackle; his outfit is of the most elaborate kind as regards its finish. He is a dapper "well got up" angler in all his appointments, and fishes much indoors over his claret and poteen, when he has a good listener. He frequently displays bad taste in his tackle, intended for fly-fishing, by having a thirty-dollar multiplying reel, filled with one of Conroy's very best relaid sea-grass lines, strong enough to hold a dolphin. If you meet him on the teeming waters of northern New York, the evening's display of his catch depends much on the rough skill of his guide.

The Rough-and-Ready Angler, the opposite of the aforenamed, disdains all "tomfoolery," and carries his tackle in an old shot bag, and his flies in a tangled mass.

We have also the Literary Angler, who reads Walton and admires him hugely; he has been inoculated with the sentiment only; the five-mile walk up the creek, where it has not been fished much, is very fatiguing to him; he "did not know he must wade the stream," and does not until he slips in, and then he has some trouble at night to get his boots off. He is provided with a stout bass rod, good strong leaders of salmon gut, and a stock of Conroy's "journal flies," and wonders if he had not better put on a shot just above his stretcher fly.

The Pretentious Angler, to use a favorite expression of the lamented Dickey Riker, once Recorder of the city of New York, is one "that prevails to a great extent in this community." This gentleman has many of the qualities attributed by Fisher, of the "Angler's Souvenir," to Sir Humphrey Davy. If he has attained the higher branches of the art, he affects to despise all sport which he considers less scientific; if a salmon fisher, he calls trout "vermin"; if he is a trout fly-fisher, he professes contempt for bait fishing. We have talked with true anglers who were even disposed to censure the eminent Divine, who has so ably, and with such labor of love, edited our American edition of Walton, for affectation, in saying of the red worm, "our hands have long since been washed of the dirty things." The servant should not be above his master, and certainly "Iz. Wa.," whose disciple the Doctor professed to be, considered it no indignity to use them, nor was he disgusted with his "horn of gentles." But the Doctor was certainly right in deprecating the use of ground bait in reference to trout, when the angler can with a little faith and less greed soon learn the use of the fly.

The Shad-roe Fisherman.—The habitat of this genus (and they are rarely found elsewhere) is Philadelphia. There are many persons of the aforesaid city, who fish only when this bait can be had, and an idea seems to possess them that fish will bite at no other. This fraternity could have been found some years back, singly or in pairs, or little coteries of three or four, on any sunshiny day from Easter to Whitsuntide, heaving their heavy dipsies and horsehair snoods from the ends of the piers, or from canal boats laid up in ordinary—the old floating bridge at Gray's Ferry was a favorite resort for them. Sometimes the party was convivial, and provided with a junk bottle of what they believed to be old rye.

Before the gas works had destroyed the fishing in the Schuylkill, I frequently observed a solitary individual of this species, wending his way to the river on Sunday mornings, with a long reed pole on his shoulder, and in his hand a tin kettle of shad roe; and his "prog," consisting of hard-boiled eggs and crackers and cheese, tied up in a cotton bandana handkerchief. Toward nightfall "he might have been seen" (as James the novelist says of the horseman), trudging homeward with a string of pan rock and white perch, or "catties" and eels, his trousers and coat sleeves well plastered with his unctuous bait, suggesting the idea of what, in vulgar parlance, might be called "a very nasty man."

But let us not turn up our scientific noses at this humble brother; nor let the home missionary or tract distributor rate him too severely, if he should meet with him in his Sunday walks; for who can tell what a quiet day of consolation it has been to him; he has found relief from the toils and cares of the week, and perhaps from the ceaseless tongue of his shrewish "old woman." If his sport has been good, he follows it up the next day, and keeps "blue Monday."

We have seen some very respectable gentlemen in our day engaged in fishing with shad roe at Fairmount Dam. The bar even had its representative, in one of our first criminal court lawyers. He did not "dress the character" with as much discrimination as when he lectured on Shakespeare, for he always wore his blue coat with gilt buttons: he did not appear to be a successful angler. "Per contra" to this was a wealthy retired merchant, who used to astonish us with his knack of keeping this difficult bait on his hooks, and his skill in hooking little white perch. Many a troller has seen him sitting bolt upright in the bow of his boat on a cool morning in May, with his overcoat buttoned up to his chin, his jolly spouse in the stern, and his servant amidship, baiting the hooks and taking off the lady's fish. The son also was an adept as well as the sire. Woe to the perch fisher, with his bait of little silvery eels, if these occupied the lower part of the swim, for the fish were all arrested by the stray ova that floated off from the "gobs" of shad roe.

As we love contrasts, let us here make a slight allusion to that sensible "old English gentleman," the Admiral, who surveyed the northwest coast of America to see, if in the contingency of the Yankees adhering to their claim of "fifty-four forty," the country about Vancouver's Island was worth contending for. He was an ardent angler, and it is reported, that on leaving his ship he provided stores for a week, which comprised of course not a few drinkables; as well as salmon rods and other tackle, and started in his boats to explore the rivers and tributaries, which, so goes the story, were so crammed in many places with salmon, that they could be captured with a boat hook; and still with all the variety of salmon flies and the piscatory skill of the admiral and his officers, not a fish could be induced to rise at the fly. He returned to his ship disheartened and disgusted, averring that the country was not worth contending for; that the Yankees might have it and be——; but it would be indecorous to record the admiral's mild expletive.

The True Angler is thoroughly imbued with the spirit of gentle old Izaak. He has no affectation, and when a fly cast is not to be had, can find amusement in catching sunfish or roach, and does not despise the sport of any humbler brother of the angle. With him, fishing is a recreation, and a "calmer of unquiet thoughts." He never quarrels with his luck, knowing that satiety dulls one's appreciation of sport as much as want of success, but is ever content when he has done his best, and looks hopefully forward to a more propitious day. Whether from boat or rocky shore, or along the sedgy bank of the creek, or the stony margin of the mountain brook, he deems it an achievement to take fish when they are difficult to catch, and his satisfaction is in proportion. If he is lazy, or a superannuated angler, he can even endure a few days' trolling on an inland lake, and smokes his cigar, chats with the boatman, and takes an occasional "nip," as he is rowed along the wooded shore and amongst the beautiful islands.

A true angler is generally a modest man; unobtrusively communicative when he can impart a new idea; and is ever ready to let a pretentious tyro have his say, and good-naturedly (as if merely suggesting how it should be done)

Man Fishing by Robert S. Duncanson, 1848. SCAD Museum of Art.

repairs his tackle, or gets him out of a scrape. He is moderately provided with all tackle and "fixins" necessary to the fishing he is in pursuit of. Is quietly self-reliant and equal to almost any emergency, from splicing his rod or tying his own flies, to trudging ten miles across a rough country with his luggage on his back. His enjoyment consists not only in the taking of fish: he draws much pleasure from the soothing influence and delightful accompaniments of the art.

With happy memories of the past summer, he joins together the three pieces of his fly rod at home, when the scenes of the last season's sport are wrapped in snow and ice, and renews the glad feelings of long summer days. With what interest he notes the swelling of the buds on the maples, or the advent of the bluebird and robin, and looks forward to the day when he is to try another cast! And, when it comes at last, with what pleasing anticipations he packs up his "traps," and leaves his business cares and the noisy city behind, and after a few hours' or few days' travel in the cars, and a few miles in a rough wagon, or a vigorous tramp over rugged hills or along the road that leads up the banks of the river, he arrives at his quarters! He is now in the region of fresh butter and mealy potatoes—there are always good potatoes in a mountainous trout country. How pleasingly rough everything looks after leaving the prim city! How pure and wholesome the air! How beautiful the clumps of sugar maples and the veteran hemlocks jutting out over the stream; the laurel; the ivy; the moss-covered rocks; the lengthening shadows of evening! How musical the old familiar tinkling of the cow-bell and the cry of the whippoorwill! How sweetly he is lulled to sleep as he hears

The waters leap and gush
O'er channelled rock and broken bush!

Next morning, after a hearty breakfast of mashed potatoes, ham and eggs, and butter from the cream of the cow that browses in the woods, he is off, three miles up the creek, a cigar or his pipe in his mouth, his creel at his side, and his rod over his shoulder, chatting with his chum as he goes; free, joyous, happy; at peace with his Maker, with himself, and all mankind; he should be grateful for this much, even if he catches no fish. How exhilarating the music of the stream! How invigorating its waters, causing a consciousness of manly vigor, as he wades sturdily with the strong current and casts his flies before him! When his zeal abates, and a few of the speckled lie in the bottom of his creel, he is not less interested in the wild flowers on the bank, or the scathed old hemlock on the cliff above, with its hawk's nest, the lady of the house likely inside, and the male proprietor perched high above on its dead top and he breaks forth lustily—the scene suggesting the song—

The bee's on its wing, and the hawk on its nest,

And the river runs merrily by.

When noon comes on, and the trout rise lazily or merely rip, he halts "*sub tegmine fagi*," or under the shadow of the dark sugar maple to build a fire and toast trout for his dinner, and wiles away three hours or so. He dines sumptuously, straightens and dries his leader and the gut of his dropper, and repairs all breakage. He smokes leisurely, or even takes a nap on the greensward or velvety moss, and resumes his sport when the sun has declined enough to shade at least one side of the stream, and pleasantly anticipates the late evening on the still waters far down the creek. God be with you, gentle angler, if actuated with the reeling of our old master! Whether you are a top fisher or a bottom fisher; whether your bait be gentles, brandling, grub, or red worm; crab, shrimp, or minnow; caddis, grasshopper, or the feathery counterfeit of the ephemera. May your thoughts be always peaceful, and your heart filled with gratitude to Him who made the country and the rivers; and "may the east wind never blow when you go a-fishing!"

CHAPTER 14

CRAZY FOR RIVERS (SELECTION)

BY BILL BARICH

The North Yuba River.

That autumn, I went a little crazy for rivers. The weather was unusually mild in northern California, where I live, and I had some time to spare and couldn't imagine a better way to spend it than in the high mountain country as the leaves began to fall. I fished the Merced and the Stanislaus, the Kings and the North Yuba, and I had some luck on them all and might have fished the Tuolumne, too, if nature hadn't dealt me a setback. It was a good period in my life, calm and reflective, even happy. The days flowed by unbroken, in perfect sunlight, and often I found myself thinking back over the years and thanking the heavens I'd come to be where I was, knee-deep in a trout stream with a fly rod in my hand.

Some people are born anglers, but I was not, even though my father had a passion for fishing. When I was a boy, I used to hear him complain about his distance from a decent lake as he dodged the traffic between our Long Island home and his office in Manhattan. He'd grown up in rural Michigan, the last of twelve children. His older brothers had taught him to love the outdoors, so he came by his longing honestly. His father—my grandfather, a stocky Slav always dressed for a wedding in a three-piece wool suit from Dubrovnik—was fond of the woods, as well, and saw no irony in decorating the tavern he owned with his cherished forest creatures (deer, moose, even hawks) stuffed and mounted.

For some reason, I'd met only a couple of my paternal uncles, so I enjoyed being told stories about them, especially about John, the eldest, who was a legendary hunter. He had shared a bed with my father for a while. That wasn't uncommon in large families in those days, and it might never have been mentioned at all, except that John talked and hunted in his sleep. In the middle of the night, he'd sit bolt upright in a trance, grab my father by the shoulders, shake him, and shout, "There's a bear in the room! Oh, no! He's going to attack us!" My father never saw the bear, of course, but it seemed real to him, and he would shiver and whimper until John stuck out an arm like a rifle, took deliberate aim, and fired a fatal shot.

"Blam! Got 'im!" he'd cry. "We're saved!" Then he would roll over and go back to sleep.

Though I couldn't have known it then, not when I was still a child myself, I understood later that my father told such stories because he missed the folks on the Upper Peninsula and felt nostalgic for his youth and its sporting pursuits. His success in business had separated him from much that he cared about and had affection for, so every summer he would saddle up his family for a two-week vacation at a fishing resort, ordinarily in Minnesota—my mother was from there—but once in darkest Maine, at Sebago Lake, where I was puzzled and a bit frightened by the taciturn, stiff-spined, pipe-smoking men in flannel shirts, who were already cutting firewood in July.

I got my first fishing lessons on those trips, but I was a lackluster student. I could swing a Louisville Slugger with aplomb and even hit the long ball, but I was terribly awkward with a spin rod. Whenever I snarled my line or tossed a Jitterbug into a tree, my father would become flustered, carrying on about the minutes he was losing as he untied the knots and retrieved the plugs from limbs. He had a temper back then and lacked the patience to be a sympathetic teacher. We hardly ever caught any fish, either, so my brother, David, and I, being enterprising lads, would amuse ourselves by liberating minnows from the minnow bucket, shooting at squirrels with a Whammo slingshot, and conducting stupid giggling fits whose sole purpose was to further annoy the old man.

The only rewarding fishing I ever had on vacation, in fact, was courtesy of Carl Peterson, my mother's father, who guided us kids around Paradise Lake in a rowboat, in 1956. Carl managed an apartment building in St. Paul and bought me my first official cowboy outfit—chaps, spurs, boots, the works. I liked him a lot, although not as much as I liked my Uncle Ned, a former star player in a semi pro baseball league, who worked as a mailman and let me walk his route with him sometimes. Ned always had a powerful thirst, and if the weather happened to be humid, we would be forced to stop at a few saloons along the way, where my uncle would polish off a quick draft beer, often paid for by an admiring fan, while I thumped the pinball machine and developed bad habits at an early age.

Carl Peterson didn't fish much himself, but he had patience in his favor and knew that children in boats are most content when they have something to do. He let us fish for easy-to-catch crappies instead of the tricky bass or pike my father went after, and we hauled in so many of them so fast that we got our picture in the local paper holding up a stringer to show off our forty or fifty victims. It still astonishes me to see how proud I look, a sophisticated East Coast youth of thirteen with his hair styled in a fashionable "Hollywood" crew cut (flat on top and slicked back at the sides), secretly imagining his future as a rock-and-roll star, even as he poses with a bunch of dead crappies at Paradise Lake.

I really hated fishing by the time I turned sixteen. I rebelled against the entire concept of a family vacation and whined and protested until my parents agreed to let me stay home alone. (Not incidentally, that was the summer I lost my virginity to a lusty cheerleader in my very own upstairs bedroom, treating her to an ice-cream pop from a circling Good Humor truck immediately afterward because I had no idea what else to do.) I thought that sitting in a boat in the middle of nowhere was the dumbest activity known to mankind and swore I would never fish again—and I might have kept my promise, too, if my brother hadn't intervened by accident, thirteen years later.

I had taken Horace Greeley's advice by then and migrated west to seek my fortune, although not to work for it. I was living in San Francisco, in a spacious Haight-Ashbury Victorian that we renters failed to dust even once during our tenancy. My hair, suffice it to say, was not in a Hollywood crew cut anymore, and I'd mastered the fine art of slacking. As for David, he had what we referred to as a "straight" job (book salesman in Manhattan), but he'd managed to finagle a transfer to California so he could savor the hippie glories I'd described to him. On a whim, he brought some of my father's old tackle with him, and we passed a comical evening sorting through it, laughing as we dredged up the names of the long forgotten lures—Hawaiian Wigglers in lurid purple skirts, an evil black Sonic, a wacky Crazy Crawler, and a single Lazy Ike, yellow with bright-red polka dots.

We stored the tackle in the basement, where it languished. It might have stayed there forever, or at least until our landlord evicted us, if I hadn't fallen for a new girlfriend and invited her on a romantic trip to the Sierra Nevada. Not that I'd ever been to the Sierra Nevada myself, but that hardly matters when you're wild about someone. I studied the maps and made the plans and knew in my heart that we would be all right wherever we landed, as long as the place had a bed. After packing the car and loading the cooler, I went downstairs at the last minute and grabbed one of the vintage spin rods and a reel, South Bend and Zebco respectively, although I wasn't truly conscious of why I might be doing it and moved about as a person does in a daze or a dream.

A lake in the Trinity Alps.

We wound up in a rustic cabin on Stuart Fork of the Trinity River, in the shadow of the Trinity Alps. The cabin resembled a packing crate inside and had an icebox instead of a fridge, but it fronted on the river and was blessed with an open-air porch, where we slept on a lumpy mattress and gazed up at the brilliant stars and moonlit peaks and felt that we must be the most fortunate couple on earth. We went hiking, played games of cribbage, and cooked steaks over the coals, and yet not once did it occur to me that I was reliving the family vacation. I was still very young then and blind to so many things, and I didn't realize how a past experience can touch us deeply, can shatter us or set us free, even though we've never reckoned with its power. But I know it now. The past is never wholly gone.

Those days in the mountains were glorious days. It was late in September, but the afternoons were still blazing hot, and we liked nothing better than a nap on the porch after lunch, with the sun falling all around us and the air rich with the scent of sun-warmed pines. One afternoon, I woke before my girlfriend and stood looking at the river, so low and clear I could count the pebbles of the streambed. Trout in there? I doubted it, but I rigged up the rod for fun, rolled up my jeans, and waded barefoot into the water. I could see the sun glinting off the spoon I'd bought at the resort's store and could hear some Steller's jays bickering in the tall trees, and I drifted so far away from Stuart Fork that when a fish hit my lure, it had the effect of yanking me out of the clouds and back into my body.

High up leaped a silvery little rainbow, as hooked in the moment as I was.

CHAPTER 15

MIDSTREAM CRISIS

BY LAMAR UNDERWOOD

Which flies will work today? Photo Credit: Jay Cassell.

As the year began, I decided to embrace the advice of my friend Sparse Grey Hackle, who told me: "Let the wolf out!" He was dead right. It was the only way to go. No more Mister Nice Guy!

My New Year's resolution was a notice served on all creatures, great and small, that in the open seasons ahead I was going to fill my hand. I was fed up with two-trout days, three-bass weekends and no-deer vacations. I'd had it with calling to bird dogs that wouldn't stand still and turkeys that would (two ridges away!). I didn't want to see another pheasant getting up 200 yards away down a corn row or another bay full of ducks and geese rafted up and preening their feathers under skies that had flown in from Palm Springs.

Government wags told me that in the previous season some 2.5 million hunters had shot 12 million ducks. The calculator that lives beside my checkbook told me that works out to five or six ducks per hunter. I didn't get any five ducks! Who the hell shot my ducks?

All around, the previous year had not just been bad; it had been a disaster. I zigged when they zagged. The northeasters and I booked into the same places at the same times. I frightened the spots off brown trout while bass slept through my offerings. The deer left the mountain country I hunt, but those from the woods alongside my house found my tulips and peas in the spring, then shredded two young pines during rubtime in the fall. Plenty of geese crossed the pit blinds I hunkered in all season, but they were so high they were a menace to aviation—and they held express tickets.

My dismal performances afield forced me to face what the late John Foster Dulles called "an agonizing reappraisal." Clearly, my tactics were lousy; my timing stank, my equipment belonged in a museum.

I knew better than to seek some all-embracing formula as my game plan. Each subject would have to be tackled separately, tactics and gear made precise. The geese, I felt, would be the simplest problem to deal with. I began squirreling away the bucks to purchase a 10-gauge magnum automatic, with which I intended to wreak havoc on the Eastern Shore. My more immediate problem—and infinitely more complex—was what to do about those trout.

Since the Romans knew nothing about splitcane rods and matching the hatch, they invented a calendar that starts the new year off from the pit of winter. For me and millions of other fishermen the real new year begins on the opening day of trout season. My usual opening-day scenario looked like this:

An already-pudgy figure, bulked further by enough clothes to outfit the Klondike gold rush, stands hip-deep in a flow of black water torn into sudsy rips by protruding rocks and bearing of the countryside what the winter snows have been holding in storage: sticks, leaves, tires, a bloated cat, the occasional beer can. Overhead the sky is a glowering mass of putty, against which the bare branches of the trees snap and creak with iron-hard stiffness as blasts of wind arrive from Siberia. For hours our man alternates making casts, peering intently at the jaunty little flies that ride the current like miniature galleons, and fumbling stiff fingers through his flybox in search of new offerings. To find a greater fool, you would have to look inside an ice fishing shanty.

The bottom of a trout stream is its food factory, and on this day it will not be violated by anything except the soles of el piscator's waders. Although he will soon abandon his dry flies (how quickly the credo fades: "I'd rather catch one on top than five down deep"), our man will make only tentative probes into the depths. His wet flies, streamers and nymphs will sweep harmlessly over the heads of the stone-hugging trout. Troutless by 3 o'clock, he will seek the solace of the lodge where fire, firewater and kindred snake-bit companions will be waiting with tales of woe and livers in various stages of distress.

Long before opening day dawned last season, I was determined to never again be a part of this demented tableau.

For weeks I hit the books with an intensity seldom mounted in my professional life. Schwiebert, Whitlock, Marinaro, Swisher-Richards, Cucci-Nastasi—the great masters of flyfishing for trout were devoured. Their instruction manifested itself in a barrage of catalogs and small packages of flies arriving daily from every corner of troutdom. My wading vest bulged with trinkets. Latin names of bugs came trippingly off the tongue.

Opening day, I stood thigh-deep at the head of a pool of black water, frigid and swollen with runoff. Coming to the stream, I had received the usual assortment of reports that the fish were in a coma. The voice on the car radio had said something about snow. None of these things intimidated me at all. This year I was ready.

To meet this early and elemental trouting condition, I pried open a box of nymphs. These were not ordinary nymphs, but masterpieces of illusion—caterpillar-like, hairy-leggy-juicy-looking. Each was weighted with enough piano wire to outfit a Steinway. Never mind that they would hit the water with the finesse of a slam-dunk. They would go down, my friend, down, down to the very noses of these frozen wisenheimers. I would fish these creations with a leader hacked to three feet. (Long leaders, I had learned, rise in the pushing and swelling of the current.) The whole outfit would ride down with high-density sinking line topped by a fluorescent strike indicator to tell me when I had a customer.

You don't cast such a rig. What you do is sort of heave the whole mess out and to one side, paying close attention that a hook in the ear is not the immediate result of the effort.

I watched the curls of line and leader straighten downstream toward a boulder that slashed the smooth flow. I tried to form a mental image of what the nymph was doing—sinking, tumbling, ticking over rocks. The line straightened past the boulder. I paid out three more long pulls from the reel, watching the strike indicator bob on downstream.

Suddenly I thought I saw it dart forward. I came back with rod and line and felt the weight of a trout. As the brown—a lovely 15-incher—darted and splashed on the way to the net, my elation soared. My patience and virtue and hard study were to be rewarded. The masters of the game were indeed wise and learned men.

After that, you can imagine my heart-hammering excitement when the next 30 minutes yielded two more fish, about the same size as the first.

Then the devil sent his disciples to descend upon me, like a plague of locusts. First one, then two, then three other anglers were crowding into my stretch of water. Not one asked what I was using. They simply assumed I had found "The Place."

Never mind, I told myself. You can afford to be generous. I waded from the stream and pointed up toward uninhabited water. In a few minutes I was sloshing, much too fast, through a bouldery run of pocket water when I felt my right foot sliding down an eel-slick ledge. I lurched hard to the left, but that leg would not bear the burden. I went down into the water on my back with a teeth jarring crash. Totally submerged for a second, I stood up and cursed my luck and the worn felt soles of my waders. I was drenched, aching-ly cold, and clearly out of action for the rest of the day.

As I waded to the edge of the stream, I discovered another result of my accident with dramatic suddenness. As I made a little sideways move with my left leg to step around a rock, I felt a nauseating wave of pain. I did not want to feel such a shock again, ever, so now I picked my way gingerly along, trying to protect the knee.

Yuk! Yuk! See the man all soaking wet and limping toward his car. Fat-ass must've fallen in. Yuk! Yuk!

A prominent physician whom I trust sentenced the knee to six weeks of healing. Because I could not wade the stream, I could not fish for trout. The great fly hatches of early spring for which I had prepared myself so diligently came and went: the Blue Quills, the Hendericksons, the Grannon caddis, the March Browns.

My mood was foul and depressed. Without my jogging program, with which I had successfully been losing weight, I quickly regained ten pounds. Going to work in New York on the train one day I was struck by a thought as morbid as any I've ever had: The obituary page of the *New York Times* named very few males in their 90s. No, the ages of the boys getting their names in the paper were in the 70s and 80s. At age 45 I had the startling realization that in all likelihood I was more than halfway to the barn. Life begins at 80? Give me a break!

Okay, my somber mood told me, so you've lost some of your good moves and speed. You can't hit a 60-yard mallard or sink a three-foot putt. On the tennis court children who can't get into an R-rated film have you gasping like a beached whale. The guide can show you a tarpon at 60 feet, and you may or may not be able to get the fly to it (probably not, given any kind of wind). But relax, buster. For the years have given you wisdom. Look at what you did with those opening-day trout!

I was still clinging to this slightly uplifting notion when I finally got back to the river in late May. One of the year's best hatches remained. According to the grapevine, the Sulphurs had arrived in tentative numbers two days earlier, and all signs pointed to their major emergence late that evening.

The hatch of *Ephemerella dorothea*, which goes on with diminishing consistency for about six weeks on good eastern streams, ranks as a favorite because it stirs smart, self-respecting trout into an unusual orgy of gluttony. Unlike some mayfly hatches, which deliver more sizzle than steak, the

appearance of the No. 16 yellow-and-dun flies in the last hour before darkness produces fishing so fast and exciting that it is the stuff for cool hands
and stout hearts.

My favorite slick-water was flat empty that evening. My recent misfortune was all forgotten as I waded into position and made a few desultory
casts while waiting for the hatch to begin. The air was heavy with humidity,
and low clouds on the ridges promised that darkness would come early and
perhaps a thunderstorm with it.

The time that passed seemed interminable. Nothing came off the darkening water, not even caddis. A kingfisher flew upstream, scolding my presence. I heard a great horned owl up on the mountain and an answering cry
from nearby. Then I saw the first delicate yellow mayfly climbing steeply
toward the trees. In a few moments there was another, then another, then another, and then I actually saw one in the instant it left the water—and beyond
it the swirl of a trout.

My line arched through the growing dusk. I saw my artificial Sulphur
begin its jaunty ride down the feeding lane where the trout had swirled. It
floated on downstream unharmed. There were other rises all over the pool
now—not splashy water-throwing slaps, but subtle bulges and swirls.

I really started worrying when my bogus Sulphur made three more rides
through the melee without interesting a trout. What was wrong? The fly? The
leader? My thoughts screamed as I watched the hatch and rises go on: You've
been out of action so long you don't know what you're doing.

In the middle of this burst of self-condemnation I saw something—
flashes of darting trout just beneath the surface. That was it! The trout were
not taking the surface duns! They were nymphing, gulping the insects as they
rose to the surface and in the film as they emerged into winged shape.

I was prepared for this, but my hands trembled as I opened the flybox
and got out a floating nymph. The light was going fast, but I managed to tie
on the fly without digging out my night light. In my excitement, however, I
dropped my reading half-glasses into the stream. Klutz! Fool! I should have
had them on a cord around my neck.

No matter. I had the right ammo now, and the fish were still going strong as I roll-cast the nymph to the top of the pool. Instantly a trout was on, and I felt a flush of ultimate satisfaction.

The fish was a strong pulsating weight as it struggled upstream for a few seconds. Then the line went slack as the trout bolted downstream almost past my legs, a momentary shadow that caused me to gasp: I was into my largest trout ever.

The reel screamed appropriately as the fish bolted downstream. He reached the lip of the falls that terminated the pool and turned to face the current. The steady pressure on the 5X felt unbelievable. I had the feeling of the fish backing up, backing to the edge of the tumbling water. He was going to be washed over the lip! I had to do something! I palmed the flange of the reel, increasing the drag, and thereby succeeded in instantly breaking off the trout as surely as though I'd been trying to.

I reeled in the sickeningly slack line and looked at the 5X tippet. So many trout were still taking the sulphur nymphs all over the pool that the excitement smothered the loss of the big fish. I quickly had another floating nymph out, ready to tie on. I felt my shirt pocket for my reading glasses and remembered where they had gone. I held the fly at arm's length against the gloom of the darkening sky. No way. I could not thread the eye of the hook in that dimness.

No problem. My night light had a magnifying glass that fit over the top of the light. No sweat, just stay cool.

I was deeply aware of the rises continuing all over the pool as I pulled the light out and draped its cord around my neck. I felt deeper into the pocket for the magnifying glass. It wasn't there! I flipped the switch on the light. Nothing! Click, click. Click, click. Still nothing! Okay, the batteries are dead. You're on your own. Now just hold the fly very still against what is left of the sky and tie it on.

My panic rose as I tried unsuccessfully to tie on the No. 16 Sulphur. I tied a No. 14. It would not go. In a final burst of madness and inspiration, I dug out a No. 10 Blonde Wulff, the biggest fly in my vest. Maybe it would work on these feeding fish.

Perhaps it would have. I don't know. I never got the Wulff tied on. My vision is 20–20, but at age 45, I could not see close up well enough to tie on a fly and resume fishing a hatch that I had waited for all winter.

I reeled in slowly, felt the end of the leader reach the reel, then broke down my rod. The splashes of feeding trout popped out from the darkness. I could not see the rises now, but they were distinctive above the murmur the current made as it tailed from the pool downstream.

Slowly the disappointment drained away. The easy moves, the good speed. Going, going with the years. Yet it was true: You were wiser, vastly richer in the things you knew. Such as realizing right now that what made fishing so great was that on any given outing, things could happen that you would remember all of your days. Few other times in life could offer that. That is the easy part of change—the knowing, the feeling. The other side is that you have left something precious behind—something you had used up and would have to go on without.

Flashes of lightning came across the ridgetop, then the roll of advancing thunder. The feeding grew quieter, then died out completely. The bursts of lightning helped me find my way up the hillside to the lane that led back to the car.

I did not know if I had reached the end of something or the beginning.

The wind blew on the high ridges, gusting along the slopes, coming down to the river.

CLASSIC FISHING STORIES

CHAPTER 16

BRANNIGAN'S TROUT

BY NICK LYONS

After the crack up, he was hospitalized for six months. Twice the doctors warned Jane that they might lose him. Then, when they saved him, they warned that there was probably brain damage. When he was released, in November, they told him he'd be paralyzed on his right side for life.

Four doctors confirmed the verdict.

There was nothing for it.

Perhaps there was a slight chance, but not likely, that regular exercise, steady exercise over a period of several years, might restore some small portion of his mobility. Not much. Possibly none. Frankly, Brannigan was not inclined to try. Why go through all the effort? So he sat silent and sullen in the wheelchair that grey afternoon and allowed the men in white to push him to the car, lift and place him into the front seat, collapse the chair and put it in the back, then tell Jane how he was to get in and out, how she was to rig the contraption and place it for him. Like a baby.

He said not a word on the long trip through the sere, dead countryside. Jane told him about the boys, and which friends had called; Mike Novak might come over that evening. He didn't even nod. His great black-haired head thrown back and tilted to one side, he watched with dead eyes the fleeting fields of withered cornstalks, leafless trees, dark scudding clouds. There was nothing for it. He was forty-six and it was over. He couldn't sell books or anything else anymore; he didn't know whether he could drink beer with his friends, chop wood, tend his garden, drive, smoke, sing, read, write; and certainly the fishing season was over for him. Permanently.

The crash in all its stark detail, the fluky chance of it, kept flashing through his brain: Johnny Wohl driving, across the seat from him saying, seconds before, "Well, Billy, we made a day of it, didn't we? I never saw the river so alive." And Mike in the back. Laughing wildly and about to say something about having caught three Hendricksons. Then the rasp of brakes, the black car coming just that moment smoothly out of the side road, the jolt of fear, his hands flying up, his back thrusting backward against the seat, the hurtling forward—and darkness, and stabbing, raw pain in his shoulders, his head. Then nothing. Johnny Wohl and the two teenagers in the black car had been killed instantly. Mike came out of it with his right pinky broken. Well, good for him. Good for old Mike.

As for himself, it would have been better to have had it over then, right then when it happened. Quick. No more pain to die than to live, then. He need merely not have come out of the coma. After that first, searing pain, poof. For good. And they all said he's only lived because he wanted to live. So he lived—like a half-squashed worm.

He saw suddenly in his mind the 20-gauge shotgun in the cabinet in his den. Would Jane have removed it? This was no time to ask. That night, when the boys were doing their homework, he'd wheel in by himself and just take a look-see. He'd take it out, break it open . . . take a look-see.

At dinner, Jane talked constantly—about the Murphy's new Brittany spaniel; the good batch of slab wood Frank had hauled from the lumber yard, piece by piece, and cut himself; the threat of an early snow. Brannigan looked up now and then from his plate, spread his lips slightly in the best he could do for a smile, and nodded. He said nothing. He was still not sure what the cracked, alien sound of his voice—what remained of speech—would be to these people, whether he could put together all the words needed for one whole sentence. Whenever he raised his head and looked toward one of his sons, Frank to his right, fifteen, Junior on his left, a year older and dark-haired too, rebellious, they were looking at their own plates. They knew everything. When he looked back at his own plate and prepared his next strategy to get a piece of meat to his mouth, he thought he saw, peripherally, their heads raise slightly and turn toward him. He didn't think he could bear it. Not that. He'd come through Normandy without a scratch; he'd never been seriously ill in his life.

Working diligently with the fork in his left hand, like they'd taught him in the hospital, he speared a piece of the steak Jane had cut for him, shifted the fork carefully in his hand, and brought it to his mouth. He chewed the meat slowly for a few moments, then lowered the fork to get another. But the prongs pressed against the gristle, slipped, and flicked the chunk of meat onto the floor. Brannigan looked after it, heard Jane say, "I'll pick it up later, dear," then slammed the fork down on his plate. Frank and Junior raised their hunched shoulders and looked up sharply. Jane took a deep breath.

"Nuff," muttered Brannigan. "Nuff." He pushed the wheelchair away, turning it, and, his hand on the wheel-rail, glided into the living and toward his den—hearing Frank say something low that ended with "like that," and Junior's heavier voice, and then Jane telling them in a normal voice to finish quickly and go upstairs: they'd talk of it later.

He negotiated the living room and came to the door of his den. His room. The door was closed but he came against it sideways, took his left hand from the wheel-rail and reached out for the knob. As he did so, the chair slipped back a few inches and he was only able to touch a bit of the knob. He gritted his teeth, pounded his left hand down on the armrest, wheeled himself close again, and tried another time. Again the chair slipped back a bit and he couldn't, hard as he strained, even touch the knob. Damned. Damned. He sat in the chair, breathing heavily for a few moment, then tried again, got it, flung the door open, gave the wheel-rail a sharp thrust forward, and was in his room. His room.

God, how many good hours he'd spent there. The soft old armchair. His own mount of the four-pound brook trout he's caught in Canada that summer with Mike and Johnny. The humidor with those long black dago-ropes he loved so much. Fireplace. Little fly-tying table—just like he'd left it. Silver rod cases in the cabinet he'd built himself. The old black-bear rug he'd bought, over Jane's hilarious objections. His room.

It was a room to which he slunk after a knockdown argument with Jane, a lousy road trip; he went there to plan his selling strategies, realign the world, read quietly in the evening or tie flies. He'd had most of his serious talks with his boys in this room; and he'd laughed and drunk beer and told stories half the night with Johnny and Mike here. Useless now. There was not one thing in the room, as he looked around, that he wanted.

The shotgun.

His eyes shifted sharply to the oak cabinet with the V-back that fitted into the corner so snugly. It was there. He went to his fly-tying table, opened the middle drawer, and felt with his hand among the capes and bobbins until his fingers found and closed tightly around the long brass key. Then, holding the key in the palm of his left hand, he used his fingers to push the chair over to the cabinet.

He had only that one gun, a beautiful 20-gauge with polished walnut stock, grey shoulder cushion, twin slate-grey barrels. He liked the feel of it in his hands, the power with which it jerked back when he shot. He'd gotten his first grouse with it last winter. Sam, Johnny's Brittany, had frozen on point, Johnny had called for the flush, and the grouse, a single, had exploded with a whirr from the underbrush. "Yours!" shouted Mike, and he'd swung, led, and watched the bird pause, sputter, and fall. He remembered the deep satisfaction he'd felt from that connection, that force which shot out from him and dropped that bird.

The shotgun.

Another moment and he'd have it in his hands, feel its sleek powerful lines, its smooth stock. The gun held power, energy, force; merely to have it in your hands was to feel some electrical current, some charge of strength shot into your veins, your body. "Look-see," he said, flinching at the cracked, strange sound of his voice, inserting the key into the lock and turning, then opening the cabinet door slowly.

It was not there. The cabinet was empty.

His eyes blazed and he slammed the door shut. It was not there. She had taken it. Grasping the wheel-rail he thrust downward and began to roll across the carpet toward the closed door to the living room. She had taken it. "Gun," he said, his voice a rasping growl. "Gun. Gun." Then, opening the door, he let his head fall, and he muttered, "Did she . . . really . . . think . . ."

"So the point is that I asked Jane for your goddamn shotgun because mine is at the gunsmith and I ain't got one to use next week," Mike said ten minutes later when they were alone in the den. "She didn't want to let me have it. Nope. 'Mike,' she says, 'Billy loves that rifle.' That's what she called it, a rifle, 'and I don't think I can let you have it.'"

Brannigan frowned. He looked intently at the bronze, hearty face of his friend, that bullish chest above toothpick legs, the straight black, always greasy and carefully combed hair, the mechanic's hands, stained black.

"I says: 'Look, Janie, he may not be out until after Christmas and I know he'd want me to put a few notches on it for him. One thing about Billy,

An artistic rendering of a brook trout.

he don't like a good rod or shotgun lying around. Offends his Scotch-Irish blood.'"

"Lie."

"I was going to take it out to the range, test it on some clays, but if you'd like it back, got some special use for it, I'll. . . ." He broke off, lowered his voice, and said: "It's been rough, ain't it, kiddo?"

"Ruh-uf."

"Yeah," said Mike, turning his back and walking across the room to look at the big, bright male brook trout on the wall. "Remember when you got that one, Billy?" he said without turning around. "You'd cast that big funny fly from New Zealand, the Red Setter, looked like a whore's hairdo, into the swirls below the falls. I was behind you. I'd gotten one about three pounds that morning and you was burning mad. Didn't even speak to me at lunch. Well, maybe I was being a bit rotten about it." He came and sat down in the soft old armchair. "I must've turned and the next thing I know your rod's bent like a crescent moon and you're yelling like a banshee. Johnny thinks you've fallen in or got bit by a snake, so he comes running up, and by this time there's the goddamnedest smug look on your face! You've got the fish well hooked, you've seen him roll, and you know the size of him—and you know you got the greatest audience any mug ever had."

He watched Brannigan's eyes. They changed as he told the story.

"You're using this ten-pound-test leader and can't possibly lose that fish unless it gets into the rapids, and you're acting just as cockeyed cool as a cock of the roost. Johnny and me, we may be a little green around the gills but we're sitting polite as you please, murmuring a few friendly words of praise now and then—like, 'Did that lemon have to get it?'—and you keep playing him gently, making maybe a bit too much of a show of fear when it heads downstream. Cool. Very cool, Billy. And when Johnny wants to net him for you, with the big net, what do you do? Wave him away, and fuss with that minnow net you carry."

The faintest trace of a smile began to struggle around the corners of Brannigan's twisted mouth and eyes.

"So this absolute monster of a brookie, the biggest trout any of us has ever seen, is beat, and over on its side, and you're swiping at it with your net—probably trying to get it to rush off so's the show can go on—and first you get the tail in, right?"

Brannigan nodded.

"Then when it flops out, you try to bend it in, from the middle, but the monster won't be bent, so you go for the head, which barely fits into that guppy net, and then you've got it head first to about the gills and sort of clamp your hand down on the rest and come yelping out of the water, the line and rod and net and you all tangled together, and you fall on it. God, that fish was gorgeous—and there he is. That the way it happened, Billy? Something like that?"

Brannigan raised his left hand in a little shrug. "Ha-pinned . . . like . . . that."

"So the point is, you got one. You got one bigger than any of us ever got, even Johnny, God rest his soul, and now you figure, 'The big bird's crapped on me. I've caught my last big fish and shot my last grouse.' That it?"

"That-z-it."

"Johnny doesn't make it and you ain't satisfied to be here. Instead of being pleased I come tonight, passing up some very possible quail, you're going to stew in your own bile, right?"

"Rrr-ight."

"There's no one in particular to hate for it, so you figure you'll spread the hate around, to Jane and the boys, and especially yourself, and maybe you'll get lucky and not be around too much longer to be a burden to anyone. Well, I see your point, Brannigan. Lot of logic to it. Then say maybe there's a chance in a couple hundred thousand that you get anything back on that right side, so you say, 'Bad odds.'" He walked to the fly-tying table, picked up one of the capes, a pale ginger, and bent back the hackle of one feather. "A good one, Billy. Firstrate dry-fly neck. Good small size, too." Then he went to the humidor and drew out one of the twisted black cigars.

"You don't mind?" Brannigan, watching him closely, did not change his expression. Mike put the cigar in the center of his mouth, struck a match, and got the tip of the cigar glowing like a little coal. "Good cigar, Billy." He puckered his lips, held the cigar in three fingers, and took a long puff.

Brannigan kept watching him. He had not moved his chair from the moment Mike had come in. Quail. Big trout. A grouse or two. Lives for that. Two wives, maybe have ten more. Funny guy. The way he holds that cigar—like he owned the world, all of it. Shotgun. Ask.

"So the point is, it would break my sweet heart if you wasn't around, kiddo. Know what I mean? You know what I did when they told me you was"—he put out his hand, palm down, and rocked it slightly—"maybe not going to make it? I prayed. Me. Prayed. I said, 'Oh, God, let old Billy come through with anything, any goddamnit thing at all, so long as he's here and I can brag to him now and then about what quail I'm snatching—anything, God, just so long as he's here where I can see his ugly black-haired head now and then'"—he puffed hard at the cigar—"when the quail ain't flying and the trout is down. It's rough, right?"

Ask about shotgun.

"Suddenly the rules is all changed."

The gun.

"So the point is," he said, puffing hard, exhaling three times in rapid succession—"Hell, I don't know what the point is, Billy, but it will be awfully lonely next May when the Hendricksons start popping not to . . . Here, catch this"—and he tossed a softball, underhand, directly at Brannigan's chest. The left hand went up and forced the ball against the right shoulder. The right shoulder, limp and loose, twitched ever so slightly toward the ball. Brannigan held the ball for a moment, then took it in his left hand and tossed it back. Then he left his right shoulder and slowly dug his fingers into the muscle. "Not . . . much left."

"You'll cast lefty," said Mike. "Once knew an old poacher name of Sven who had to learn because there was bad brush on the right side. Dry-fly purist of a poacher." And the story went on for twenty minutes, and included a patrol dog named Wolf, five pound rainbows, two delicious young women, the true origin of "Sven's left curve drop cast," which only lefties could use, and then, just before the point of it all, Mike simply said, "It's eleven. The quail will have flown. I'll bring the 20-gauge tomorrow, eh?"

Brannigan smiled, a slow, deep smile that spread into his cheeks and eyes, and stayed, even when the twitch started. He nudged his right hand out with his left, so Mike could take and hold it, and Mike took it and held it in both of his own, rubbing the lifeless thing vigorously, then turning quickly for the door. Before he got there, Brannigan said: "The gun . . . yours."

The limbs remember, he thought, working the rake lightly across the soil he'd just fitted with seed, and so does the earth. It remembers what it must do to these seeds, and the seeds, someplace deep within them, knew what they must do.

Back and forth he moved the rake, holding it firmly in his left hand, using his nearly useless right to steady it. The May sun was warm but not bright, and kneaded his broad naked shoulders. He could walk without the cane now—somewhat. With that bizarre arc. His hair had gone snow white, which he liked, but otherwise, if he didn't move and didn't talk, he looked nearly the same.

Everyone else had planted a week or two ago but he'd worked more slowly, as he had to—long patient hours, setting his fertilizer, running the hand plow steadily across the small garden he'd staked out last spring, seeding the soil. This would be a good year. He could feel it. He's learned how to coax green from the brown soil, how important it was, always, to be patient—to lay the proper foundation, however long that took, before you could expect anything to grow. Tomatoes, cucumbers, carrots, radishes, onions—he'd had these last year; now he added kale, zucchini, tarragon, other herbs. Each day now he would work on his garden for several hours, bending down to it, plucking, feeling, watering, watching. It all mattered. Even the watching. Every day. He'd increased the size of his garden by a third this year. It would require more work but he could do it. He still forgot many things—names, events, people he had known; but he forgot nothing connected to his garden. It would be a good garden this year, as fruitful as anyone's garden. Maybe better.

Got it all now, he thought, leaning against the rake, and Mike will be here soon to take us a-fishing. It would be good to be in the car, on a trip, listening to Mike's excited patter, it would be good to try the river again. Mike had said the Hendricksons had started.

Three years. Days, weeks, months had ticked by, minute by minute, and imperceptibly the changes had come. The insurance had kept them from bankruptcy, Jane had begun to work for a real-estate agent in town—and had blossomed with it. Junior was earning his way in college, his own man, and Frank was a senior in high school and working part-time at Mike's garage.

They didn't need what he'd once earned; he knew that what they needed most he could give them only after he had given it to himself.

He had done the exercises the men in white advised, with barbells and bicycle—over and over and again; he hated to do them and stopped when it came time to work in his garden. Several times last spring Mike had taken him to the West Branch, which they'd often fished together, before he got wracked. At first he merely found a rock, sat down, and watched. But he had not been able to resist the tug, deep inside him, to be on the stream, part of it, fishing. Wasn't that really why he'd done all those endless, tedious exercises, up and down, back and forth, hour after hour, all those months?

It had been impossible at first, after nearly two years. He had slipped twice on the rocks before he even reached the river. Even with the cane his right leg would not hold on broken terrain. Then he slipped again when he took his first tentative step into the water, careening badly, catching himself on his left arm. "No help, no help," he'd said when Mike stepped toward him.

Then he'd been unable to strip line and cast left-handed, and finally, after several mad minutes he had given it up and fallen again on his way out, slamming his chin into a rock, cutting it sharply. No. It was not possible. He could not do it.

But it was a warm May morning and Mike would be there soon and it would be better this year. He'd earned it. Perhaps he'd even take his first trout since the crash.

Mike came promptly at twelve, and in a few minutes they were in the car racing toward the West Branch. "Magnificent day, Billy," Mike said, pushing the pedal harder. "The Hendricksons will be on in all their glory. They'll be popping out and the birds will be working, and we're going to get us a few. The cornfield run. I can feel a certain fat old brownie just waiting for you there today."

Mike parked along a small dirt turnoff and they got out and began to rig their rods, put on the waders. Mike was suited up and ready before Brannigan had worked one leg into his hip boots. "Go on, Mike. I'll be there . . . when I'm there."

"So you're tired of my company. Fine. I'm going upstream, you take the middle of the run. Where the current slows. Take your time: we're a half hour early. Lousy luck, kiddo."

Brannigan watched him stride off, his bull back bouncing even in waders. Then he finished raising his boots, strapped them to his belt, and got out his vest. He could use his right hand as a support now, to hold one section of the rod firmly enough for his left to insert the other section; he managed it, with guides aligned, on only the second try. Then he strung the line slowly through the guides until the end of the fly line and all of the leader were outside the tip top. It was well he had practiced all winter.

He got out a Hendrickson he'd tied before the crash, kept in mothballs, and held it as firmly as he could with his right fingers. Then he tried to insert the point of the leader. It would not go. He kept shoving it off to the side, or shaking the fly. Finally he dropped the fly in the grass and had to bend down, slowly, to look for it. When he found it, he stayed on the ground in the shadow of the car and held the fly up to the sky so that the light-blue would show through the hole and he could better fit in the leader. The operation took him five minutes.

As he began to walk along the edge of the cornfield toward the river, his right leg came up in a large, jerky arc, and then down again, one step after the other. Slowly. There was no rush. There was plenty of time. Mike had coaxed him out several more times last summer and fall, and each time he fell but there was some slight improvement. Not much. Not enough for him to know he could do it, like he could garden, not enough to get a line out far enough to tempt a trout—but some. You had to connive. You had to be cunning and crafty, and to forget how it once was. You had to remember always that it would not all come back, not ever. You had to work within the fixed knowledge that you continue to improve, always, and that this counted, but that even at your very best, some day, you would be, by the world's standards, a lemon.

Perhaps he'd get one today. His first. It would be wonderful if he could get into a really large trout, perhaps seventeen or eighteen inches. You didn't have to make many casts, just the right one at the right time. He'd practiced on the lawn and he knew he now could get enough distance to reach the lip of the current in the cornfield pool. He'd once fished it many times. There was room for a decent backcast, and the shallow bar on his side of the run was hard earth and rubble, with only a few rocks that might trip him up. Mike had made a good choice; he'd be fishing upstream, in the fast water where the Hendricksons hatched, but there'd be plenty of fish falling back into the pool to pick up the duns as they floated down, especially once the hatch really got going.

One step at a time—the right leg out first, and down, out and down. No hurry. You couldn't rush a walk anymore than you could a garden. You couldn't rush anything. Anyway, you saw more when you walked this slow— those crows pecking at corn seeds, that huge growth of skunk cabbage, lush and green and purple, the fuzzy green on the boughs of the willows. A gorgeous day, only slightly overcast now, perfect for Hendricksons.

As he neared the row of trees that bordered the river, he could see Mike upstream, wading deep; his rod was held high and had a sharp arc. Good old Mike. Got one already. Up and out, then down. Then again. And again. He worked his way through the alders to the edge of the river. The water was perfect—dark and alive, flecked with bubbles and eddies where the current widened and slowed. Like he'd dreamed it all winter. Yes, that was a fish. And another. He looked to the sky and saw four or five tan flies flutter and angle off into the trees. Yes. Yes.

He took a tentative step into the water and felt a touch of fear as he left the firmness of the earth. No matter. It would pass. All the old feeling was there; he could still feel, deep within him, something in him reaching out to the life of the river—its quick faceted run above the long flat pool below; its translucent dark green and gliding shadows. Flowing, always moving. Changing. The same and not the same. He picked out a dun and watched it bound, like a tiny tan sailboat, over the tail of the riffle, then swirl and float into slower water where it vanished in a sudden pinching of the surface.

Yes, they were moving today. He could see six, seven fish in fixed feeding positions, rising steadily. There was plenty of time. Don't rush. Do it very, very slowly. They'd be going good for another hour; he wanted to pick out one good fish, near enough for him to reach with his short cast. Only one good fish. He didn't want a creelful. Only one.

Upstream, Mike was into another trout, and a few minutes later while Brannigan still eased slowly, steadily into deeper water, inch by inch, Mike had another. We've caught one of those magical days, he thought. Another foot or so . . . At last, deep as he dared go, he stood on firm hard rubble in water up to his thighs. He stripped line deliberately by raising and lowering his right hand; then, holding the loose line as best he could, he made an extremely short cast. Good. Much better this year. Then he stood, rod poised, watching the spreading circles of feeding fish. There were two twelve-inchers in the middle current lane, feeding freely, and two small fish back ten feet; he couldn't reach any of those anymore, though they'd once have been easy enough casts. He could never have finished to that rise in the far eddy, though: the currents were too tricky, the cast too long. Too bad. That was a large fish.

Then he saw the steady sipping rise directly upstream from him, not thirty feet away. Sometimes the largest fish rose like that, but so did fingerlings. It was time to try. He could reach that fish.

His first cast was too short and too hard. His next was off to the right and too hard. The next two were not bad but the fish both times rose to a natural a second before his fly floated past. On his next cast, the trout rose freely, took, and, gripping line and handle with his left hand, as he'd practiced, he struck and had the fish on. A good one. A bright, large leaper that came out, shaking its spots at him and falling back, and then streaking up into the current, across to the far bank, boring deep, and then leaping again.

"Mike!" He usually didn't talk while he fished but he wanted his friend to see this. He hadn't shouted very loud and above him, Mike, busy with still another fish, did not hear. Again the fish came out. "A beauty," he said audibly. "A fine brown." Again the fish raced across the current, stripping line from the reel, arching the rod sharply. Got to get it. Can't lose this one.

In ten minutes he could tell the trout was tiring. But it was still on the opposite side of the current. As he began to retrieve the line slowly, the fish came into the current and allowed itself to be carried downstream. Then, suddenly, it bolted directly toward him and the line went slack. "No, no," he said, struggling but unable to strip back line quickly enough.

When he regained control, the fish was gone. He drew the line back slowly until he could see the bedraggled fly. The fish had merely pulled out on the slack line—because of his goddam right arm. His right arm—which might as well not be there.

He was sitting in the car, all his equipment packed away, when Mike came back. Mike had caught seven fish, all of size but none as large as the one Brannigan had lost, and said it was the best day he could remember, except of course the day he'd gotten the three-pound brookie in Canada and Brannigan that lucky male. Brannigan offered a weak smile but said nothing, and Mike looked at him and then said nothing as he took off his vest and waders.

In the car, heading home, he turned to Brannigan and asked quietly, "How'd you do, Billy? Take any?"

"I lost one . . . Mike. Pretty good fish. Then I decided I'd better quit because at least I hadn't fallen in. Like every other time. So I headed . . . out. Slowly. Praising myself all the time . . . that at least I hadn't taken . . . a bath this time."

"You took some bad ones last year, Billy."

"I'd lost a good one, a really good fish, and that didn't make . . . me feel too cheery . . . Yet I'd hooked it and played it a long time . . . which I . . . never did before, not since I got wrecked, and I figured . . . if I could get out without a spill, I'd . . . still be ahead."

"Was it really a good fish, Billy?" "Big. Very big brown."

"Sixteen inches." "More."

"That's a big fish."

"So I was one step or two from the bank, smiling and praising myself . . . that I . . . hadn't fallen, when . . . I went into a pothole."

"Hell!"

"So I went down and over, ass . . . over teakettle. Almost drowned."
"Billy!"

"Almost. My head went under . . . and I was on my right side and couldn't . . . get leverage, and sort of forced my head out, and went under again, and gagged. Know I was going to die. I felt the grasp of brakes . . . in my brain. I suddenly . . . did not want to die. The water was shallow . . . but it was deep enough. Deep enough. Mike. I did not want to die," he said quietly. "So finally I managed to twist over onto my left side. Broke my rod. Slammed my bone badly. Barely . . . got out of it."

Mike looked over at this friend who had lost his fish, nearly ended it all. He had not one word to cheer him with. Brannigan was sitting in the same seat he'd been in when the accident smashed him, and there was a curious grin on his face. "Maybe we . . . really shouldn't go anymore, Billy," Mike said soberly. "Know what I mean?" He had hoped desperately that Brannigan would get one good trout, that this day might be a new beginning. He had for three years said everything he knew to say. He had no words left.

Faintly, as a slight pressure first and then a firm grip, Mike felt his friend's left hand on his shoulder. "No," he heard Brannigan say. And when he turned: "We're going . . . to keep going . . . back."

CHAPTER 17

ON DRY-COW FISHING AS A FINE ART

BY RUDYARD KIPLING

Wivenhoe Park by John Constable, 1816.

It must be clearly understood that I am not at all proud of this performance. In Florida men sometimes hook and land, on rod and tackle a little finer than a steam-crane and chain, a mackerel-like fish called "tarpon," which sometime run to 120 pounds. Those men stuff their captures and exhibit them in glass cases and become puffed up. On the Columbia River sturgeon of 150 pounds weight are taken with the line. When the sturgeon is hooked the line is fixed to the nearest pine tree or steamboat-wharf, and after some hours or days the sturgeon surrenders himself, if the pine or the line do not give way. The owner of the line then states on oath that he has caught a sturgeon, and he, too, becomes proud.

These things are mentioned to show how light a creel will fill the soul of a man with vanity. I am not proud. It is nothing to me that I have hooked and played seven hundred pounds weight of quarry. All my desire is to place the little affair on record before the mists of memory breed the miasma of exaggeration.

The minnow cost eighteen-pence. It was a beautiful quill minnow, and the tackle-maker said that it could be thrown as a fly. He guaranteed further in respect to the triangles—it glittered with triangles—that, if necessary, the minnow would hold a horse. A man who speaks too much truth is just as offensive as a man who speaks too little. None the less, owing to the defective condition of the present law of libel, the tackle-master's name must be withheld.

The minnow and I and a rod went down to a brook to attend to a small jack who lived between two clumps of flags in the most cramped swim that he could select. As a proof that my intentions were strictly honorable, I may mention that I was using a light split-cane rod—very dangerous if the line runs through the weeds, but very satisfactory in clean water, inasmuch as it keeps a steady strain on the fish and prevents him from taking liberties. I had an old score against the jack. He owed me two live-bait already, and I had reason to suspect him of coming up-stream and interfering with a little bleak-pool under a horse-bridge which lay entirely beyond his sphere of legitimate influence. Observe, therefore, that my tackle and my motives pointed clearly to jack, and jack alone; though I knew that there were monstrous big perch in the brook.

The minnow was thrown as a fly several times, and, owing to my peculiar, and hitherto unpublished, methods of fly throwing, nearly six pennyworth of the triangles came off, either in my coat-collar, or my thumb, or the back of my hand. Fly fishing is a very gory amusement.

The jack was not interested in the minnow, but towards twilight a boy opened a gate of the field and let in some twenty or thirty cows and half-a-dozen cart-horses, and they were all very much interested. The horses galloped up and down the field and shook the banks, but the cows walked solidly and breathed heavily, as people breathe who appreciate the Fine Arts.

By this time I had given up all hope of catching my jack fairly, but I wanted the live-bait and bleak-account settled before I had quite made up my mind to borrow a tin of chloride of lime from the farm-house—another triangle had fixed itself in my fingers—I made a cast which for pure skill, exact judgment of distance, and perfect coincidence of hand and eye and brain, would have taken every prize at a bait-casting tournament. That was the first half of the cast. The second was postponed because the quill minnow would not return to its proper place, which was under the lobe of my left ear. It had done thus before, and I supposed it was in collision with a grass tuft, till I turned around and saw a large red and white bald faced cow tying to rub what would be withers in a horse with her nose. She looked at me reproachfully, and her look said as plainly as words: "The season is too far advanced for gadflies. What is this strange disease?"

I replied, "Madam, I must apologize for an unwarrantable liberty on the part of my minnow, but if you will have the goodness to keep still until I can reel in, we will adjust this little difficulty."

I reeled in very swiftly and cautiously, but she would not wait. She put her tail in the air and ran away. It was a purely involuntary motion on my part: I struck. Other anglers may contradict me, but I firmly believe that if a man had foul-hooked his best friend through the nose, and that friend ran, the man would strike by instinct. I struck, therefore, and the reel began to sing just as merrily as though I had caught my jack. But had it been a jack, the minnow would have come away. I told the tackle-maker this much afterwards, and he laughed and made allusions to the guarantee about holding a horse.

Because it was a fat innocent she-cow that had done me no harm the minnow held—held like an anchor-fluke in coral moorings—and I was forced to dance up and down an interminable field very largely used by cattle. It was like salmon fishing in a nightmare. I took gigantic strides, and every stride found me up to my knees in marsh. But the cow seemed to skate along the squashy greens by the brook, to skim over the miry backwaters, and to float like a mist through the patches of rush that squirted black filth over my face. Sometimes we whirled through a mob of her friends—there were no friends to help me—and they looked scandalized; and sometimes a young and frivolous cart-horse would join in the chase for a few miles, and kick solid pieces of mud into my eyes; and through all the mud, the milky smell of kine, the rush and the smother, I was aware of my own voice crying: "Pussy, pussy, pussy! Pretty pussy! Come along then, puss-cat!" You see it is so hard to speak to a cow properly, and she would not listen—no, she would not listen.

Then she stopped, and the moon got up behind the pollards to tell the cows to lie down; but they were all on their feet, and they came trooping to see. And she said, "I haven't had my supper, and I want to go to bed, and please don't worry me." And I said, "The matter has passed beyond any apology. There are three courses open to you, my dear lady. If you'll the common sense to walk up to my creel I'll get my knife and you shall have all the minnow. Or, again, if you'll let me move across to your near side, instead of keeping me so coldly on your off side, the thing will come away in one tweak. I can't pull it out over your withers. Better still, go to a post and rub it out, dear. It won't hurt much, but if you think I'm going to lose my rod to please you, you are mistaken." And she said, "I don't understand what you are saying. I am very, very unhappy." And I said, "It's your fault for trying to fish. Do go to the nearest gate-post, you nice fat thing, and rub it out."

For a moment I fancied she was taking my advice. She ran away and I followed. But all the other cows came with us in a bunch, and I thought of Phaeton trying to drive the Chariot of the Sun, and Texan cowboys killed by stampeding cattle, and "Green Grow the Rushes, O!" and Solomon and Job, and "loosing the bands of Orion," and hooking Behemoth, and Wordsworth who talks about whirling around with stones and rocks and trees, and "Here we go round the Mulberry bush," and "Pippin Hill," and "Hey Diddle Diddle," and most especially the top joint of my rod. Again she stopped—but nowhere in the neighborhood of my knife—and her sisters stood moonfaced round her. It seemed that she might, now, run towards me, and I looked for a tree, because cows are very different from salmon, who only jump against the line, and never molest the fisherman. What followed was worse than any direct attack. She began to buckjump, to stand on her head and her tail alternately, to leap to the sky, all four feet together, and to dance on her hind legs. It was so violent and improper, so desperately unladylike, that I was inclined to blush, as one would blush at the sight of a prominent statesman sliding down a dire escape, or a duchess chasing her cook with a skillet. That flop-some abandon might go on all night in the lonely meadow among the mists, and if it went on all night—this was pure inspiration—I might be able to worry through the fishing line with my teeth.

Those who desire an entirely new sensation should chew with all their teeth, and against time, through a best waterproofed silk line, one end of which belongs to a mad cow dancing fairy rings in the moonlight; at the same time keeping one eye on the cow and the other on the top joint of a split-cane rod. She buck-jumped and I bit on the slack just in front of the reel; and I am in a position to state that that line was cored with steel wire throughout the particular section which I attacked. This had been formally denied by the tackle-maker, who is not to be believed.

The wheep of the broken line running through the rings told me that henceforth the cow and I might be strangers. I had already bidden good-bye to some tooth or teeth; but not price is too great for freedom of the soul.

"Madam," I said, "the minnow and twenty feet of very superior line are your alimony without reservation. For the wrong I have unwittingly done to you I express my sincere regret. At the same time, may I hope that Nature, the kindest of nurses, will in due season—"

She or one of her companions must have stepped on her spare end of the line in the dark, for she bellowed wildly and ran away, followed by all the cows. I hoped the minnow was disengaged at last; and before I went away looked at my watch, fearing to find it nearly midnight. My last cast for the jack was made at 6:23 p.m. There lacked still three and a-half minutes of the half-hour; and I would have sworn that the moon was paling before the dawn!

"Simminly someone were chasing they cows down to bottom o' Ten Acre," said the farmer that evening. "'Twasn't you, sir?"

"Now under what earthly circumstances do you suppose I should chase your cows? I wasn't fishing for them, was I?"

Then all the farmer's family gave themselves up to jam-smeared laughter for the rest of the evening, because that was a rare and precious jest, and it was repeated for months, and the fame of it spread from the farm to another, and yet another at least three miles away, and it will be used again for the benefit of visitors when the freshets come down in spring.

But to the greater establishment of my honor and glory I submit in print this bald statement of fact, that I may not, through forgetfulness, be tempted later to tell how I hooked a bull on a Marlow Buzz, how he ran up a tree and took to water, and how I played him along the London-road for thirty miles, and gaffed him at Smithfield. Errors of this kind may creep in with the lapse of years, and it is my ambition ever to be a worthy member of that fraternity who pride themselves on never deviating by one hair's breadth from the absolute and literal truth.

CHAPTER 18

THE HOLE

BY GUY DE MAUPASSANT

Ardèche River, France.

"Cuts and wound that caused death"—That was the heading of the charge which brought Leopold Renard, upholsterer, before the Assize Court.

Round him were the principal witnesses, Madame Flameche, widow of the victim, Louis Ladureau, cabinetmaker, and Jean Durdent, plumber.

Near the criminal was his wife, dressed in black, a little ugly woman, who looked like a monkey dressed as a lady.

This is how Renard described the drama:

"Good heavens, it is a misfortune of which I am the first and last victim, and with which my will has nothing to do. The facts are their own commentary, Monsieur le President. I am an honest man, a hard-working man, an upholsterer in the same street for the last sixteen years, known, liked, respected, and esteemed by all, as my neighbors have testified, even the porter, who is not folatre every day. I am fond of work, I am fond of saving, I like honest men, and respectable pleasures. That is what has ruined me, so much the worse for me; but as my will had nothing to do with it, I continue to respect myself.

"Every Sunday for the last five years, my wife and I have spent the day at Passy. We get fresh air, not to say that we are fond of fishing—as fond of it as we are of small onions. Melie inspired me with that passion, the jade; she is more enthusiastic than I am, the scold, and all the mischief in this business is her fault, as you will see immediately.

"I am strong and mild-tempered, without a pennyworth of malice in me. But she, oh la la! She looks insignificant, she is short and thin, but she does more mischief than a weasel. I do not deny that she has some good qualities; she has some, and those very important to a man in business. But her character! Just ask about it in the neighborhood; even the porter's wife, who has just sent me about my business—she will tell you something about it.

"Every day she used to find fault with my mild temper: 'I would not put up with this! I would not put up with that.' If I had listened to her, Monsieur le President, I should have had at least three bouts of fisticuffs a month."

Madame Renard interrupted him: "And for good reasons too; they laugh best who laugh last."

He turned toward her frankly: "Oh! very well, I can blame you, since you were the cause of it."

Then, facing the President again he said:

"I will continue. We used to go to Passy every Saturday evening, so as to be able to begin fishing at daybreak the next morning. It is a habit which has become second nature with us, as the saying is. Three years ago this summer I discovered a place, oh! such a spot! There, in the shade, were eight feet of water at least and perhaps ten, a hole with a retour under the bank, a regular retreat for fish and a paradise for any fisherman. I might look upon that hole as my property, Monsieur le President, as I was its Christopher Columbus. Everybody in the neighborhood knew it, without making any opposition. They used to say: 'That is Renard's place'; and nobody would have gone to it, not even Monsieur Plumsay, who is renowned, be it said without any offense, for appropriating other people's places.

"Well, I went as usual to that place, of which I felt as certain as if I had owned it. I had scarcely got there on Saturday, when I got into Delila, with my wife. Delila is my Norwegian boat, which I had built by Fourmaise, and which is light and safe. Well, as I said, we got into the boat and we were going to bait, and for baiting there is nobody to be compared with me, and they all know it. You want to know with what I bait? I cannot answer that question; it has nothing to do with the accident; I cannot answer, that is my secret. There are more than three hundred people who have asked me; I have been offered glasses of brandy and liquors, fried fish, matelotes, to make me tell! But just go and try whether the chub will come.

"Ah! they have patted my stomach to get at my secret, my recipe. Only my wife knows, and she will not tell it, any more than I shall! Is not that so, Melie?"

The President of the Court interrupted him: "Just get to the facts as soon as you can."

The accused continued: "I am getting to them; I am getting to them. Well, on Saturday, July 8, we left by the five twenty-five train, and before dinner we went to ground-bait as usual. The weather promised to keep fine, and I said to Melie: 'All right for to-morrow!' And she replied: 'It looks like it.' We never talk more than that together.

"And then we returned to dinner. I was happy and thirsty, and that was the cause of everything. I said to Melie: 'Look here Melie, it is fine weather, so suppose I drink a bottle of Casque a meche. That is a little white wine which we have christened so, because if you drink too much of it, it prevents you from sleeping and is the opposite of a nightcap. Do you understand me?

"She replied: 'You can do as you please, but you will be ill again, and will not be able to get up to-morrow.' That was true, sensible, prudent, and clear-sighted, I must confess. Nevertheless, I could not withstand it, and I drank my bottle. It all comes from that.

"Well, I could not sleep. By Jove! It kept me awake till two o'clock in the morning, and then I went to sleep so soundly that I should not have heard the angel shouting at the Last Judgment.

"In short, my wife woke me at six o'clock and I jumped out of bed, hastily put on my trousers and jersey, washed my face and jumped on board Delila. But it was too late, for when I arrived at my hole it was already taken! Such a thing had never happened to me in three years, and it made me feel as if I were being robbed under my own eyes. I said to myself, Confound it all! confound it! And then my wife began to nag at me. 'Eh! What about your Casque a meche! Get along, you drunkard! Are you satisfied, you great fool?' I could say nothing, because it was all quite true, and so I landed all the same near the spot and tried to profit by what was left. Perhaps after all the fellow might catch nothing, and go away.

"He was a little thin man, in white linen coat and waistcoat, and with a large straw hat, and his wife, a fat woman who was doing embroidery, was behind him.

"When she saw us take up our position close to their place, she murmured: 'I suppose there are no other places on the river!' And my wife, who was furious, replied: 'People who know how to behave make inquiries about the habits of the neighborhood before occupying reserved spots.'

"As I did not want a fuss, I said to her: 'Hold your tongue, Melie. Let them go on, let them go on; we shall see.'

"Well, we had fastened Delila under the willow-trees, and had landed and were fishing side by side, Melie and I, close to the two others; but here, Monsieur, I must enter into details.

"We had only been there about five minutes when our male neighbor's float began to go down two or three times, and then he pulled out a chub as thick as my thigh, rather less, perhaps, but nearly as big! My heart beat, and the perspiration stood on my forehead, and Melie said to me: 'Well, you sot, did you see that?'

"Just then, Monsieur Bru, the grocer of Poissy, who was fond of gudgeon fishing, passed in a boat, and called out to me: So somebody has taken your usual place, Monsieur Renard? And I replied: 'Yes, Monsieur Bru, there are some people in this world who do not know the usages of common politeness.'

"The little man in linen pretended not to hear, nor his fat lump of a wife, either."

Here the President interrupted him a second time: "Take care, you are insulting the widow, Madame Flameche, who is present.

Renard made his excuses: "I beg your pardon, I beg your pardon, my anger carried me away . . . Well, not a quarter of an hour had passed when the little man caught another chub and another almost immediately, and another five minutes later.

"The tears were in my eyes, and then I knew that Madame Renard was boiling with rage, for she kept on nagging at me: 'Oh! how horrid! Don't you see that he is robbing you of your fish? Do you think that you will catch anything? Not even a frog, nothing whatever. Why, my hands are burning, just to think of it.'

"But I said to myself: 'Let us wait until twelve o clock. Then this poaching fellow will go to lunch, and I shall get my place again. As for me, Monsieur le President, I lunch on the spot every Sunday; we bring our provisions in 'Delila.' But there! At twelve o'clock, the wretch produced a fowl out of a newspaper, and while he was eating, actually he caught another chub!

"Melie and I had a morsel also, just a mouthful, a mere nothing, for our heart was not in it.

"Then I took up my newspaper, to aid my digestion. Every Sunday I read the Gil Blas in the shade like that, by the side of the water. It is Columbine's day, you know, Columbine who writes the articles in the Gil Blas. I generally put Madame Renard into a passion by pretending to know this Columbine. It is not true, for I do not know her, and have never seen her, but that does not matter; she writes very well, and then she says things straight out for a woman. She suits me, and there are not many of her sort.

"Well, I began to tease my wife, but she got angry immediately, and very angry, and so I held my tongue. At that moment our two witnesses, who are present here, Monsieur Ladureau and Monsieur Durdent, appeared on the other side of the river. We knew each other by sight. The little man began to fish again, and he caught so many that I trembled with vexation, and his wife said: 'It is an uncommonly good spot, and we will come here always, Desire.' As for me, a cold shiver ran down my back, and Madame Renard kept repeating: 'You are not a man; you have the blood of a chicken in your veins'; and suddenly I said to her: 'Look here, I would rather go away, or I shall only be doing something foolish.'

"And she whispered to me as if she had put a red-hot iron under my nose: 'You are not a man. Now you are going to run away, and surrender your place! Off you go, Bazaine!'

"Well, I felt that, but yet I did not move, while the other fellow pulled out a bream, Oh! I never saw such a large one before, never! And then my wife began to talk aloud, as if she were thinking, and you can see her trickery. She said: 'That is what one might call stolen fish, seeing that we baited the place ourselves. At any rate, they ought to give us back the money we have spent on bait.'

"Then the fat woman in the cotton dress said in turn: 'Do you mean to call us thieves, Madame?' And they began to explain, and then they came to words. Oh! Lord! those creatures know some good ones. They shouted so loud, that our two witnesses, who were on the other bank, began to call out by way of a joke: 'Less noise over there; you will prevent your husbands from fishing.'

"The fact is that neither of us moved any more than if we had been two tree-stumps. We remained there, with our noses over the water, as if we had heard nothing, but by Jove, we heard all the same. 'You are a mere liar.'

" 'You are nothing better than a street-walker.'

" 'You are only a trollop.'

" 'You are a regular strumpet.'

"And so on, and so on; a sailor could not have said more.

"Suddenly I heard a noise behind me, and turned round. It was the other one, the fat woman who had fallen on to my wife with her parasol. Whack! Whack! Melie got two of them, but she was furious, and she hits hard when she is in a rage, so she caught the fat woman by the hair and then, thump, thump. Slaps in the face rained down like ripe plums. I should have let them go on—women among themselves, men among themselves—it does not do to mix the blows, but the little man in the linen jacket jumped up like a devil and was going to rush at my wife. Ah! no, no, not that, my friend! I caught the gentleman with the end of my fist, crash, crash, one on the nose, the other in the stomach. He threw up his arms and legs and fell on his back into the river, just into the hole.

"I should have fished him out most certainly, Monsieur le President, if I had had the time. But unfortunately the fat woman got the better of it, and she was drubbing Melie terribly. I know that I ought not to have assisted her while the man was drinking his fill, but I never thought that he would drown, and said to myself: 'Bah, it will cool him.'

"I therefore ran up to the women to separate them, and all I received was scratches and bites. Good Lord, what creatures! Well, it took me five minutes, and perhaps ten, to separate those two viragoes. When I turned round, there was nothing to be seen, and the water was as smooth as a lake. The others yonder kept shouting: 'Fish him out!' It was all very well to say that, but I cannot swim and still less dive!

"At last the man from the dam came, and two gentlemen with boat-hooks, but it had taken over a quarter of an hour. He was found at the bottom of the hole in eight feet of water, as I have said, but he was dead, the poor little man in his linen suit! There are the facts, such as I have sworn to. I am innocent, on my honor."

The witnesses having deposed to the same effect, the accused was acquitted.

CHAPTER 19

A WEDDING GIFT

BY JOHN TAINTOR FOOTE

Boy Fishing by Winslow Homer, 1892. San Antonio Museum of Art.

George Baldwin Potter is a purist. That is to say, he either takes trout on a dry fly or he does not take them at all. He belongs to a number of fishing clubs, any member of which might acquire his neighbor's wife, beat his children, or poison a dog and still cast a fly, in all serenity, upon club waters; but should he impale on a hook a lowly though succulent worm and immerse the creature in those same waters it would be better that he send in his resignation at once, sooner than face the shaken committee that would presently wait upon him.

George had become fixed in my mind as a bachelor. This, of course, was a mistake. I am continually forgetting that purists rush into marriage when approaching or having just passed the age of forty. The psychology of this is clear.

For twenty years, let us say, a purist's life is completely filled by his efforts to convert all reasonable men to his own particular method of taking trout. He thinks, for example, that a man should not concern himself with more than a dozen types of standard flies. The manner of presenting them is the main consideration. Take any one of these flies, then, and place, by means of an eight-foot rod, a light, tapered line, and a mist-colored leader of reasonable length, on fast water—if you want trout. Of course, if you want to listen to the birds and look at the scenery, fish the pools with a long line and an eight-foot leader. Why, it stands to reason that—

The years go by as he explains these vital facts patiently, again and again, to Smith and Brown and Jones. One wet, cold spring, after fighting a muddy stream all day, he re-explains for the better part of an evening and takes himself, somewhat wearily upstairs. The damp and chill of the room at whatever club he may be fishing is positively tomblike. He can hear the rain drumming on the roof and swishing against the windows. The water will be higher than ever tomorrow, he reflects, as he puts out the lights and slides between the icy sheets. Steeped to the soul in cheerless dark, he recalls numbly that when he first met Smith and Brown and Jones they were fishing the pools with a long line. That was, let's see—fifteen—eighteen—twenty years ago. Then he must be forty. It isn't possible! Yes, it is a fact that Smith and Brown and Jones are still fishing the pools with a long line.

In the first faint light of dawn he falls into an uneasy, muttering slumber. The dark hours between have been devoted to intense thought and a variety of wiggles which have not succeeded in keeping the bedclothes against his shoulder blades.

Some time within the next six months you will remember that you have forgotten to send him a wedding present.

George, therefore, having arrived at his fortieth birthday, announced his engagement shortly thereafter. Quite by chance I ran across his bride-to-be and himself a few days before the ceremony, and joined them at lunch. She was a blonde in the early twenties, with wide blue eyes and a typical rose-and-white complexion. A rushing, almost breathless account of herself, which she began the moment we were seated, was curious, I thought. It was as though she feared an interruption at any moment. I learned that she was an only child, born and reared in Greater New York; that her family had recently moved to New Rochelle; that she had been shopping madly for the past two weeks; that she was nearly dead, but that she had some adorable things.

At this point George informed me that they would spend their honeymoon at a certain fishing club in Maine. He then proceeded to describe the streams and lakes in that section at some length—during the rest of the luncheon, as a matter of fact. His fiancée, who had fallen into a wordless abstraction, only broke her silence with a vague murmur as we parted.

Owing to this meeting I did not forget to send a wedding present. I determined that my choice should please both George and his wife through the happy years to come.

If I had had George to consider, I could have settled the business in two minutes at a sporting-goods store. Barred from these for obvious reasons, I spent a long day in a thoroughly exhausting search. Late in the afternoon I decided to abandon my hopeless task. I had made a tremendous effort and failed. I would simply buy a silver doodad and let it go at that.

As I staggered into a store with the above purpose in view, I passed a show case devoted to fine china, and halted as my eyes fell on a row of fish plates backed by artfully rumpled blue velvet. The plates proved to be hand painted. On each plate was one of the different varieties of trout, curving up through green depths to an artificial fly just dropping on the surface of the water.

In an automatic fashion I indicated the plates to a clerk, paid for them, gave him my card and the address, and fled from the store. Some time during the next twenty-four hours it came to me that George Potter was not among my nearest and dearest. Yet the unbelievable sum I had left with that clerk in exchange for those fish plates could be justified in no other way.

I thought this fact accounted for the sort of frenzy with which George flung himself upon me when next we met, some two months later. I had been weekending in the country and encountered him in the Grand Central Station as I emerged from the lower level. For a long moment he wrung my hand in silence, gazing almost feverishly into my face. At last he spoke:

"Have you got an hour to spare?"

It occurred to me that it would take George an hour at least to describe his amazed delight at the splendor of my gift. The clock above Information showed that it was 12:45. I therefore suggested that we lunch together.

He, too, glanced at the clock, verified its correctness by his watch, and seized me by the arm.

"All right," he agreed, and was urging me toward the well-filled and somewhat noisy station café before I grasped his intention and tried to suggest that we go elsewhere. His hand only tightened on my arm.

"It's all right," he said; "good food, quick service—you'll like it."

He all but dragged me into the café and steered me to a table in the corner. I lifted my voice above an earnest clatter of gastronomical utensils and made a last effort.

"The Biltmore's just across the street."

George pressed me into my chair, shoved a menu card at me and addressed the waiter.

"Take his order." Here he jerked out his watch and consulted it again. "We have forty-eight minutes. Service for one. I shan't be eating anything; or, no—bring me some coffee—large cup—black."

Having ordered mechanically, I frankly stared at George. He was dressed, I now observed, with unusual care. He wore a rather dashing gray suit. His tie, which was an exquisite shade of gray-blue, was embellished by a handsome pearl. The handkerchief, appearing above his breast pocket, was of the same delicate gray-blue shade as the tie. His face had been recently and closely shaven, also powdered; but above that smooth whiteness of jowl was a pair of curiously glittering eyes and a damp, beaded brow. This he now mopped with his napkin.

"Good God," said I, "what is it, George?"

His reply was to extract a letter from his inside coat pocket and pass it across the table, his haunted eyes on mine. I took in its few lines at a glance:

"Father has persuaded me to listen to what you call your explanation. I arrive Grand Central 2:45, daylight saving, Monday." Isabelle.

Poor old George, I thought; some bachelor indiscretion; and now, with his honeymoon scarcely over, blackmail, a lawsuit, heaven only knows what.

"Who," I asked, returning the letter, "is Isabelle?"

To my distress, George again resorted to his napkin. Then, "My wife," he said.

"Your wife!" George nodded.

"Been living with her people for the last month. Wish he'd bring that coffee."

"You don't happen to have a flask with you?"

"Yes, I have a flask." George brightened. "But it's empty."

"Do you want to tell me about your trouble? Is that why you brought me here?"

"Well, yes," George admitted. "But the point is—will you stand by me? That's the main thing.

"She gets in"—here he consulted his watch—"in forty-five minutes, if the train's on time." A sudden panic seemed to seize him. His hand shot across the table and grasped my wrist. "You've got to stand by me, old man—act as if you knew nothing. Say you ran into me here and stayed to meet her. I'll tell you what—say I didn't seem to want you to stay. Kid me about wanting her all to myself, or something like that. Get the point? It'll give me a chance to sort of—well, you understand."

"I see what you mean, of course," I admitted. "Here's your coffee. Suppose you have some and then tell me what this is all about—if you care to, that is."

"No sugar, no cream," said George to the waiter; "just pour it. Don't stand there waving it about—pour it, pour it!" He attempted to swallow a mouthful of steaming coffee, gurgled frightfully and grabbed his water glass. "Great jumping Jehoshaphat!" he gasped, when he could speak, and glared at the waiter, who promptly moved out into the sea of diners and disappeared among a dozen of his kind.

"Steady, George," I advised as I transferred a small lump of ice from my glass to his coffee cup.

George watched the ice dissolve, murmured "Idiot" several times, and presently swallowed the contents of the cup in two gulps.

"I had told her," he said suddenly, "exactly where we were going. She mentioned Narragansett several times—I'll admit that. Imagine—Narragansett! Of course I bought her fishing things myself. I didn't buy knickers or woolens or flannel shirts—naturally. You don't go around buying a girl breeches and underwear before you're married. It wouldn't be—well, it isn't done, that's all. I got her the sweetest three-ounce rod you ever held in your hand. I'll bet I could put out sixty feet of line with it against the wind. I got her a pair of English waders that didn't weigh a pound. They cost me forty-five dollars. The rest of the outfit was just as good. Why, her fly box was a Truxton. I could have bought an American imitation for eight dollars. I know a lot of men who'll buy leaders for themselves at two dollars apiece and let their wives fish with any kind of tackle. I'll give you my word I'd have used anything I got for her myself. I sent it all out to be packed with her things. I wanted her to feel that it was her own—not mine. I know a lot of men who give their wives a high-class rod or an imported reel and then fish with it themselves.

"What time is it?"

"Clock right up there," I said. But George consulted his watch and used his napkin distressingly again.

"Where was I?"

"You were telling me why you sent her fishing things out to her."

"Oh, yes! That's all of that. I simply wanted to show you that from the first I did all any man could do. Ever been in the Cuddiwink district?"

I said that I had not.

"You go in from Buck's Landing. A lumber tug takes you up to the head of Lake Owonga. Club guides meet you there and put you through in one day—twenty miles by canoe and portage up the west branch of the Penobscot; then nine miles by trail to Lost Pond. The club's on Lost Pond. Separate cabins, with a main dining and loafing camp, and the best squaretail fishing on earth—both lake and stream. Of course, I don't fish the lakes. A dry fly belongs on a stream and nowhere else. Let me make it perfectly clear."

George's manner suddenly changed. He hunched himself closer to the table, dropped an elbow upon it and lifted an expository finger.

"The dry fly," he stated, with a new almost combative ring in his voice, "is designed primarily to simulate not only the appearance of the natural insect but its action as well. This action is arrived at through the flow of the current. The moment you move a fly by means of leader you destroy the—

I saw that an interruption was imperative.

"Yes, of course," I said; "but your wife will be here in—"

It was pitiful to observe George. His new-found assurance did not flee— flee suggests a withdrawal, however swift—it was immediately and totally annihilated. He attempted to pour himself some coffee, take out his watch, look at the clock, and mop his brow with his napkin at one and the same instant.

"You were telling me how to get to Lost Pond," I suggested.

"Yes, to be sure," said George. "Naturally you go in light. The things you absolutely have to have—rods, tackle, waders, wading shoes, and so forth, are about all a guide can manage at the portages in addition to the canoe. You pack in extras yourself—change of underclothes, a couple of pairs of socks, and a few toilet articles. You leave a bag or trunk at Buck's Landing. I explained this to her. I explained it carefully. I told her either a week-end bag or one small trunk.

Herb Trescott was my best man. I left everything to him. He saw us on the train and handed me tickets and reservations just before we pulled out. I didn't notice in the excitement of getting away that he'd given me three trunk checks all stamped 'Excess.' I didn't notice it till the conductor showed up, as a matter of fact. Then I said, 'Darling, what in heaven's name have you brought three trunks for?' She said—I can remember her exact words—'Then you're not going to Narragansett?'

"I simply looked at her. I was too dumbfounded to speak. At last I pulled myself together and told her in three days we'd be whipping the best squaretail water in the world. I took her hand, I remember, and said, 'You and I together, sweetheart,' or something like that."

George sighed and lapsed into a silence which remained unbroken until his eye happened to encounter the face of the clock. He started and went on:

"We got to Buck's Landing, but way of Bangor, at six in the evening of the following day. Buck's Landing is a railroad station with grass growing between the ties, a general store and hotel combined, and a lumber wharf. The store keeps canned peas, pink-and-white candy, and felt boots. The hotel part is—well, it doesn't matter except that I don't think I ever saw so many deer heads; a few stuffed trout but mostly deer heads. After supper the proprietor and I got the three trunks up to the largest room: We just go them in and that was all. The tug left for the head of the lake at seven next morning. I explained this to Isabelle. I said we'd leave the trunks there until we came out, and offered to help her unpack the one her fishing things were in. She said, 'Please go away!' So I went away. I got out a rod and went down to the wharf. No trout there, I knew; but I thought I'd limber up my wrist. I put on a Cahill Number Fourteen—or was it Sixteen—"

George knitted his brows and stared intently but unseeingly at me for some little time.

"Call it a Sixteen," I suggested.

George shook his head impatiently and remained concentrated in thought. "I'm inclined to think it was a Fourteen," he said at last. "But let it go; it'll come to me later. At any rate, the place was alive with big chub—a foot long, some of 'em. I'll bet I took fifty—threw 'em back, of course. They kept on rising after it got dark. I'd tell myself I'd go after one more cast. Each time I'd hook a big chub, and—well, you know how the time slips away.

"When I got back to the hotel all the lights were out. I lit matches until I got upstairs and found the door to the room. I'll never forget what I saw when I opened that door—never! Do you happen to know how many of the kind of things they wear a woman can get into one trunk? Well, she had three and she'd unpacked them all. She had used the bed for the gowns alone. It was piled with them—literally piled; but that wasn't a starter. Everywhere you looked was a stack of things with ribbons in 'em. There were enough shoes and stockings for a girl's school; silk stockings, mind you, and high-heeled shoes and slippers." Here George consulted clock and watch. "I wonder if that train's on time," he wanted to know.

"You have thirty-five minutes, even if it is," I told him; "go right ahead." "Well, I could see something was wrong from her face. I didn't know what, but I started right in to cheer her up. I told her all about the chub fishing I'd been having. At last she burst into tears. I won't go into the scene that followed. I'd ask her what was the matter and she'd say, 'Nothing,' and cry frightfully. I know a lot of men who would have lost their tempers under the circumstances, but I didn't; I give you my word. I simply said, 'There, there,' until she quieted down. And that isn't all. After a while she began to show me her gowns. Imagine—at eleven o'clock at night, at Buck's Landing! She'd hold up a dress and look over the top of it at me and ask me how I liked it, and I'd say it was all right. I know a lot of men who wouldn't have sat there two minutes.

"At last I said, 'They're all all right, darling,' and yawned. She was hold-ing up a pink dress covered with shiny dingle-dangles, and she threw the dress on the bed and all but had hysterics. It was terrible. In trying to think of some way to quiet her it occurred to me that I'd put her rod together and let her feel the balance of it with the reel I'd bought her—a genuine Fleetwood, mind you—attached. I looked around for her fishing things and couldn't find them. I'll tell you why I couldn't find them." George paused for an impressive instant to give his next words the full significance due them. "They weren't there!"

"No?" I murmured weakly.

"No," said George. "And what do you suppose she said when I ques-tioned her? I can give you her exact words—I'll never forget them. She said, 'There wasn't any room for them.'" Again George paused. "I ask you," he inquired at last, "I ask you as man to man; what do you think of that?"

I found no adequate reply to this question and George, now thoroughly warmed up, rushed on.

"You'd swear I lost my temper then, wouldn't you? Well, I didn't. I did say something to her later, but I'll let you be the judge when we come to that. I'll ask you to consider the circumstances. I'll ask you to get Old Faithful in your mind's eye."

"Old Faithful?" I repeated. "Then you went to the Yellowstone later?"

"Yellowstone! Of course not! Haven't I told you we were already at the best trout water in America? Old Faithful was a squaretail. He'd been in the pool below Horseshoe Falls for twenty years, as a matter of record. We'll come to that presently. How are we off for time?"

"Thirty-one minutes," I told him. "I'm watching the clock—go ahead."

"Well, there she was, on a fishing trip with nothing to fish with. There was only one answer to that—she couldn't fish. But I went over everything she'd brought in three trunks and I'll give you my word she didn't have a garment of any sort you couldn't see through.

"Something had to be done and done quick, that was for sure. I fitted her out from my own things with a sweater, a flannel shirt, and a pair of knickerbockers.

Then I got the proprietor up and explained the situation. He got me some heavy underwear and two pairs of woolen stockings that belonged to his wife. When it came to shoes it looked hopeless, but the proprietor's wife, who had got up, too, by this time, thought of a pair of boy's moccasin's that were in the store and they turned out to be about the right size. I made arrangements to rent the room we had until we came out again to keep her stuff in, and took another room for the night—what was left of it after she'd repacked what could stay in the trunks and arranged what couldn't so it wouldn't be wrinkled.

"I got up early, dressed, and took my duffle down to the landing. I wakened her when I left the room. When breakfast was ready I went to see why she hadn't come down. She was all dressed, sitting on the edge of the bed. I said, 'Breakfast is ready, darling,' but I saw by her face that something was wrong again. It turned out to be my knickers. They fitted her perfectly—a little tight in spots—except in the waist. They would simply have fallen off if she hadn't held them up.

"Well, I was going in so light that I only had one belt. The proprietor didn't have any—he used suspenders. Neither did his wife—she used—well, whatever they use. He got me a piece of clothesline and I knotted it at each and ran it through the what-you-may-call-'ems of the knickers and tied it in front. The knickers sort of puckered all the way around, but they couldn't come down—that was the main thing. I said, 'There you are, darling.' She walked over and tilted the mirror of the bureau so that she could see herself from head to foot. She said, 'Who are going to be at this place where we are going?' I said, 'Some of the very best dry-fly men in the country.'

She said, 'I don't mean them; I mean the women. Will there be any women there?'

"I told her, certainly there would be women. I asked her if she thought I would take her into a camp with nothing but men. I named some of the women: Mrs. Fred Beal and Mrs. Brooks Carter and Talcott Ranning's sister and several more.

"She turned around slowly in front of the mirror, staring into it for a minute. Then she said, 'Please go out and close the door.' I said, 'All right, darling; but come right down. The tug will be here in fifteen minutes.'

"I went downstairs and waited for ten minutes, then I heard the tug whistle for the landing and ran upstairs again. I knocked at the door. When she didn't answer I went in. Where do you suppose she was?"

I gave it up.

"In bed!" said George in an awe-struck voice. "In bed with her face turned to the wall; and listen, I didn't lose my temper as God is my judge. I rushed down to the wharf and told the tug captain I'd give him twenty-five dollars extra if he'd hold the boat till we came. He said all right and I went back to the room.

"The breeches had done it. She simply wouldn't wear them. I told her that at a fishing camp in Maine clothes were never thought of. I said, 'No one thinks of anything but trout, darling.' She said, 'I wouldn't let a fish see me looking like that.'" George's brow beaded suddenly. His hands dived searchingly into various pockets. "Got a cigarette? I left my case in my other suit."

He took a cigarette from me, lighted it with shaking fingers and inhaled deeply.

"It went on like that for thirty minutes. She was crying all the time, of course. I had started down to tell the tug captain it was all off, and I saw a woman's raincoat hanging in the hall. It belonged to someone up in one of the camps, the proprietor told me. I gave him seventy-five dollars to give to whoever owned it when he came out, and took it upstairs. In about ten minutes I persuaded her to wear it over the rest of her outfit until we got to camp. I told her one of the women would be able to fix her up all right when we got there. I didn't believe it, of course. The women at camp were all old-timers; they'd gone in as light as the men, but I had to say something.

"We had quite a trip going in. The guides were at the head of the lake all right—Indian Joe and a new man I'd never seen, called Charlie. I told Joe to take Isabelle—he's one of the best canoemen I ever saw. I was going to paddle bow for my man, but I'd have to bet a cookie Indian Joe could stay with us on any kind of water. We had to beat it right through to make camp by night. It's a good stiff trip, but it can be done. I looked back at the other canoe now and then we struck about a mile of white water that took all I had. When we were through the other canoe wasn't in sight. The river made a bend there, and I thought it was just behind and would show up any minute.

"Well, it didn't show up and I began to wonder. We hit our first portage about ten o'clock and landed. I watched downstream for twenty minutes, expecting to sight the other canoe every instant. Then Charlie, who hadn't opened his head, said, 'Better go back,' and put the canoe in again. We paddled downstream for all that was in it. I was stiff with fright. We saw 'em coming about three miles lower down and back-paddled till they came up. Isabelle was more cheerful-looking than she'd been since we left New York, but Joe had that stony face an Indian gets when he's sore.

"I said, 'Anything wrong?' Joe just grunted and drove the canoe past us. Then I saw it was filled with wild flowers. Isabelle said she'd been picking them right off the banks all the way long. She said she'd only had to get out of the boat once, for the blue ones. Now, you can't beat that—not in a thousand years. I leave it to you if you can. Twenty miles of stiff current, with five portages ahead of us and a nine-mile hike at the end of that. I gave that Indian the devil for letting her do such a thing, and tipped the flowers into the Penobscot when we unloaded for the first portage. She didn't speak to me on the portage, and she got into her canoe without a word.

"Nothing more happened going in, except this flower business had lost us two hours, and it was so dark when we struck the swamp at Loon Lake that we couldn't follow the trail well and kept stumbling over down timber and stepping into bog holes. She was about fagged out by then, and the mosquitoes were pretty thick through there. Without any warning she sat down on the trail. She did it so suddenly I nearly fell over her. I asked her what was the matter and she said, 'This is the end'—just like that—'this is the end!' I said, 'The end of what, darling?' She said, 'Of everything!' I told her if she sat there all wet and muddy she'd catch her death. She said she hoped so. I said, 'It's only two miles more, darling. Just think, tomorrow we'll be on the best trout water in the world!' With that she said, 'I want my mother, my darling mother,' and bowed her head in her hands. Think it over, please; and remember, I didn't lose my temper. You're sure there's nothing left in your flask?"

"Not a drop more, George," I assured him. "Go ahead; we've only twenty-five minutes."

George looked wildly at the clock, then at his watch.

"A man never has it when he wants it most. Have you noticed that? Where was I?"

"You were in the swamp."

"Oh, yes! Well, she didn't speak after that, and nothing I could say would budge her. The mosquitoes had got wind of us when we stopped and were coming in swarms. We'd be eaten alive in another ten minutes. So I told Joe to give his pack to Charlie and help me pick her up and carry her. Joe said, 'No, by damn!' and folded his arms. When an Indian gets sore he stays sore, and when he's sore he's stubborn. The mosquitoes were working on him good and plenty, though, and at last he said, 'Me carry packs. Charlie help carry—

that.' He flipped his hand over in the direction of Isabelle and took the pack from Charlie.

"It was black as your hat by now, and the trail through there was only about a foot wide with swamp on each side. It was going to be some job getting her out of there. I thought Charlie and I would make a chair of our arms and stumble along with her some way; but when I started to lift her up she said, 'Don't touch me!' and got up and went on. A blessing if there ever was one. We got to camp at ten that night.

"She was stiff and sore the next morning—you expect it after a trip like that—besides, she'd caught a little cold. I asked her how she felt, and she said she was going to die and asked me to send for a doctor and her mother. The nearest doctor was at Bangor and her mother was in New Rochelle. I carried her breakfast over from the dining camp to our cabin. She said she couldn't eat any breakfast, but she did drink a cup of coffee, telling me between sips how awful it was to die alone in a place like that.

"After she'd had the coffee she seemed to feel better. I went to the camp library and got *The Dry Fly on American Waters*, by Charles Darty. I considered him the soundest man in the country.

He's better than Pell or Fawcett. My chief criticism of him is that in his chapter on Streams East of the Alleghenies—east of the Alleghenies, mind you—he recommends the Royal Coachman. I consider the Lead-Wing Coachman a serviceable fly on clear, hard-fished water; but the Royal—never! I wouldn't give it a shade over the Professor or the Montreal. Just consider the body alone of the Royal Coachman—never mind the wings and hackle—the body of the Royal is—"

"Yes, I know, George," I said; "but—"

I glanced significantly at the clock. George started, sighed, and resumed his narrative.

"I went back to the cabin and said, 'Darling, here is one of the most intensely interesting books ever written. I'm going to read it aloud to you. I think I can finish it to-day. Would you like to sit up in bed while I read?' She said she hadn't strength enough to sit up in bed, so I sat down beside her and started reading. I had read about an hour, I suppose, when she did sit up in bed quite suddenly. I saw she was staring at me in a queer, wild way that was really startling. I said, 'What is it, darling?' She said, 'I'm going to get up. I'm going to get up this instant.'

"Well, I was delighted, naturally. I thought the book would get her by the time I'd read it through. But there she was, as keen as mustard before I'd got well into it. I'll tell you what I made up my mind to do, right there. I made up my mind to let her use my rod that day. Yes, sir—my three-ounce Spinoza, and what's more, I did it."

George looked at me triumphantly, then lapsed into reflection for a moment.

"If ever a man did everything possible to—well, let it go. The main thing is, I have nothing to reproach myself with—nothing. Except—but we'll come to that presently. Of course, she wasn't ready for dry flies yet. I borrowed some wet flies from the club steward, got some cushions for the canoe and put my rod together. She had no waders, so a stream was out of the question. The lake was better, anyway, that first day; she'd have all the room she wanted for her back cast.

"I stood there on the landing with her before we got into the canoe and showed her just how to put out a fly and recover it. Then she tried it." A sort of horror came into George's face. "You wouldn't believe any one could handle a rod like that," he said huskily. "You couldn't believe it unless you'd seen it. Gimme a cigarette.

"I worked with her a half hour or so and saw no improvement—none whatever. At last she said, 'The string is too long. I can't do anything with such a long string on a pole.' I told her gently—gently, mind you—that the string was an eighteen-dollar double-tapered Hurdman line, attached to a Gebhardt reel on a three-ounce Spinoza rod. I said, 'We'll go out on the lake now. If you can manage to get a rise, perhaps it will come to you instinctively.'

"I paddled her out on the lake and she went at it. She'd spat the flies down and yank them up and spat them down again. She hooked me several times with her back cast and got tangled up in the line herself again and again. All this time I was speaking quietly to her, telling her what to do. I give you my word I never raised my voice—not once—and I thought she'd break the tip every moment.

"Finally she said her arm was tired and lowered the rod. She'd got everything messed up with her last cast and the flies were trailing just over the side of the canoe. I said, 'Recover your cast and reel in, darling.' Instead of using her rod, she took hold of the leader close to the flies and started to pull them into the canoe. At that instant a little trout—couldn't have been over six inches—took the tail fly. I don't know exactly what happened, it was all over so quickly. I think she just screamed and let go of everything. At any rate, I saw my Spinoza bounce off the gunwale of the canoe and disappear. There was fifty feet of water just there. And now listen carefully: not one word did I utter—not one. I simply turned the canoe and paddled to the landing in absolute silence. No reproaches of any sort. Think that over!"

I did. My thoughts left me speechless. George proceeded:

"I took out a guide and tried dragging for the rod with a gang hook and heavy sinker all the rest of the day. But the gangs would only foul on the bottom. I gave up at dusk and paddled in. I said to the guide—it was Charlie—I said, 'Well, it's all over, Charlie.' Charlie said, 'I brought Mr. Carter in and he had an extra rod. Maybe you could borrow it. It's a four-ounce Meecham.' I smiled. I actually smiled. I turned and looked at the lake. 'Charlie,' I said, 'somewhere out there in that dark water, where the eye of man will never behold it again, is a three-ounce Spinoza—and you speak of a Meecham.' Charlie said, 'Well, I just thought I'd tell you.' I said, 'That's all right, Charlie. That's all right.' I went to the main camp, saw Jean, the head guide and made arrangements to leave the next day. Then I went to our cabin and sat down before the fire. I heard Isabelle say something about being sorry. I said, 'I'd rather not talk about it, darling. If you don't mind, we'll never mention it again.' We sat there in silence, then, until dinner.

"As we got up from dinner, Nate Griswold and his wife asked us to play bridge with them that evening. I'd told no one what had happened, and Nate didn't know, of course. I simply thanked him and said we were tired, and we went back to our cabin. I sat down before the fire again. Isabelle seemed restless. At last she said, 'George.' I said, 'What is it, darling?' She said, 'Would you like to read to me from that book?' I said, 'I'm sorry, darling; if you don't mind I'll just sit here quietly by the fire.'

"Somebody knocked at the door after a while. I said, 'Come in.' It was Charlie. I said, 'What is it, Charlie?' Then he told me that Bob Frazer had been called back to New York and was going out the next morning. I said, 'Well, what of it?' Charlie said, 'I just thought you could maybe borrow his rod.' I said, 'I thought you understood about that, Charlie.' Charlie said, 'Well, that's it. Mr. Frazer's rod is a three-ounce Spinoza.'

"I got up and shook hands with Charlie and gave him five dollars. But when he'd gone I began to realize what was before me. I'd brought in a pint flask of prewar Scotch. Prewar—get that! I put this in my pocket and went over to Bob's cabin. Just as I was going to knock I lost my nerve. I sneaked away from the door and went down to the lake and sat on the steps of the canoe landing. I sat there for quite a while and took several nips. At last I thought I'd just go and tell Bob of my loss and see what he said. I went back to his cabin and this time I knocked. Bob was putting a few odds and ends in a shoulder pack. His rod was in its case, standing against the wall.

"I said, 'I hear you're going out in the morning.' He said, 'Yes, curse it, my wife's mother has to have some sort of damned operation or other.' I said, 'How would a little drink strike you, Bob?' He said, 'Strike me! Wait a minute! What kind of drink?' I took out the flask and handed it to him. He unscrewed the cap and held the flask to his nose. He said, 'Great heavens above, it smells like—' I said, 'It is.' He said, 'It can't be!' I said, 'Yes, it is.' He said, 'There's a trick in it somewhere.' I said, 'No, there isn't—I give you my word.' He tasted what was in the flask carefully. Then he said, 'I call this white of you, George,' and took a good stiff snort. When he was handing back the flask he said, 'I'll do as much for you some day, if I ever get the chance.' I took a snifter myself.

"Then I said, 'Bob, something awful has happened to me. I came here to tell you about it.' He said, 'Is that so? Sit down.' I sat down and told him. He said, 'What kind of rod was it?' I said, 'A three-ounce Spinoza.' He came over and gripped my hand without a word. I said, 'Of course, I can't use anything else.' He nodded, and I saw his eyes flicker toward the corner of the room where his own rod was standing. I said, 'Have another drink, Bob.' But he just sat down and stared at me. I took a good stiff drink myself. Then I said, 'Under ordinary circumstances, nothing on earth could hire me to ask a man to—' I stopped right there.

"Bob got up suddenly and began to walk up and down the room. I said, 'Bob, I'm not considering myself—not for a minute. If it was last season, I'd simply have gone back tomorrow without a word. But I'm not alone any more. I've got the little girl to consider. She's never seen a trout taken in her life—think of it, Bob! And here she is, on her honeymoon, at the best water I know of. On her honeymoon, Bob!' I waited for him to say something, but he went to the window and stared out, with his back to me. I got up and said good-night and started for the door. Just as I reached it he turned from the window and rushed over and picked up his rod. He said, 'Here, take it,' and put the rod case in my hands. I started to try to thank him, but he said, 'Just go ahead with it,' and pushed me out the door."

The waiter was suddenly hovering above us with his eyes on the dishes.

"Now what do you want?" said George.

"Never mind clearing here," I said. "Just bring me the check. Go ahead, George."

"Well, of course, I can't any more than skim what happened finally, but you'll understand. It turned out that Ernie Payton's wife had an extra pair of knickers and she loaned them to Isabelle. I was waiting outside the cabin while she dressed next morning, and she called out to me, 'Oh, George, they fit!' Then I heard her begin to sing. She was a different girl when she came out to go to breakfast. She was almost smiling. She'd done nothing but slink about the day before. Isn't it extraordinary what will seem important to a woman? Gimme a cigarette."

"Fifteen minutes, George," I said as I supplied him.

"Yes, yes, I know. I fished the Cuddiwink that day. Grand stream, grand. I used a Pink Lady—first day on a stream with Isabelle—little touch of sentiment—and it's a darn good fly. I fished it steadily all day. Or did I try a Seth Green about noon? It seems to me I did, now that I recall it. It seems to me that where the Katahdin brook comes in I—"

"It doesn't really matter, does it, George?" I ventured.

"Of course, it matters!" said George decisively. "A man wants to be exact about such things. The precise details of what happens in a day's work on a stream are of real value to yourself and others. Except in the case of a record fish, it isn't important that you took a trout; it's exactly how you took him that's important."

"But the time, George," I protested.

He glanced at the clock, swore softly, mopped his brow—this time with the blue-gray handkerchief—and proceeded.

A pink lady.

"Isabelle couldn't get into the stream without waders, so I told her to work along the bank a little behind me. It was pretty thick along there, second growth and vines mostly; but I was putting that Pink Lady on every foot of good water and she kept up with me easily enough. She didn't see me take many trout, though. I'd look for her, after landing one, to see what she thought of the way I'd handled the fish, and almost invariably she was picking the ferns or blueberries, or getting herself untangled from something. Curious things, women. Like children, when you stop to think of it."

George stared at me unseeingly for a moment.

"And you never heard of Old Faithful?" he asked suddenly. "Evidently not, from what you said a while ago. Well, a lot of people have, believe me. Men have gone to Cuddiwink district just to see him. As I've already told you, he lay beside a ledge in the pool below Horseshoe Falls.

"Almost nothing else in the pool. He kept it cleaned out. Worst sort of cannibal, of course—all big trout are. That was the trouble—he wanted something that would stick to his ribs. No flies for him. Did his feeding at night.

"You could see him dimly if you crawled out on a rock that jutted above the pool and looked over. He lay in about ten feet of water, right by his ledge. If he saw you he'd back under the ledge, slowly, like a submarine going into dock. Think of the biggest thing you've ever seen, and that's the way Old Faithful looked, just laying there as still as the ledge. He never seemed to move anything, not even his gills. When he backed in out of sight he seemed to be drawn under the ledge by some invisible force.

"Ridgway—R. Campbell Ridgway—you may have read his stuff. Brethren of the Wild, that sort of thing—claimed to have seen him move. He told me about it one night. He said he was lying with just his eyes over the edge of the rock, watching the trout. Said he'd been there an hour, when down over the falls came a young red squirrel. It had fallen in above and been carried over. The squirrel was half drowned, but struck out feebly for shore. Well, so Ridgway said—Old Faithful came up and took Mister Squirrel into camp. No hurry; just came drifting up, sort of inhaled the squirrel and sank down to the ledge again. Never made a ripple, Ridgway said; just business.

"I'm telling you all this because it's necessary that you get an idea of that trout in your mind. You'll see why in a minute. No one ever had hold of him. But it was customary, if you fished the Cuddiwink, to make a few casts over him before you left the stream. Not that you ever expected him to rise. It was just a sort of gesture. Everybody did it.

"Knowing that Isabelle had never seen trout taken before, I made a day of it—naturally. The trail to camp leaves the stream just at the falls. It was pretty late when we got to it. Isabelle had her arms full of—heaven knows what—flowers and grass and ferns and fir branches and colored leaves. She'd lugged the stuff for hours. I remember once that day I was fighting a fourteen-inch blackberry—I think it was—she'd found. How does that strike you? And listen! I said, 'It's a beauty, darling.' That's what I said—or something like that . . . Here, don't you pay that check! Bring it here, waiter!"

"Go on, George!" I said. "We haven't time to argue about the check. You'd come to the trail for camp at the falls."

"I told Isabelle to wait at the trail for a few minutes, while I went below the falls and did the customary thing for the edification of Old Faithful. I only intended to make three or four casts with the Number Twelve Fly and the hair fine leader I had on, but in getting down to the pool I hooked the fly in a bush. In trying to loosen it I stumbled over something and fell. I snapped the leader like a thread, and since I had to put on another, I tied on a fairly heavy one as a matter of form.

"I had reached for my box for a regulation fly of some sort when I remembered a fool thing that Billy Roach had given me up on the Beaverkill the season before. It was fully two inches long; I forget what he called it. He said you fished it dry for bass or large trout. He said you worked the tip of your rod and made it wiggle like a dying minnow. I didn't want the contraption, but he'd borrowed some fly oil from me and insisted on my taking it. I'd stuck it in the breast pocket of my fishing jacket and forgotten it until then.

"Well, I felt in the pocket and there it was. I tried it on and went down to the pool. Now let me show you the exact situation." George seized a fork. "This is the pool." The fork traced an oblong figure on the tablecloth. "Here is Old Faithful's ledge." The fork deeply marked this impressive spot. "Here are the falls, with white water running to here. You can only wade to this point here, and then you have an abrupt six-foot depth. 'But you can put a fly from here to here with a long line,' you say. No, you can't. You've forgotten to allow for your back cast. Notice this bend here? That tells the story. You're not more than twenty feet from a lot of birch and whatnot, when you can no longer wade. 'Well then, it's impossible to put a decent fly on the water above the sunken ledge,' you say. It looks like it, but this is how it's done: right here is a narrow point running to here, where it dwindles off to a single fat rock. If you work out on the point you can jump across to this rock—situated right here—and there you are, with about a thirty-foot cast to the sunken ledge. Deep water all around you, of course, and the rock is slippery; but—there you are. Now notice this small cove, right here. The water from the falls rushes past it in a froth, but in the cove it forms a deep eddy, with the current moving round and round like this." George made a slow circular motion with the fork. "You know what I mean?"

I nodded.

"I got out on the point and jumped to the rock; got myself balanced, worked out the right amount of line and cast the dungaree Bill had forced on me, just above the sunken ledge. I didn't take the water lightly and I cast again, but I couldn't put it down decently. It would just flop in—too much weight and too many feathers. I suppose I cast it a dozen times, trying to make it settle like a fly. I wasn't thinking of trout—there would be nothing in there except Old Faithful—I was just monkeying with this doodle-bug thing, now that I had it on.

"I gave up at last and let it lie out where I had cast it. I was standing there looking at the falls roaring down, when I remembered Isabelle, waiting up on the trail. I raised my rod preparatory to reeling in and the what-you-may-call-'em made a kind of dive and wiggle out there on the surface. I reached for my reel handle. Then I realized that the thingamajig wasn't on the water. I didn't see it disappear, exactly; I was looking at it, and then it wasn't there. 'That's funny,' I thought, and struck instinctively. Well, I was fast—so it seemed—and no snags in there. I gave it the butt three or four times, but the rod only bowed and nothing budged. I tried to figure it out. I thought perhaps a water-logged timber had come diving over the falls and upended right there. Then I noticed the rod take more of a bend and the line began to move through the water. It moved out slowly, very slowly, into the middle of the pool. It was exactly as though I was hooked on to a freight train just getting under way.

"I knew what I had hold of then, and yet I didn't believe it. I couldn't believe it. I kept thinking it was a dream, I remember. Of course, he could have gone away with everything I had any minute if he'd wanted to, but he didn't. He just kept moving slowly, round and round the pool. I gave him what pressure the tackle would stand, but he never noticed a little thing like that; just kept moving around the pool for hours, it seemed to me. I'd forgotten Isabelle; I admit that. I'd forgotten everything on earth. There didn't seem to be anything else on earth, as a matter of fact, except the falls and the pool and Old Faithful and me. At last Isabelle showed up on the bank above me, still lugging her ferns and whatnot. She called down to me above the noise of the falls. She asked me how long I expected her to wait alone in the woods, with night coming on.

"I hadn't had the faintest idea how I was going to try to land the fish until then. The water was boiling past the rock I was standing on, and I couldn't jump back to the point without giving him slack and perhaps falling in. I began to look around and figure. Isabelle said, 'What on earth are you doing?' I took off my landing net and tossed it to the bank. I yelled, 'Drop that junk quick and pick up that net!' She said, 'What for, George?' I said, 'Do as I tell you and don't ask questions!' She laid down what she had and picked up the net and I told her to go to the cove and stand ready.

"She said, 'Ready for what?' I said, 'You'll see what presently. Just stand there.' I'll admit I wasn't talking quietly. There was the noise of the falls to begin with, and—well, naturally, I wasn't.

"I went to work on the fish again. I began to educate him to the lead. I thought if I could lead him into the cove he would swing right past Isabelle and she could net him. It was slow work—a three-ounce rod—imagine! Isabelle called, 'Do you know what time it is?' I told her to keep still and stand where she was. She didn't say anything more than that.

"At last the fish began to come. He wasn't tired—he'd never done any fighting, as a matter of fact—but he'd take a suggestion as to where to go from the rod. I kept swinging him nearer and nearer the cove each time he came around. When I saw he was about ready to come I yelled to Isabelle. I said, 'I'm going to bring him right past you, close to the top. All you have to do is to net him.'

"When the fish came round again I steered him into the cove. Just as he was swinging past Isabelle the stuff she'd been lugging began to roll down the bank. She dropped the landing net on top of the fish and made a dive for those leaves and grasses and things. Fortunately the net handle lodged against the bank, and after she'd put her stuff in a nice safe place she came back and picked up the net again. I never uttered a syllable. I deserve no credit for that. The trout had made a surge and shot out into the pool and I was too busy just then to give her any idea of what I thought.

"I had a harder job getting him to swing in again. He was a little leery of the cove, but at last he came. I steered him toward Isabelle and lifted him all I dared. He came up nicely, clear to the top. I yelled, 'Here he comes! For God's sake, don't miss him!' I put everything on the tackle it would stand and managed to check the fish for an instant right in front of Isabelle.

"And this is what she did: it doesn't seem credible—it doesn't seem humanly possible; but it's a fact that you'll have to take my word for. She lifted the landing net above her head with both hands and brought it down on top of the fish with all her might!"

George ceased speaking. Despite its coating of talcum powder, I was able to detect an additional pallor in his countenance.

"Will I ever forget it as long as I live?" he inquired at last.

"No, George," I said, "but we've just exactly eleven minutes left." George made a noticeable effort and went on.

"By some miracle the fish stayed on the hook; but I got a faint idea of what would have happened if he'd taken a real notion to fight. He went around the pool so fast it must have made him dizzy. I heard Isabelle say, 'I didn't miss him, George'; and then—well, I didn't lose my temper; you wouldn't call it that exactly. I hardly knew what I said. I'll admit I shouldn't have said it. But I did say it; no doubt of that; no doubt of that whatever."

"What was it you said?" I asked. George looked at me uneasily.

"Oh, the sort of thing a man would say impulsively—under the circumstances."

"Was it something disparaging about her?" I inquired.

"Oh, no," said George, "nothing about her. I simply intimated—in a somewhat brutal way, I suppose—that's she'd better get away from the pool—er—not bother me anymore is what I meant to imply."

For the first time since George had chosen me for a confidant I felt a lack of frankness on his part.

"Just what did you say, George?" I insisted.

"Well, it wasn't altogether my words," he evaded. "It was the tone I used, as much as anything. Of course, the circumstances would excuse—Still, I regret it. I admit that. I've told you so plainly."

There was no time in which to press him further. "Well, what happened then?" I asked.

"Isabelle just disappeared. She went up the bank, of course, but I didn't see her go. Old Faithful was still nervous and I had to keep my eye on the line. He quieted down in a little while and continued to promenade slowly around the pool. I suppose this kept up for half an hour more. Then I made up my mind that something had to be done. I turned very carefully on the rock, lowered the tip until it was on the line with the fish, turned the rod under my arm until it was pointing behind me and jumped.

"Of course, I had to give him slack; but I kept my balance on the point by the skin of my teeth, and when I raised the rod he was still on. I worked to the bank, giving out line, and crawled under some bushes and things and got around to the cove at last. Then I started to work again to swing him into the cove, but absolutely nothing doing. I could lead him anywhere except into the cove. He'd had enough of that; I didn't blame him, either.

"To make a long story short, I stayed with him for two hours. For a while it was pretty dark; but there was a good-sized moon that night, and when it rose it shone right down on the pool through a gap in the trees fortunately. My wrist was gone completely, but I managed to keep some pressure on him all the time, and at last he forgot about what had happened to him in the cove. I swung him in and the current brought him past me. He was on his side by now. I don't think he was tired even then—just discouraged. I let him drift over the net, heaved him out on the bank and sank down beside him, absolutely all in. I couldn't have got to my feet on a bet. I just sat there in a sort of daze and looked at Old Faithful, gleaming in the moonlight.

"After a half-hour's rest I was able to get up and go to camp. I planned what I was going to do on the way. There was always a crowd in the main camp living room after dinner. I simply walked into the living room without a word and laid Old Faithful on the center table.

"Well, you can imagine faintly what happened. I never got any dinner— couldn't have eaten any, as a matter of fact. I didn't even get a chance to take off my waders. By the time I'd told just how I'd done it to one crowd, more would come in and look at Old Faithful; and then stand and look at me for a while; and then make me tell it all over again. At last everybody began to dig up anything they had with a kick in it. Almost everyone had a bottle he'd been hoarding. There was Scotch and gin and brandy and rye and a lot of experimental stuff. Art Bascom got a tin dish pan from the kitchen and put in on the table beside Old Faithful. He said, 'Pour your contributions right in here, men.' So each man dumped whatever he had into the dish pan and everybody helped himself.

"It was great, of course. The biggest night of my life, but I hope I'll never be so dog-tired again. I felt as though I'd taken a beating. After they'd weighed Old Faithful—nine pounds five and a half ounces; and he'd been out of water two hours—I said I had to go to bed, and went.

"Isabelle wasn't in the cabin. I thought, in a hazy way, that she was with some of the women, somewhere. Don't get the idea I was stewed. But I hadn't had anything to eat, and the mixture in that dish pan was plain TNT.

"I fell asleep as soon as I hit the bed; slept like a log till daylight. Then I half woke up, feeling that something terrific had happened. For a minute I didn't know what; then I remember what it was. I had landed Old Faithful on a three-ounce rod!

"I lay there and went over the whole thing from the beginning, until I came to Isabelle with the landing net. That made me look at where her head should have been on the pillow. It wasn't there. She wasn't in the cabin. I thought perhaps she'd got up early and gone out to look at the lake or the sunrise or something. But I got up in a hurry and dressed.

"Well, I could see no signs of Isabelle about camp. I ran into Jean just coming from the head guide's cabin and he said, 'Too bad about your wife's mother.' I said, 'What's that?' He repeated what he'd said, and added, 'She must be an awful sick woman.' Well, I got out of him finally that Isabelle had come straight up from the stream the evening before, taken two guides and started for Buck's Landing. Jean had urged her to wait until morning, naturally; but she'd told him she must get to her mother at once, and took on so, as Jean put it, that he had to let her go.

"I said, 'Let me have Indian Joe, stern, and a good man, bow. Have 'em ready in ten minutes.' I rushed to the kitchen, drank two cups of coffee and started for Buck's Landing. We made the trip down in seven hours, but Isabelle had left with her trunks on the 10:40 train.

"I haven't seen her since. Went to her home once. She wouldn't see me; neither would her mother. Her father advised not forcing things—just waiting. He said he'd do what he could. We'll, he's done it—you read the letter. Now you know the whole business. You'll stick, of course, and see me through just the first of it, old man. Of course, you'll do that, won't you?

"We'd better get down to the train now. Track nineteen."

"George," I said, "one thing more: just what did you say to her when she—"

"Oh, I don't know," George began vaguely.

"George," I interrupted, "no more beating about the bush. What did you say?"

I saw his face grow even more haggard, if possible. Then it mottled into a shade resembling the brick on an old colonial mansion.

"I told her—" he began in a low voice. "Yes?" I encouraged.

"I told her to get the hell out of there."

And now a vision was presented to my mind's eye; a vision of twelve fish plates, each depicting a trout curving up through green waters to an artificial fly. The vision extended on through the years. I saw Mrs. George Baldwin Potter ever gazing upon those rising trout and recalling the name on the card which had accompanied them to her door.

I turned and made rapidly for the main entrance of the Grand Central Station. In doing so I passed the clock above Information and saw that I still had two minutes in which to be conveyed by a taxicab far, far from the entrance to Track Nineteen.

I remember hearing the word "quitter" hurled after me by a hoarse, despairing voice.

CHAPTER 20

MR. THEODORE CASTWELL

BY G. E. M. SKUES

Mr. Theodore Castwell, having devoted a long, strenuous and not unenjoyable life to hunting to their doom innumerable salmon, trout, and grayling in many quarters of the globe, and having gained much credit among his fellows for his many ingenious improvements in rods, flies, and tackle employed for that end, in the fullness of time died and was taken to his own place.

St. Peter looked up from a draft balance sheet at the entry of the attendant angel.

"A gentleman giving the name of Castwell. Says he is a fisherman, your Holiness, and has 'Fly-Fishers' Club, London' on his card."

"Hm-hm," says St. Peter. "Fetch me the ledger with his account." St. Peter perused it.

"Hm-hm," said St. Peter. "Show him in."

Mr. Castwell entered cheerfully and offered a cordial right hand to St. Peter.

"As a brother of the angle—" he began.

"Hm-hm," said St. Peter. "I have been looking at your account from below."

"I am sure I shall not appeal to you in vain for special consideration in connection with the quarters to be assigned to me here."

"Hm-hm," said St. Peter.

"Well, I've seen worse accounts," said St. Peter. "What sort of quarters would you like?"

"Do you think you could manage something in the way of a country cottage of the Test Valley type, with modern conveniences and, say, three quarters of a mile of one of those pleasant chalk streams, clear as crystal, which proceed from out the throne, attached?"

"Why, yes," said St. Peter. "I think we can manage that for you. Then what about your gear?

"You must have left your fly rods and tackle down below. I see you prefer a light split cane of nine foot or so, with appropriate fittings. I will indent upon the Works Department for what you require, including a supply of flies. I think you will approve of our dresser's productions. Then you will want a keeper to attend you."

"Thanks awfully, your Holiness," said Mr. Castwell. "That will be first-rate. To tell you the truth, from the Revelations I read, I was inclined to fear that I might be just a teeny-weeny bit bored in heaven."

"In h-hm-hm," said St. Peter, checking himself.

It was not long before Mr. Castwell found himself alongside an enchantingly beautiful clear chalk stream, some fifteen yards wide, swarming with fine trout feeding greedily: and presently the attendant angel assigned to him had handed him the daintiest, most exquisite, light split-cane rod conceivable—

perfectly balanced with the reel and line—with a beautifully damped tapered cast of incredible fineness and strength, and a box of flies of such marvelous tying as to be almost mistakable for the natural insects they were to simulate. Mr. Castwell scooped up a natural fly from the water, matched it perfectly from the fly box, and knelt down to cast to a riser putting up just under a tussock ten yards or so above him. The fly lit like gossamer, six inches above the last ring; and next moment the rod was making the curve of beauty. Presently, after an exciting battle, the keeper netted out a beauty of about two and a half pounds. "Heavens," cried Mr. Castwell. "This is something like."

"I am sure his Holiness will be pleased to hear it," said the keeper.

Mr. Castwell prepared to move upstream to the next riser when he noticed that another trout had taken up the position of that which he had just landed, and was rising. "Just look at that," he said, dropping instantaneously to his knee and drawing off some line. A moment later an accurate fly fell just above the neb of the fish, and instantly Mr. Castwell engaged in battle with another lusty fish. All went well, and presently the landing net received its two and a half pounds. "A very pretty brace," said Mr. Castwell, preparing to move on to the next string of busy nebs which he had observed putting up around the bend. As he approached the tussock, however, he became aware that the place from which he had just extracted so satisfactory a brace was already occupied by another busy feeder.

"Well, I'm damned," said Mr. Castwell. "Do you see that?"

"Yes, sir," said the keeper.

The chance of extracting three successive trout from the same spot was too attractive to be forgone, and once more Mr. Castwell knelt down and delivered a perfect cast to the spot. Instantly it was accepted and battle was joined. All held, and presently a third gleaming trout joined his brethren in the creel.

Mr. Castwell turned joyfully to approach the next riser round the bend. Judge, however, his surprise to find that once more the pit beneath the tussock was occupied by a rising trout, apparently of much the same size as the others.

"Heavens," exclaimed Mr. Castwell. "Was there ever anything like it?" "No, sir," said the keeper.

"Look here," said he to the keeper, "I think I really must give this chap a miss and pass on to the next."

"Sorry, it can't be done, sir. His Holiness would not like it."

"Well, if that's really so," said Mr. Castwell, and knelt rather reluctantly to his task.

Several hours later he was still casting to the same tussock.

"How long is this confounded rise going to last?" inquired Mr. Castwell. "I suppose it will stop soon."

"No, sir," said the keeper.

"What, isn't there a slack hour in the afternoon?" "No afternoon, sir."

"What? Then what about the evening rise?" "No evening rise, sir," said the keeper.

"Well, I shall knock off now. I must have had about thirty brace from that corner."

"Beg pardon, sir, but his Holiness would not like that." "What?" said Mr. Castwell. "Mayn't I even stop at night?"

"No night here, sir," said the keeper.

"Then do you mean that I have got to go on catching these damned two-and-a-half-pounders at this corner forever and ever?"

The keeper nodded. "Hell!" said Mr. Castwell. "Yes," said his keeper.

MODERN CLASSICS

CHAPTER 21

ROMANCING THE FALLS

BY JAMES R. BABB

Helen Falls.

"Romance," said the amoral Mrs. Cheveley in Oscar Wilde's *An Ideal Husband*, "should never begin with sentiment. It should begin with science and end with a settlement." This is not quite how my ten-year romance with Helens Falls played out.

My first encounter came through the science of radio in a northern Quebec caribou camp, where a deflating inflatable and wrath-o-God weather had sent guide Chris Turcotte and me searching for food and shelter; instead, we found vandalizing bears and a shredded tent. Four long days we waited for flying weather and the rescue Otter while living on salvage from our abbreviated float trip of the Lefevre River and crumbs of culinary radio chatter between

Marlene, who cooked for the arctic char camp at Weymouth Inlet, and her mother Shirley, who cooked for the Atlantic salmon camp at Helens Falls.

"Oh, t'wedder's awful," Shirley told Marlene. "T'sports was catchin' lotsa salmon, but den t'weather turns ugly and now t'sports is hangin' round t'kitchen an' gettin' underfoot, and dere's been seven bears here doin' t'same. One had 'is face pressed right up against t'dinin' room window, all slobberin' an' moanin'."

"Shoot 'em," said Marlene. "Remember las' year when they had t'kill t'polar bear come sniffin' round up here?"

"Well," said Shirley, "they comes 'roun moi kitchen I'll get after'm wit' t'broom. So what you got on for suppah?"

This was the part Chris and I were waiting for. We had our own bear stories. What we didn't have was food.

"Oim makin' roast turkey and cheesecake. You?"

"Oi've got stuffed pork chops and lemon pie."

Chris looked down at the salvaged salami from which he'd been trimming furry green spots. I looked at the oil heater, where our sole half-loaf of waterlogged bread lay drying.

"Mmmmmmmmmmmm," we said in our best Homer Simpson voices. "Helens Falls."

Fast-forward nine years, and I was sitting in a half-century-old de Havilland Beaver flying down the rugged valley of the George River and heading for Helens Falls, an entirely accidental zigzag from a brook trout trip to Three Rivers Lodge in central Labrador.

As the story goes, Sammy Cantafio of Ungava Adventures invited Three Rivers partners Kevin Barry Junior and Robin Reeve to come visit Helens Falls with the idea of forming some sort of business relationship—an extra-cost option for sports who might want to fly north to Helens Falls to fish some of North America's best Atlantic salmon water or fly south to Three Rivers to fish some of North America's best brook trout water.

This all sounds properly businesslike until you factor in Marco Valcourt, who piloted the Three Rivers Beaver and subtly and perhaps underhandedly instigated this expedition, and Trina Wellman, who cooked at Helens Falls and on whom, unbeknownst to everyone including Trina, Marco had romantic designs.

And me? Well, I was just along for the ride—a last-minute seat-filler for Robin, who was recalled to Massachusetts to settle some business affairs.

Settlement? Thank you Mrs. Cheveley.

It's a long flight from Three Rivers to Helens Falls. We stopped en route to fish Arctic char on Mistastin Lake, a large asteroid-impact crater so sacred to the Innu that they can't even look at the small croissant-shaped island at its head. After a cold, wet afternoon of fishing for Arctic char, icing several to take back to Three Rivers, we flew on into the gray dusk to Lac Cananée, where we spent the night at a caribou camp Marco's father used to own. In the morning we topped off the Beaver's gas tanks from fifty-five-gallon drums by dipping with a five-gallon detergent pail and straining the gas through panty hose of unknown provenance, and then we flew off into the mist skimming just beneath the clouds at three hundred feet above the unending Arctic landscape until we found the George River. For two hours we followed it downriver, turning left and right as the river willed, until finally we zoomed over the falls and past Cantafio's famous salmon camp that I had been longing to see for the past nine years.

Marco circled, scouting the swirling eddies below the falls for a smooth place to set down the Beaver, and as we pivoted on one wingtip I frantically filled my tattered notebook with adjectives in a vain attempt to capture the setting's sheer romance.

Helens Falls—sources differ on the presence or absence of an apostrophe, and some even dispute the possessive s altogether, perhaps alluding to the original Greek tragedy—are more a series of falls stretching over several miles than a single sharp drop, and the river looks less like standard-issue

Atlantic salmon water than a high mountain trout stream somehow grown to the size of the Ohio or the Tennessee flowing through as wild a country as you will find on this earth yet possessing a tender, almost delicate beauty that veils, but doesn't entirely conceal, a savage core.

We climbed the stairway from the roaring falls up onto the gravelly bench past a cluster of neat frame cabins and into the magnetic dining room, which was as large and bright and comfortable as Chris and I had imagined it years ago while we were quietly starving in a weather-bound caribou camp. Inside, its picture windows looked out on a vista that could stop your heart.

From the kitchen emerged the smells of cooking that drew both bears and t'sports from far and wide, and then Trina—like the original Helen, a heart-stopper and voyage launcher in her own right—entered from the kitchen bearing a platter of sandwiches and mint-chocolate-chip brownies so rich you could happily infarct at the first bite. Trina didn't look like a typical northwoods camp cook, who tend to be as rugged, burly, and raw as bears; she looked like a ballerina, as refined and ethereal as her cinnamon rolls—a proper Helen of the Falls.

Kevin and I exchanged glances, understanding finally why Marco the Lothario and unrepentant gourmand had engineered this trip. But we weren't here, camp owner Sammy Cantafio reminded us, to ogle his cook and eat all his food. We were here to fish for salmon, or at least Kevin and I were—or at least I was, Kevin having business affairs to settle. So after a quick and elegant lunch we pushed off upriver and powered through the falls in a jut-jawed old freighter canoe through some of the most dramatically magnificent water you could ever hope to see.

The romantic thing about Atlantic salmon fishing is its utter uncertainty coupled with the wealth of unsupportable theories that attempt to explain the uncertainty. As serious anglers all know, Atlantic salmon don't eat anything in freshwater, but they do take flies—though not for reasons anyone entirely understands. This maddens the scientific wing of angler-dom just as it delights the romantically inclined. Discovering the precise why of the thing is to improve efficiency at the expense of sentiment. What begins as enigma becomes merely ant-like industry that crushes the thrill of surprise beneath a ream of informative instruction and relentlessly repeated activity.

I have fished Atlantic salmon a fair amount and know too well why they're called both the fish of kings and the fish of a thousand casts—the wild, exclusive water they inhabit and those wild, heart-stopping leaps you see just often enough to keep you coming back but not so often that you ever feel entitled. So I was more than a little surprised, my first afternoon on the George, to hook and land a couple of tail-walking eight-pound grilse and a fourteen-pound salmon as bright as a silver ingot, as well as to hook and not land two others in the ten- to twelve-pound range thanks to the brutal current and my wimpy seven-weight trout rod. And I was even less surprised the next morning to find the salmon completely indifferent to the fly they had wanted so badly the previous afternoon.

The river level didn't change. The weather, soft and misty and autumnal, didn't change. My persistent presentation of small dark wet flies didn't change. Only the salmon changed, and the mystery of why they suddenly changed is part of why we fish for them. Whatever is most difficult becomes

An Atlantic salmon.

most interesting if you're doing it right. A properly romantic fly fisher doesn't want his fish to come easy; he wants them playing hard to get.

And they were. Once, imagining yesterday's teeming river somehow gone barren of fish, I waded onto a barbell-shaped boulder of pink and gray serpentine polished to glass by a current so overwhelming that it shot chest-high waves into my face, and a hen salmon close to three feet long swam across my bootlaces—a flashing silver heartthrob pursuing a hot date who ignored me as part of the landscape, the inevitable fate of all middle-aged men.

Young and handsome Marco—politely, cordially, but firmly rebuffed in his own great pursuit—shortly scored compensation in another when he landed a high-jumping male, bright from the sea and heading uphill from twenty pounds.

Kevin, too, tied into a couple of good fish, his first Atlantic salmon despite living his whole life in central Labrador. Finally my morning's drought was broken by a pity strike from an electrocuted grilse, and just as I released him it was time to head downriver, pile back into the Beaver, and set a course for home while stuffing ourselves along the way with a liberated pan of Trina's cinnamon rolls so light they nearly floated away. As did, for various reasons, our hearts.

As we buzzed the camp at Helens Falls, Marco waggling the old Beaver's wings like some madcap Waldo-Pepper barnstormer from the biplane days, I pressed my face against the window and wondered if I'd ever again see what I had waited so long to see and saw all too briefly.

Sometimes if you sit back and allow life to develop its own map for the future instead of trying to impose your own myopic views, things have a way of settling out because a year and two weeks later on a sunny morning in late August, I was climbing out of an Air Inuit Twin Otter and heading down the trail from the airstrip toward Helens Falls. This time I was going salmon fishing not for an afternoon and a morning but for a whole week thanks to a midwinter invitation from Sammy and a fortuitous cavity in my editorial calendar the very week he had free.

Trina waited in the dining room dispensing hugs and brownies, and we—we being two retired doctors from New Jersey, a real-estate guy from Manhattan and another from Boston who were traveling as a pack and had been here before, and two guys from New Brunswick who can only be described as salmon bums and hadn't been here before—sat down to eat, fill out the paperwork for licenses, and engage in the usual pregame banter of fish camp.

Then it was into the canoes, up the river, and back into the rhythmic waltz of Atlantic salmon fishing: cast, cast, cast, step-step-step; cast, cast, cast, step-step-step. *Whaaaaaaaaaang!*

For such an immense river, the George is surprisingly easy to fish. Most of the salmon lie close to the bank; only a few lies require casts longer than fifty feet, and most can be covered with a thirty-foot lob. Only a few pools require deft wading, and many can be fished in knee boots. It's a bit of a hike to the top of the falls and the last pool, but the first pool is only ten feet from the boat landing. In many ways, the George is almost remedial salmon fishing.

Not that this helped us catch fish our first afternoon. Frenchy—one of the New Brunswick salmon bums who lives on the Miramichi and fishes it daily—landed a good one using a very large and flashy fly, a counterintuitive approach for this river, where the fish are said to prefer small dark flies, riffle-hitched and waked like water-skiers. But then, with Atlantic salmon, slavishly following conventional science is only wise if sentiment fails to direct you elsewhere.

The trouble, as usual, was the weather: bright and warm and unapologetically sunny, which for salmon fishing is good news but for salmon catching it isn't. What we wanted were clouds and drizzle and wind, and as Marco the pilot found out last year, when you really want something is exactly when you don't get it.

Yet we didn't suffer for salmon over the warm and sunny week. Everyone caught fish from Peter, who was fishing for only the second week of his life, to Frenchy—he insists on being called that, honest—who has fished virtually every week of his life.

I, who fish a fair amount, caught two grilse in the eight-pound range right off by riffle-hitching a small Black Bear-Green Butt through the pocket water near the bank. To see me in action with that first grilse, however, you would never believe I've fished a day in my life.

Sammy, who was guiding me—or interfering with me or amusing himself with me, depending on your viewpoint—was laughing too hard to breathe as the fish, brought in too hot and too soon, set about amusing himself with me, too. I reached for his tail, and he darted between my legs and jumped head-high behind me. When I reached again for his tail he darted back through my legs and jumped head-high in front of me. Just as he was making his third pass through my legs, crossing the tee on the clove hitch, Sammy grabbed him by the tail and prevented what might have been the first hog-tying of a salmon fisher by a salmon in angling history.

After lunch Sammy and I took the canoe across the river to the east bank and walked up the old portage trail, the path followed by centuries of caribou and caribou-hunting Inuit and, a hundred years ago that very August, by a young woman from Ontario called Mina Benson Hubbard.

Back in 1903, Leonidas Hubbard, a New York-based editor for *Outing* magazine, tried to find these falls and thence Ungava Bay in a long canoe expedition by following much the same route from Labrador that we flew last year in Marco's Beaver. Only Hubbard's expedition didn't make it to the George. Hubbard took a wrong turn in the braid of channels leading from Northwest River into Michikamau Lake and starved to death. He left behind, back in the States, a young wife.

Mina Hubbard felt that her husband and his sense of direction had been unfairly maligned in *Lure of the Labrador Wild*, a book written by another expedition member, Dillon Wallace, and so in 1905 she set out to make things right by completing her husband's expedition to chart the inland path from coastal Labrador to Ungava Bay. Moreover, she did so while racing a parallel expedition led by Wallace.

And she won, leading the expedition the whole way and writing, in 1908, a remarkable book called *A Woman's Way Through Unknown Labrador*, describing for the very first time this land of terrible beauty.

"And still the river roared on down through its narrow valley, at Helen Falls dropping by wild and tempestuous cascades, and then by almost equally wild rapids, to a mile below where it shoots out into an expansion with such terrific force as to keep this great rush of water above the general level for some distance out into the lake. Here we made the longest portage of the journey down the George River, carrying the stuff one and a quarter mile."

Walking along this trail a century later, I found it difficult to think about anything except Mrs. Hubbard and the kind of romance that will spur a young woman to lead an expedition through untracked land at a time when society compressed young women into roles typically allowing no leadership at all.

At least it was difficult to think about anything else until the portage trail led back down to the river with a whole new array of pools and seams holding great salmon awaiting their own romantic spur to goad them out into the current and on upstream to fulfill their biological imperatives.

And yet we didn't catch a thing, Sammy and I, although we saw plenty of fish. But with the river so high, we couldn't get a good drift or wade out to the right spots on this eastern shore, as geologically and topographically different from the west bank as though the George were an ocean separating two continents.

It fell to Frenchy and Steve, on their last day and with water levels down a couple of feet, to come fish the east bank's tough pools and to take five bright salmon, including the fish of the week, an eighteen-pounder that tail-walked like a tarpon, and to lose the fish of the year, a twenty-five-pounder, according to Chris the guide, that bulldogged Steve for half an hour before finally disappearing downstream—trailing his entire fly line.

As for my last day, unattended and wandering beneath a welcome new veil of clouds, I decided that after a week of waking riffle-hitched wet flies in the glaring sun and catching two or three eight-pound grilse each day—and getting skunked yesterday—that I ought to diverge from accepted science and rely entirely on sentiment.

I opened my fly box and spied in a dusty corner an electric green cigar with a hackle wound through it that looked less like a proper fishing fly than like something ejected from the Jolly Green Giant's nostril: a small Green Machine leftover from a trip to the Miramichi.

After lunch I knotted one on, greased it to float, and headed for the topmost pool. On the third swing, a fourteen-pound cockfish nailed it and tore the pool to foam. As I tweezed out the fly and watched the salmon melt away, I remember thinking: All right. I'm onto something here.

Which of course meant that I wasn't, as for the next hour I waked the Green Machine across splendid water without one pull. But at least I had the whole river to myself with Frenchy and Steve on the east bank, Sammy off in the Cessna to Kuujjuaq to attend to business, and everyone else gone char fishing in the nearby Ford River. With no salmon showing I reverted to type and trout fished my way down to the canoe, dead-drifting the little Green Machine in all the places I would be if I were a brook trout.

And there they were. By the time I reached the canoe I'd taken better than a dozen bright orange brookies to twenty inches and a bonus grilse of maybe six pounds. Down at the boat pool at a dark little eddy within a foot of shore, I cast toward a perfect brook trout lie, and the instant the fly hit the water a twelve-pound salmon plucked it from the surface and rocketed across the river.

After releasing him and resting the pool—well, resting me, more accurately, as the salmon was fresh from the sea and wild as a wolf—I cast again to the same spot, and five salmon rose simultaneously for the fly. An eight-pound grilse got there first, but as he somersaulted across the pool and came to hand, fiercely snapping and freshly peppered with sea lice, it was hard to be disappointed even though he barely won the race for the fly against three salmon around twelve pounds and another that easily bested twenty, according to my notebook—though in my sleepless dreams he's gaining weight by the week.

And in those same dreams I envision somehow engineering a return to Helens Falls, and in this dream I do everything right. I always arrive in the dining room just as Trina's evening platter of gravlax makes its first appearance and before it makes its rapid disappearance, and when we see bears they're always picturesquely sequestered on the far side of the river. I always cast perfectly and fish my drifts precisely. I choose the right fly by knowing my quarry's mind and not by simply following conventional wisdom or my own unsubstantiated whims. I land what I hook and hook what I cast to, and it's always the biggest fish that takes my fly. And when I cleanly release those big salmon they all swim away unmarred, psychically or psychologically, by the experience.

In my dreams of Helens Falls, sentiment and science combine to form the very core of romance, and there is no talk anywhere of a settlement.

Of course that's how I fish in my dreams, not in real life. For an honest assessment of my fishing I must borrow a line from Mrs. Cheveley's polar opposite, brave Mina Hubbard: "The work was imperfectly done, yet I did what I could."

"I did what I could." It's such a keen, useful phrase from an intrepid soul like brave Mina Hubbard and such a self-important bloat from that most unuseful of all possible parasites, a professional fish-writer. And yet. . . .

Once upon a time I went to Helens Falls in northern Ungava, and I did something worthwhile because eight years after my last visit there I received an e-mail from Trina. She wrote:

I'm sure you don't remember me. I used to work as a cook at the beautiful Helens Falls salmon camp on the George River in Quebec, Canada. You visited us there in 2005 and later wrote an article for *Gray Sporting Journal* called "Romancing the Falls." If you remember this, then you must remember the Beaver pilot who flew you there, Marco Valcourt. The article was great, by the way. I read it a few months after it was published and thought it was quite flattering, especially the part that suggested Marco had romantic designs on the cook. To make a long story short, Marco and I started dating in the spring of 2008, we fell very much in love, which was easy because you spilled the beans about our love through writing this article. I never thought it could be possible for a guy like Marco to like me, but after reading your article I did, and it helped to move things to another level for us: Ha!

I thank you for that. Your article has been such a big part of my love story with Marco that I've shared it with many people we've met over these past five and a half years. Although, today, I'm saddened to the depths of my being to tell you that Marco has passed away. He died suddenly on September 20, 2013, of a massive heart attack, when we were both working together at a caribou camp in northern Quebec. I just ordered a copy of Gray's Feb/March 2006 issue to have in my safekeeping your wonderfully written article that I will keep with me forever in memory of my beautiful Marco. So thank you so much for that. I believe if it weren't for your article I may never have believed he could have loved me and I possibly would have missed out on the absolute best part of my life, which was spent with him.

Thank you,
Trina

CHAPTER 22

SASHIMI

BY HENRY HUGHES

I had been in Japan just one week, and I was thinking about Eugene and my brother on Long Island, how we could fish together for hours, speaking very few words over the water in early light, but feeling very close. Then I thought of silent days fishing alone—sometimes sad, troubled, or unsure—when angling became the language of asking, the fish a hoped-for answer, as easy, elusive, or complicated as any deep truth. Some days there were no fish, some days there were many.

Here, at dusk, the fishing party of fifteen men shouted back and forth above the roar of the engine, rigging outrageously long poles with sabiki rigs, consisting of five small hooks dressed in capes of pearlescent plastic and tinsel that twinkled like holiday lights. "Like Christmas," I said, singing a bit of Jingle Bells. The men laughed. I was aboard the fifty-five foot *Yutaka Maru*. "It means boat of plenty," explained Usami Manabu, one of the English teachers I would be working with that year. The school was in Niigata Prefecture on a river-crossed rice plain twenty minutes from the Sea of Japan and fishing ports like Teradomari, where we sailed from that evening. Usami and a few other teachers from the junior high had offered to take me *sakana tsuri*, fishing, when they heard it was my *shumi*, my hobby, said to be an important part of everyone's identity in Japan. Unlike the duties of family and job, which are often foisted upon us, a hobby was something one pursued for pure pleasure, which may have been particularly important in a culture where social forms and responsibilities seemed greater and stricter. Wherever and however we live, it's good to have a *shumi*.

The steel boat plowed north beyond the jetty, the mountainous mainland creased in cedar ravine shadows behind us. Japan was greener than I imagined, but this was the first foreign port from which I ever sailed. I had never been abroad, hadn't yet learned a word of Japanese, but I understood the familiar pitch of the boat, the smell of salt air, the rods and reels ready in their holders.

We cruised a couple miles offshore, the engine idled down, and the whole deck lit up like a baseball stadium under large, clear bulbs swinging from a wire running the length of the boat. The captain set the anchor, and then lowered four submersible lamps into the sea, igniting a glowing emerald ring around us. Within ten minutes I started seeing small fish drawn to the chum of our light.

I was told to fish the bottom, but I stopped on the way down and jigged a little—I knew it as a way of locating fish. The man next to me said "*dame*," no good, "*tana o awasete*," on the bottom. He gestured with his fist pressed hard against the gunnel and reached over to flip the clutch on my reel. I pulled away, a little annoyed. *I know how to fish*, I thought. A few minutes later, the first fish were caught, and true enough, it wasn't until I bounced the bottom that I hooked one myself, an eight-inch silver *aji* that I swung over the railing.

I studied the *aji* that were now being caught in great numbers. Usami pulled a paperback dictionary from his bag and said, "Horse mackerel." I knew it wasn't a mackerel, but it certainly shared its schooling and feeding behavior and was caught in a similar fashion. One of the science teachers approached holding another book. "Jackusu famuly," he said.

"Jacuzzi family?" I cocked my head.

"This fish is jacku's family," Usami peered at the book and tried to help.

"Who's Jack?" I asked.

But when I looked at the page it became clear. There was the Japanese word, *aji*; the Latin, *Trachurus japonicus*; and the English with a study sentence, "Jack mackerel (Japanese horse mackerel), belonging to the family

Aji.

of jacks, among them the amberjack and trevally." "Okay," I smiled. "It's a jack." The relieved and joyous faculty repeated "jacku, jacku, okay."

As the evening progressed a wild arena unfolded in the green glow below us. Schools of small mackerel and yellowtail (another species of jack) skittered across the surface, squid and swimming crabs hunted the shadows, and a pair of gulls sat at the light's soft edge. It was a magical world surrounding our boat and we started catching fish at various depths, sometimes a bonus squid groping an imperiled *aji*.

The captain, a short sinewy man who wore a cap eerily similar to Japanese naval officers in World War II, came down to chat with me through Usami. The captain told of a huge sea turtle that once swam into the light of the *Yutaka Maru*, its swollen flippers entangled in fishing line. He tried to net the turtle so it could be brought on board and the lines cut away, but the alarmed creature dove and he never saw it again. "That's sad," I said, telling him about a dead swan I once found, its beautiful, long neck choked in fishing line. "*Hakucho*," swan, the captain raised his hands into the sky, telling us that they came every fall from Siberia to winter in Niigata.

"*Taihen, nē*," that's terrible, he acknowledged the fate of our turtle and swan. Although such casualties may seem insignificant in the face of vast human interferences on the planet, we nodded solemnly, knowing that every angler has lost harmful line, hooks, and lead; every angler has released fish that would not survive; everyone has injured and killed creatures unintentionally.

With the captain watching, I reeled in two *aji* and suddenly felt a fierce strike. Something like a dragon broke into the glowing arena. "*Tachiuo, tachiuo,*" the men called from the deck. The long, bright fish had swallowed one of my hooked *aji* and hooked itself. The captain swept down a landing net and scooped up the yard-long beast. *Tachi* means "long sword," a much better name than ribbonfish, as the species is commonly called in English. Stretched over a bladelike body the fish's skin was preternaturally silver, brilliantly reflecting the lights on deck, and its dragon head narrowed into a mouth of long, needle teeth. It twisted powerfully out of the net, the live *aji* still fluttering in its jaws.

As the fishing slowed, a few of the men sat around the stern drinking Asahi beer and cutting squid and *aji* into sashimi, thin strips of raw fish dipped in soy sauce. I had never eaten raw fish before. Watanabe Jun, a broad-shouldered, handsome teacher with a crew cut, pulled a knife from his bag. He held up my stiffening *tachiuo* and gestured, bringing the two beams of silver together, creating a triangle between us. "Okay?" he asked. "Okay, okay," I affirmed. He slit the fish lengthwise and skinned it. Then he sliced the pale flesh into thin ribbons, handed me a pair of chopsticks and asked, "*Sashimi oishī desu ka?*" Is sashimi delicious? I sampled the flesh of the dragon. It was tender and delicate. "*Oishī desu,*" Delicious, I said, learning my first bit of Japanese.

One of the men aboard the *Yutaka Maru* that night was the tall, thin, and very fishy Kanamaru Mitsuru, who asked me to call him Ken. Ken often took me fishing along the Niigata coast, where we cast from rocks and tetrapod jetties for tai, a bottom dwelling sea bream that reminded me of its cousin in the *Sparidae* family, the Long Island porgy. For twelve hours we would stand, slip, sit, talk, or stare silently into the waves, angling long rods and strange baits, Ken chirping "*kita-kita-kita*" when he felt a bite, which wasn't very often. The first time out we each caught one *kurodai*, the black sea bream, about the size and shape of an average freshwater sunfish, and Ken said it was wonderful. "One fish is worth twenty dollars."

"No way," I said.

"Way," he countered with a smile, having watched and loved the new movie, *Wayne's World.*

Ken insisted we eat the fish the next day, explaining that it takes hours for the flavor of some fish to develop. I was incredulous, thinking the fresher the better, but with dictionaries and patience, he explained that the proteins had to break down into mouthwatering amino acids. I told him about aging beef and he said, "Fish, too. But not too long." The following afternoon at his house, Ken filleted the *kurodai* with surgical precision. He then set out small dipping dishes with his preferred mixture of soy sauce, a sweet cooking sake called mirin, and a broth called dashi made with the flakes of a cured bonito. His wife, young son, and I all had a slice of *kurodai* that we dipped gently in the sauce. Firm, almost crunchy, imparting the subtle flavors of the ocean, it seemed the epitome of seafood sophistication and yet required no cooking. "Oishī amino acids," I said. Ken didn't catch my joke and asked, "Okay?" with brow-lined concern. "*Oishī desu,*" I smiled. Never had I eaten a fish with such a heightened awareness of its delicacy and value.

Around the Kanamaru house were *gyotaku* ink prints of trophy fish Ken had landed over the years, and in the family room alcove hung a scroll featuring an ink painting of a carp rising in a lotus pond. The tapestries of the Sistine Chapel and Coventry Cathedral could not have felt more holy.

Ken may have exaggerated the value of the little black bream, but its red-skinned relative, the famous tai, often called "red snapper" in America, was a truly precious fish; I saw four pounders on ice at the market for 6,000 yen, about sixty dollars. When I attended the elaborate wedding of a friend, each guest was served a whole cooked tai in a lacquered box, the very name of the fish the tail end of "*omedetai,*" meaning "congratulations." Honored at shrines, pursued by emperors, revered by the people, the tai seemed almost sacred. But it was also being fished to death. The difficulty of catching a single tai indicates not only the rocky elusiveness of these creatures but also their relative scarcity in many areas. Even on a bad day off Long Island, we could catch a few porgies. Japan's seas have been supporting human predators for thousands of years, but the population density and industrialization of the twentieth century had taken a serious toll. The thought of a hundred, well-armed Japanese men and women dropping lines down on a few lonely tai hiding in their mossy grottoes was discomfiting. I angled Ken toward the more abundant aji and yellowtail, feeling better, but perhaps just hiding my own head from the truth of man's deep reaching predations.

"Don't get too deep," the dive master warned before we rolled off the side of the fiberglass skiff. Scuba diving around Niigata's Sado Island, a couple friends and I chased a football-sized octopus that changed color and shape as it gloved into a new cave. I followed another octopus into seventy feet of water before the cold and darkness turned me around. We swam with the honored bream and the famous *fugu*, a blowfish with delicious or, if improperly prepared, deadly flesh. And a huge, bulb-headed *kobudai*, an Asian sheepshead, dogged us around the rocks, eating squid from our hands.

Sado Island.

On the boat ride back to the island we also saw the Japanese fishing fleet chasing bluefin tuna, *kuro maguro*. As Japan and the West craved fattier melting bites of sushi, the bluefin's value exceeded the snapper, sole, swordfish, and every other fish in the sea. In the 1990s, bluefin prices were already on the rise at hundreds of dollars per pound; in January, 2013, a 489 pound bluefin tuna sold for $1.8 million, more than $3,600 a pound. At these rates, very few Japanese or American sport anglers will ever catch a bluefin tuna on rod and reel like Hemingway and Zane Gray.

"Imagine hooking one those giants?" I prompted Ken.

"They're too expensive to play with," he said.

"That's a crazy way of looking at it," I argued. "If we stop fishing commercially for bluefin tuna, or any rare fish, they're likely to recover." I'd happily give up eating any fish for a few years or forever if it meant the species' survival. And if the big fleets would lay off the bluefin maybe the average sport angler could, one day, catch one. "The schools would return," I said, dreamy-eyed.

"Like the great herds of buffalo."

"Japanese don't like buffalo," Ken snorted, fluffing up his tight curly hair with a pick. "They like Kobe beef."

Under the cover of a language misunderstanding or by poetic tangent, Ken would often evade my questions and contrary opinions.

One afternoon, under a beautiful October sky, I saw salmon leaping and rolling up the Shinano River not far from where I lived. A fisherman casting for mullet told me only commercial netters could pursue them. Fuck that, I thought to myself, making plans to cast some big spinners. When I told Ken, he snapped: "You must never!" His face red, his tight hair vibrating.

"Just catch-and-release," I shrugged. "I'll say I'm mullet fishing. What's the problem?"

"It's against the law and Japanese people obey the law. You have no right."

It was the first time Ken got upset with me and I backed down. But I thought it wrong to deny a few anglers the experience of pursuing, hooking, and battling a salmon while gill nets hung across the river. Why should commercial operations have exclusive rights to the tuna and salmon, especially when these rights were abused? Ken was a passionate angler, but sheepishly obedient to customs, systems, and laws that favored government-supported industrial fishing over sport angling. And he almost blew a gasket when I told him I was going to fake a few sick days and fish in the mountains.

"Are you sick?"

"No," I laughed.

"Then you shouldn't do that."

"I haven't used any of my sick days, and they're in my contract. Just a couple days."

"You're a teacher. That's not right."

Despite some cultural differences, Ken and I got along. A hair stylist who had studied in England, Ken ran a salon that became an after-hours fishing social club. Ken's English was excellent, but two languages as different as Japanese and English are prone to pratfalls, and I smiled at his expensive sign, "Hair Craps," depicting two friendly looking crabs with scissoring claws. Even if spelled correctly, "Hair Crabs" is not a great English name for any sort of salon. Sitting in state-of-the-art styling chairs, drinking beer and sake, and eating dried squid and miso mackerel, we would discuss hair, women, pornography, food, fishing, travel—everything under the rising sun.

Through Ken and the salon, I made more friends, including Teiko, a beautiful woman in her early thirties who seemed, nonetheless, to carry sadness in her dark eyes. I sat in her pottery studio one afternoon, watching her hands press and pull a dull mound of spinning clay into the cylindrical form of a sake flask. "You love to drink," she said. "So I make you a *chōsi*. But this one will have fish." Teiko called herself a "modern" Japanese woman. An artist who graduated from the Women's Art College in Tokyo, she attended English conversation clubs, watched new movies, listened to cool music, and dated me, a twenty-six-year-old American. But she confided her increasing problems at home. "Now I embarrass my parents. They want me to marry. Then I will have no time for this," she said, shaving the inside of the *chō*si with a long wooden tool.

"My father gets very mad. He say I'm wasting my time with art and you."
She picked up a wide, wet paintbrush and groomed the outer walls, leaving
them smooth and unreflective; then took another wooden stylus, and with
a few lines, engraved a lovely fish. "I'm sorry," I said. She suddenly smiled,
flaring the *chōsi*'s mouth and pinching a pouring spout where the fish rose.

Teiko liked the water. We took trips to the sea and walked along the
beach. Beaches in Japan are full of delights: people swimming, flying kites,
surfing, and racing motorcycles. There were interesting dead creatures and
debris printed in bright characters. But I was always surprised by the tide of
garbage—bottles, cans, tires, plastic wrappers, even a washed-up female man-
ikin, entirely nude but for a piece of kelp across her eyes, as if she were a sea
bandit turned to plastic by the dragon, Ryūjin, for trying to steal his jewels.
Every culture has its paradoxes, and the law abiding Japanese with all their
civic mindfulness, their order, cleanliness and efficiency, their cultivated arts,
and an obvious love of natural beauty, were still capable of trashing the sea.

"Maybe it comes from Korea," Teiko said. And though oceanic garbage
can travel thousands of miles, this empty can of Asahi beer had the stamp of
a local distributor.

Teiko would often stay the night at my apartment. We'd wake on the futon,
I'd make tea and slide open the *shōgi* screens to a field and marsh waving
gently with new rushes. Spared by the plow and bulldozer, the wedge of
land behind my apartment provided a small sanctuary for egrets, warblers,
and shrikes. The waters teemed with frogs, crayfish, dragonfly larvae, and
small fish. Stepping onto the gravel along the train tracks directly behind
my building, a cock pheasant warily pecked. We noted the iridescent blue-
green neck without a white ring and the long gray tail striped in black. I
told Teiko about the ring-necked pheasants of South Dakota and Indiana,
how they'd been introduced to America from the far fields of China and

Japan. She put her hands around my neck and said, "You go the other way, *nē?*"

Some mornings I would get up early and fish the town's river and canals. One drizzly dawn I saw a man riding his bicycle down the cinder path under a line of ash trees, once grown to support bamboo poles for drying rice. Very old, wearing a shoulder cape and a round hat of woven rushes, he may, indeed, have dried rice stalks on these very trees before the war.

Dismounting from his rusted one-speed, I noticed his mitten style rubber boots, which separated the big toe from the other digits. From the rear basket he pulled out a bag and a plastic bucket, and then assembled a long, two-piece bamboo handle and attached a semicircular net. He began dipping for *funa*, small crucian carp abundant in the warm rivers, muddy irrigation ditches, and polluted canals of East Asia. *Funa*, like all carp, seem to flourish almost anywhere, swimming through murky debris, feeding on vegetation, plankton, and small insects. Carp are tough, enduring fish, perhaps that is why they named Hiroshima's major league baseball team the Hiroshima Carp, just four years after the devastation of the atomic bomb dropped on that city in August, 1945.

Following the example of the young boys in town, I was also *funa* fishing, but with a light wand, hair-thin line, and tiny hooks baited with maggots plucked from a dead cat. Catching finger-size fish from an irrigation ditch may not sound like great angling, but it brought me out into the fields where I could watch birds and insects, follow water, and bring home enough tiddlers for Teiko to make *kanroi*. Back in my apartment, I scaled and gutted the little fish, and then Teiko grilled them lightly over the gas burner and placed them in a pot with soy sauce, sugar, and mirin. The fish simmered all day while we played around, drank sake, watched a movie, until late afternoon when the *funa* became soft and dark. Served in Teiko's elegant little bowls, with sides of white rice and pickled eggplant, we picked up our chopsticks and ate the sweet stewed fish of the fields.

Up at school during the week, I was frequently visited by one of our textbook salesmen, Mr. Masugata, the characters in his name meaning "trout inlet." "I must take you *ayu* fishing," he said over and over. "*Tomo zuri, ne*" Friend fishing, okay? I had no idea what he was talking about, but his snapshots of the beautiful trout-like fish and the sparkling rocky rivers were enticing.

It was late July and Masugata picked me up early in the morning. He knew little English and my Japanese was basic, but we had a fishing language between us until he popped in a cassette tape of Kabuki, his other hobby, and tried to explain what was going on. We stopped at a 7–11, the popular mini-mart of Japan, and bought some canned coffee and *onigiri*, hand-size triangles of rice stuffed with salmon or pickled plum, and wrapped with crispy seaweed. I loved *onigiri*. We ate and drove to the river, stopping on a bridge so he could eye the water level and strategize our approach. At a nearby bait shop, Masugata parked the car and said, "Now buy *ayu*."

"Aren't we fishing for *ayu*?" I asked.

Masugata laughed. "I'll show you 'Friend catch friend fishing.' Okay?"

"Okay," I said.

I had gotten used to entering into events or taking trips where I really wasn't sure what was going on. One of the young teachers once brought me to a "Beach Love Party" that I thought would be a blast, only to discover I was captive among a dozen missionaries from Kansas, sipping Coke and eating *yaki* soba while they discussed the Lord's work in Japan. I saw sharks in the waves and feigned stomach upset, getting home and calling Teiko for some sake and a long surf on the blue futon.

The tackle shop was busy but the proprietor greeted us with a smile and netted ten live *ayu*, about nine inches in length, from a bubbling cement tank, securing them in Masugata's hi-tech aerated cooler. We drove down to a river looking very much like a North American trout stream, clear water braiding over rocks with riffles and blue-green pockets. The banks and islands bloomed in violet wildflowers and small bright bushes. There was very little garbage and birds flitted through the willows.

At streamside, we assembled the rods, incredible lances some thirty feet long. "Samurai fished *ayu*," Masugata spoke in deep charcoal tones. "Instead of sword when no more war." I watched an angler downriver. There was, indeed, something of the *nodachi*, the long sword, in the grace and power of his motions, and I could imagine a scarred warrior finding solace in a summer day wielding a bamboo rod below the cascades. Like Hemingway's Nick Adams, trying to heal after the horrors of World War I, mindfully preparing his gear and casting for trout on Michigan's Big Two-Hearted River, sometimes one had to practice deliberately at peace in order to find and keep it.

"No reel, but many lines," Masugata instructed, handing me about a foot of top line that I tied directly to the rod tip and then to about fifteen feet of aerial line running to a marker, and a new ten-foot length of underwater line made of fine monofilament to minimize the strain on the bait.

The bait, decoy, or "friend," was a live *ayu*, detained by a braided line leading to a nose ring snapped through the fish's nostrils. From the nose ring, another span of braid runs along the body of the unfortunate hostage, ending in a monofilament leader and a single hook pierced through its anus, another treble hook trailing an inch behind.

Would you do this to a trout? Live minnows for trout, maybe, but never a live trout to catch a trout, though artificial lures are manufactured to mimic small trout, and I've had a large brown trout attack a little rainbow I was reeling in. Trout are cannibals, but we still grant them respect. When it comes to speciesism, we differ, sometimes arbitrarily, in the way we treat animals. We love and pamper our dogs and cats, yet slaughter and eat cows and pigs. As an angler, I have happily snagged bunker and shad, jerking weighted treble hooks through their bright schools, yet I'd never dream of doing that to trout. Why not? Sportsmen extol the ethics of "fair chase," thus we ban snagging and restrict the baits and lures that may be deployed on those game fish we privilege. In some cases, these laws make catching more challenging and less injurious to wild species whose numbers are threatened. That's good conservation. But even in a pond stocked with hatchery-raised trout, it would be considered very unsporting and downright savage to snag fish or use baby trout for bait. Fishing laws and attitudes often reflect the way we feel about certain fish. So how should we feel about *ayu*?

Ayu are cousins to the smelt, I reasoned, associated in America with creel limits by the ton, fund-raising fish fries, cheap beer, bowling alleys, and Michigan all-nighters. So in the end, however spurious my logic, I felt okay lowering this store-bought smelt into the river for his friends to attack.

The territorial, wild *ayu* becomes "angry," Masugata said. The fish rams the intruder's flanks and belly, possibly hooking himself. "So they are not friends?" I retorted. Earlier, Masugata had acted out this drama with finny gestures and butts of the head, and now it was making sense. We both smiled, walked out into the river, and dropped our fake friends into likely living rooms. Masugata was a master angler, and with his conical straw paddy hat, red neckerchief, techy vest, and the graceful motions of his lance, he conjured the time-traveling samurai cowboy, or perhaps the mysterious conductions of the ribbon-wanded Kabuki actor.

Emitting deep humming sounds and holding firm, he swam the leashed *ayu* upriver a few feet. His rod tip pulsed with the living decoy, and then suddenly he felt the pull of another fish and swung back, launching two gold rockets through the air and into his fine-meshed net.

The name *ayu* nicely translates as "sweet fish," and it has the lovely golden colors and grace of a trout. In winter, *ayu* hatch upriver and head out to sea, returning in spring and early summer and continuing to feed on vegetation and small insects, growing up to thirteen inches.

Masugata took the tired decoy off the hooks and creeled it in a little floating bow-nosed holder he towed like a toy boat behind him. The freshly caught wild *ayu* was hooked as the new bait and the show went on. The water was deep and swift, and I knifed my hips into the current, found some sure footing, and swung my flipping friend into a likely lie. But I had trouble knowing if the wiggling action was my bait, the rushing flow, or an ensnared quarry, and I pulled up too often to check, wrecking my set and, in a couple cases, knocking off a nearly hooked wild fish. Masugata coached the best he could, but I exhausted a couple baits and had to start fresh. This time when I felt something like an attack, I yanked fiercely and shot two fish way over my head onto the gravel.

We waded and fished until early afternoon. Small sculpins fled from our steps and sulfur butterflies fanned the mud. Masugata landed *ayu* like a lacrosse goalie stopping double shots with ease, while I caught only one more, admiring the sunburst on its side and the orange trimmed adipose fin. "Smell it," Masugata urged. "Maybe melon, *nĕ?*" There was something fruity to the *ayu*'s skin. The subtle and various smells of fresh fish were always pleasing to me. Fresh bluefish smelled of garden cucumbers, and grayling earned their Latin name, *Thymallus*, from their air of thyme. Oregon writer Ben Hur Lampman found smallmouth bass "as fragrant as flowers," and old Izaak Walton wrote that English smelt "smell like violets." The *Oxford English Dictionary* notes the peculiar odor of smelt, but does not suggest a connection to "smell." With words, I say, it's not so much where you begin, but where you end up, and this sweet smelt smelled swell.

We built a small fire on the bank, and as the wood burned down, we drank sake from pull-cap glass cups. Masugata drank little, observing the enforced zero-tolerance for alcohol and driving in Japan. The Japanese were really good about this—they loved to drink and party, but knew enough to arrange a ride or call a cab. Today I could drain a few cups of sake, eat strawberries his wife packed, sit back, and watch the river and the other anglers.

Down at the water's edge, Masugata splashed some river on himself and me, and said "River spirit." I asked if it was a Shinto rite and he laughed and said "cheap shower." The Japanese seemed to be the most and least religious people in the world, but either way, they worshipped the spirit of all things fishy.

I helped Masugata clean the fish, friends and all; and he reminded me to carefully scrape the "bloodline," the dark purple artery and kidney in the body cavity along the spine. I then followed as he raked his knife back against the tiny scales, patting the fish dry with a clean rag. He pushed a long metal skewer longways through each one, salted them, and like an installation artist, positioned the fish over the fire in a way that suggested a swimming school. The perfectly fatted fish sizzled and twisted, turning golden brown. With a pair of gloves, Masugata pulled out a couple stakes and pushed off the cooked fish on black plastic plates. Ah, sweetfish, I thought, chewing slowly. The skin was salty and crisp, the flesh extraordinarily moist and, yes, slightly melony—indeed, some wild fruit, some sweet sacrament of the river.

In November of 1992, my old friend Eugene Jones came to visit me in Japan. I picked him up at Narita airport and we rode the Shinkansen, the bullet train, back to Niigata, sipping *fugu* sake from cans that activated a heater upon opening, gently warming the fish infused brew. "Not bad," Eugene said. Many of my gaijin friends reviled treats like *fugu* sake, sea urchin sushi, jellyfish salad, roasted squid on a stick, or savory bar snacks of nuts and minnows called *iriko*. "Bait" was the common joke. Japan was, indeed, a fishy place, but Eugene was a fishy guy and I figured he'd like *fugu* sake. Opening up the English edition of *The Daily Yomiuri*, he started asking questions about Japan, and then said, "Holy shit," pointing to a small headline: "Man Dies of Fugu Poisoning." But this *fugu* sake had only positive effects that we chased with a couple beers, arriving in the Tsubame-Sanjo station where Teiko and her friend, Yuko, met us with a car.

Teiko hugged me, put on her hip blue-framed glasses, and drove us to a local *izakaya* for more drinks and food. Cushioned on tatami, Eugene and I were getting pretty loaded, eating *gyōza*, *yakitori*, and fried crickets, croaking karaoke, pawing our dates, and at one point reaching into a large aquarium to grab a dinner-fatted carp. We paid our bill and Teiko was herding us toward the door when Eugene stumbled. I tried to steady him and also lost balance, both of us crashing through a *shōgi* screen and into a room of celebrating businessmen who found the intrusion hilarious, unlike sober Teiko and the tavern keeper.

The next day demanded recovery. "Did we really eat crickets?" Eugene rasped as I poured cups of green tea. In the morning mail I received a long letter from Caitlin that reminded me of her beauty and brilliance. She was flourishing in graduate school, excited about new books and her own writing. I read parts of the letter to Eugene and he said, "She's pretty amazing. But so is Teiko."

Hungover but dutiful, we made it up to the junior high where Eugene was a big hit with the kids, talking, asking simple questions, and handing out half dollars, *I Love New York* stickers, and little tin models of the Statue of Liberty. This went a long way, especially since my principal received a phone call from the *izakaya* owner reporting that Hendy sensei and his big gaijin *tomodachi* had trashed his tavern last night. My supervisor, Sagi, was not happy, but he deftly repaired the situation. "You pay nothing this time," he told me. "Bring present and say, 'Sorry.' Next big teachers party, we have there." I brought the tavern keeper a good bottle of sake and bowed in apology. He smiled and said, "Okay."

Sagi was a wise and warm friend, and he and his wife hosted Eugene and me at his home with a feast, including superbly grilled wedges of salmon, and a seemingly endless sampling of fine Niigata sakes. A year later, Sagi and his wife visited New York, and Eugene and I took them out dining, drinking, and porgy fishing.

During Eugene's stay in Japan, Sagi arranged for the two of us to go cod fishing with his old friend who ran a boat out of Teradomari. I never got the man's name, but everyone called him Senchō san, Mr. Captain, and we stepped aboard his creaky boat on a cold, drizzly November morning. The seas were rough, the tops of big swells blowing off like snow in a stormy Hokusai print. Eugene and I sat in the cabin with two silent fishermen, rolling and tossing, unable to do or say much of anything. Senchō san was probably in his early sixties but he jumped around the deck like a teenager. We stopped, anchored, picked up the heavy rods and reels, pierced bits of squid on a set of three hooks, and sent them down into the dark. I could feel the lead hit bottom, but it was hard to keep it there with the high pitch and fall of the boat. Senchō san smiled and showed us how to click the rod butts into the holders. "Sit down and watch the poles," he said in Japanese. Eugene and I were both feeling cold and queasy, and it was one of those rare moments when I wasn't entirely happy to be fishing. At Senchō san's command, we reeled in and tried another spot, catching a couple tiny fish, including a small *fugu*, its pectoral fins buzzing away like a hummingbird. The little spotted puffer inflated in my hand as I unhooked and tossed it back, floating for a moment until the waves washed it away. Finally Eugene's rod showed some life and he reeled up from a hundred feet, with hardly a fight, an eighteen-inch tara, codfish, that I netted. It didn't look like much, but the captain was delighted. Within the next four hours, the other three fishermen and I caught one cod each of identical size. I had to wonder if, like the Atlantic stocks off North America and Europe, these cod were pursued beyond the brink of survival? Should the Japanese, like the Canadians, put a moratorium on catching cod before it was too late? Should we even be out here?

When the boat turned back toward land, Eugene and I felt relief. And when we got into the calm harbor, we felt damn good, cracking a couple beers and eyeing the sights. Senchō san tied up and invited us into his dock-side house. Past the runkled tin exterior, the wooden two-story displayed an impressive timbering of cedar and smelled strongly of fish, the bottom floor a kind of shop with nets, rods, tools, and large boiling cauldrons. We climbed wooden steps to a loft that served as a casual parlor where we sat on cushions beside a kerosene heater. The captain's wife appeared. A short, thick woman, gold-toothed and friendly, she poured us sake and set down a dish of shredded dried fish. Eugene and I looked around. There were old family portraits in tortoise shell frames tilting down from the wall: a young man in a Japanese naval uniform; a handsome couple in formal yukata and kimono, perhaps a wedding photo. When Senchō san returned we asked him about the photos and he said, "Father and mother," and nothing more. I was fascinated by Japan's World War II history, but most Japanese were reluctant to discuss those dark times. After a couple more sakes, I asked Senchō san about his father. Was he in the war? "Yes. His ship went down at Leyte. I was just a boy." Eugene and I both said we were sorry. Eugene spoke briefly of his father, a surviving veteran of D-Day, wounded at Battle of the Bulge. I mentioned my father's service in Korea. "To our fathers," Eugene raised his glass. I translated and we drank.

The captain's wife brought three steaming bowls of soup on a lacquered tray. "*Tara jiru*," cod soup, she said over the yellowish broth amalgamated with leaks, white radishes, and big hunks of cod. Mine contained a head. We lifted the bowls to slurp the misoed broth, then chivied out bits with our chopsticks. Working on the head, I pulled lovely white meat from behind the cheeks then plucked out one of the eyeballs. "*Oishī*," delicious, pointed Senchō san, his face reddened by the sake. So I put it in my mouth, the lens was a bit chewy, the ball bursting briny between my teeth. The captain clapped his hands and laughed in approval. Eugene downed his sake and said, "Okay, bring me a head."

CHAPTER 23

OBLIVIOUS

BY RICHARD CHIAPPONE

"I'm gonna knock his head clean off!"
—Br'er Bear, *Song of the South*

Catch a monster rainbow like this one, and you'll remember it for the rest of your life. Photo Credit: Jay Cassell.

One of the earliest memories I have is of my mother reading to me from a Little Golden Book designed to teach preschoolers the alphabet by way of the Noah's Ark story. On page one, Noah gathered two apes—or aardvarks maybe, something starting with the letter A. I don't remember.

On the last page two zebras climbed up the gangplank to the big boat under Noah's benevolent, animal-loving gaze just as the rain clouds opened up for the first of forty extremely wet days and nights. What I remember most is the letter B, spoken for by two enormous brown bears, which, according to this version, Noah acquired in a place called the Great North Woods. The Great North Woods! I was a goner. Along with Never Never Land and that island where the little boys in Pinocchio went to gamble and smoke cigars, the Great North Woods became a fantasy destination I had to see, had to live in.

The artwork for that page in the little book remains in my heart and mind today: Behind those two lucky bruins who got the species-saving boat ride from Noah, a forest of pointy topped conifers was rendered iconically as tall, green, Christmas tree triangles. I hadn't even been bitten by the fishing bug yet (that would come one or two years later), but I wanted to go to the Great North Woods. I wanted to see brown bears. It would have to wait. I was four years old with no way to get there. Besides, my mother didn't allow me to get close to dangerous wild animals.

At that time, we hadn't yet moved to the house near the river, and we still lived in an old neighborhood in downtown Niagara Falls. While Western New York State indeed sits at a relatively northerly latitude, there was nothing "great" about what few wooded vacant lots remained in the old industrial city, and there were no bears at all in Niagara County by the 1950s. What there was however was the Great Bear Market on Pine Avenue in the middle of the ethnic Italian neighborhood. The Great Bear was a family-owned place, but it was large and rather ambitious, a precursor to the big chain supermarkets that would replace it a few decades later. It stood out as something quite modern among the more traditional mom-and-pop stores catering to the immigrant population there. Take the Stinky Store, for example. This is the name my little sister Claudia and I had for Latina Italian Imports. Each time our mother took us in there our tiny, sensitive noses were assaulted by the stench of hard cheeses and sopressata salamis and God only knows what other odiferous Old World products they had hanging from the ceiling of the crammed little store. We preferred the clean, modern Great Bear Market filled with familiar

Campbell soups and Wonder Bread and Maxwell House coffee that our generation embraced and preferred over the pig's feet and Sicilian snails that
Latina Italian Imports offered. Mostly, I loved the sign over the Great Bear
Market's door featuring a giant bear standing on its hind legs. It might have
been a polar bear, now that I think of it, but who cares? I wanted to see real
bears. Wild bears. Big ones. I wanted to get close to them, just like Noah—
who I considered a lucky bastard for having a whole boatful of wild animals
of his own. It would be almost thirty years before I moved to Alaska to fish its
great northern rivers and had my wish come true many times over.

If you are going to fish coastal Alaskan rivers, you are going to fish with
bears. Whether you see them or not, they're somewhere nearby. And how
you feel about that is going to fall somewhere on a scale between paranoid
white-knuckle terror that makes your every hour on a salmon-filled stream an
endless nail-biting nightmare and, at the other extreme, a foolish oblivious-
ness that puts you and everyone around you in danger of death by tooth and
claw. I hate to admit it, but I'm pretty much the best example of the fool at
the latter end of the scale you'll ever find. One of the reasons I fish is because
it is very cheap therapy. When I'm up to my wader belt in a trout stream,
casting, I tend to forget about everything and anything even potentially un-
pleasant in my life or around me. Unfortunately, that includes bears. Which
is why I've ended up close to bears more times than my four-year-old self ever
dreamed I would.

There is no such thing as being simply "close" to coastal Alaskan brown
bears. There is only "far far away" from them or "way too fucking close." In
June of 1989, on a trip to the Brooks River in Katmai National Park, I got
way too close to a brown bear for the first time. I had just tangled with a
Katmai rainbow trout far too heavy and rambunctious for the light line I had
brought with me. I was sitting by myself on a grassy bankside tussock, tying
on a new tippet, my neoprene-clad legs dangling in the water at the foot of a
tall cutbank. A few hundred yards upstream, the famous Brooks Falls—often
pictured on calendars lined with enormous bears snapping at leaping sockeye
salmon—rushed and rumbled in the sunny afternoon air, lulling me into

the kind of stupefied serenity that river music and sunshine can produce. Distracted by the possibility of hooking another big rainbow, I was lost in thought, as the cliché goes—but, more accurately, lack of thought is probably closer—when, over the rushing water, I heard a snort above and behind me. I turned and looked up the steep cutbank. An enormous bear, whom I would later learn was the dominant bear on the river and had been named Diver by the rangers, stood at the brink of the cutbank, about ten feet above me, looking down. At me.

Diver, now long deceased, was estimated to weigh eight hundred pounds when he emerged from hibernation each spring, and well over a thousand by autumn after consuming sixty or seventy pounds of salmon each day all summer. Sitting on the ground as I was, looking up at him from that low angle, he looked like a dirigible in a fur coat. He pulled his lips back and showed me his teeth, in what I hoped was a smile. I could almost hear him doing the math: one 180-pound fly fisherman equals thirty sockeye salmon averaging six pounds apiece. Plus, he wouldn't even have to dive for the meat. Hmmm.

Being the "dominant" bear on the river meant that he was the biggest, toughest, scariest animal within a community of thirty or forty very big, tough, and scary animals. It also meant that he could walk, swim, or fish anywhere he wanted to, whenever he wanted to—unless, of course, somebody cared to challenge him.

I stood, my intestines twisting, recalling the park rangers' rule: Do not run when confronted by a bear. Run? I was wearing chest waders, standing in fast water at the base of a dirt cliff. There was nowhere to run. My natural inclination was to plunge downstream and let the river carry me away from the monster, but there was nothing but deep water in that direction, and I can't swim wearing a bathing suit, let alone in waders. So, I stepped aside and slogged a few yards upstream against the current, yanking out handfuls of grasses from the base of the cutbank with one hand, gripping my fly rod in the other. Diver waited for me to move out of his way, slid down the bank in an avalanche of pebbles, walked right over the tussock I had been sitting on a moment before, and dropped into the river. I could have touched him with the tip of my rod. Another rule: Stay fifty yards away from any bear, a hundred yards from a sow with cubs. My fly rod is exactly three yards long. I could see I was going to have to be a little more vigilant. I could also see that vigilance was not my strongest trait. It's still not.

Last month, I went camping in Katmai again for the twentieth time (I missed one year in the '90s for some reason I now forget). It should be no surprise that I have not become a whole lot more careful in those intervening two decades. In fact, twenty years of camping alongside the Brooks River bears has only made me even more foolishly comfortable with them, and I'll admit right now that my luck is going to run out one of these days. Unlike the late, now famous, Timothy Treadwell, I do not think that the bears are my buddies or my pets, but I do love seeing them again and again—especially up way too close. They are a big reason I came to Alaska in the first place—one of the things that make living and fishing in the Great Land great.

The Brooks Rivers, Alaska.

So, this summer I got to see some big bears again up way too close. My wife and I flew out to Katmai for our twentieth Brooks River anniversary. There we met up with old friends already settled into the campground. When we first camped in the lovely cottonwood grove there on the shore of Naknek Lake twenty-one years ago, the bears roamed among us at will. They appeared suddenly, showing up at the picnic tables, disrupting our dinners; they stomped past our tents in the middle of the night, sniffing and huffing and sending jolts of adrenaline shooting through us as we huddled in our sleeping bags. It was good scary fun.

One night in the early years, I fished until the near-dark twilight of the Alaskan summer threw long shadows across the forest path around midnight. All the others in our party had given up and gone to bed hours before, but I was still young and in my "more is better" mode. Exhausted from a very long day of wading and fishing, I stumbled back to camp, alone, head down, wading shoes dragging. Apparently, some bears are no more cautious than I am. I was within sight of our tent—in which my wife was lying in her sleeping bag, reading, and possibly wondering where I was so late, and how much of my remains my life insurance policy required as proof of death—when I ran right into a big bear, also bumbling along, head down. It could have been Diver. It was too dark to tell, and not the right moment for introductions. We both yelped, and jumped back. I froze. The bear ran the other way, missed our tent by a couple feet, and stopped. It stood on its hind legs, looming over the tent trying to see what the heck it had collided with. I called out to my wife, "Honey, don't come out of the tent right now." Later she said that when the bear dropped down onto its front paws, maybe six feet away from her on the other side of the thin nylon wall, she felt the ground shake under its weight.

As I said: good, scary fun.

Today an electric fence surrounds the tent camping area, offering a feeling of security—no matter how close the bears come to the camp. We sleep much more soundly, but some of the thrill is gone too. Inside the fence we are the caged animals; the bears wander past freely, like zoo-goers. Maybe it's better this way.

This year, on our first evening in camp, a young sow with a single cub visited. The rangers said the big cub is two and a half years old; he is nearly as big as his mother and obviously needs to be sent out into the world, but the mom is apparently not ready to let go of her first child. (I was a first child myself—I know how charming we can be.) The sow and the huge cub stopped to roll around on the sandy beach in front of the campground. We stood inside the fence and oohed and ahhed and took pictures of them. They soon ambled off toward the river, probably checking to see if the salmon had started running yet.

The first night celebrations ran a little long and the whiskey a little low, and the next morning I awoke very late to find that my friends had already had breakfast and set off to the river to fish for trout. All the fly rods in camp and every pair of waders but mine were gone from the gear shelter. I was moving slowly, aching from the night on the ground in spite of the high-tech Therm-a-Rest pads beneath my none-too-fit body. I took my morning painkillers. (Almost everyone in camp is on the unfortunate side of sixty now; there are enough meds in our tents to start a M*A*S*H unit.) I was putting on my waders when the same sow and cub walked past along the beach, once more heading toward the Brooks River, a quarter mile away. I watched them again, with that same mix of awe and dread and gratitude for the chance to see them, another feeling I get whenever the big bears are near. By the time I left the campground and walked to the river I had forgotten they were in the area. The sun was shining and I was going fishing. My friends were already out there somewhere catching trout like mad, I believed. Who cares if some giant omnivores are roaming around in the brush? I'm talking about fat, wild Alaskan rainbows. I hurried the quarter mile from the campground to the river.

Standing on the footbridge at the mouth of the Brooks River where it flows into Naknek Lake, I could see my friend Bill and his wife Deb fishing a little ways upstream. Instead of following the gravel bars along the winding river, I decided to take a shortcut through the tall grass in a direct path to them. On the other side of the river, at the far end of the bridge, there is a bear-viewing platform about ten feet high for visitors who want to look at the bears but have no desire to climb into the river and fish alongside them for some reason. In other words, the sane visitors. The platform was full of such bear-viewers and photographers. There were a couple rangers.

I left the path and strode out into the tall grass on a beeline for the ox-bow where my friends were fishing, but I only got about halfway to the river when Deb saw me approaching and began shouting: "Rich! Bear! Rich! Bear!" I have to say that hearing your name urgently placed in the same sentence fragment as the word "bear" is not comforting. Not when you are knee-deep in boot-sucking mud and can't see over the grass in front of you. I hit the brakes. The sow and the big cub—which all the people on the platform had been watching me approach, but not warning me about—stood up on their hind legs a few yards in front of me. Without the electric fence between us, they looked a lot bigger and far less cuddly. The platform erupted with laughter as I backtracked and took a roundabout route to the oxbow. Forget the hundred yards from a sow and her cubs rule; I had foolishly come within a couple dozen feet of them. Now, I don't mind being the class clown, or the comic relief character, and I do realize that the rangers can't prevent every careless idiot such as myself from getting chewed to shreds because of our own stupidity, but a little shout-out from the platform about the bears I was heading for might have been in order in this case.

That particular sow with the oversized cub was a single mom raising the bruin equivalent of a teenage boy, and she looked it. She was haggard and sort of weary-looking and seemed like she might be ready for an argument with anyone dumb enough to start one. Put yourself in her paws. She was getting no support from the father (doesn't even know who the father was), and worse, in fact knew that the father—or any other large male bear for that matter—would far more likely eat her teenage son than offer to help rearing him. She looked like she would certainly bite your head off if you rubbed her the wrong way. And in this case, those are not metaphors. A brown bear will often grab its victim by the head during an attack. And there is no right way to rub one.

A little fear of bears and other large carnivores is obviously a good idea when fishing in bear country. But you can't let it keep you home. In 1972 I went to the nearest thing to the Great North Woods I could reach at that time in my life. I was still living in Niagara Falls, married with one child, working in a paint store, painting houses on weekends for extra money. I was not going to Alaska any time soon. My young brother Marty and I did go camping in Algonquin Provincial Park on the Laurentian Plateau of Central Ontario, Canada, that spring. It was a place where a black bear had killed a couple young boys the year before. We were intrigued and more than a little frightened. But it was our first remote backcountry fishing trip and nothing as minor as a man-eating bear could stop us.

We canoed and portaged our way across a lake system until we were far from the one road that cuts across the southernmost corner of the big park. We fished, and we cooked trout on a wood fire, and slept in a cheap plastic tent in Army Surplus sleeping bags—no Therm-a-Rests—on the hard Precambrian bedrock. The condensation from our breath dripped on us all night long. It was May, and it got very dark in the middle of the night, and when we heard the chewing sounds start, just outside the tent, we knew that the killer black bear was working through our food supply on his way to us. We had no flashlight.

Marty was sixteen years old. Being his older brother, a married man and a father, I felt responsible for him. More senseless than brave, I led the way from the tent into the absolutely opaque blackness, lighting wooden matches and cupping them one after another in front of me trying to throw a little light on the fearsome beast that had come for us. We nearly tripped over the porcupine before we saw him, hunched under the overturned canoe, nibbling on one paddle. We did not have a gun. I have no idea what we thought we were going to do, or perhaps say, to the animal if it had, in fact, been a bear.

In my twenty trips to the Brooks River, and in all my foolishly close encounters with those bears there, I have never had a gun on my person. That is partly because I have no training and very little experience with guns (I hunted small game when I was a younger man), but it is also because guns have been prohibited in national parks. Only recently, as I got older and less able to convince myself that I could climb a spruce tree if I needed to, have I begun carrying bear-repellent pepper spray. But this past winter the National Park regulations were amended to allow guns in the parks—to the extent that state laws allow them wherever the park is situated. That means guns are now permitted in all Alaska national parks. You are not allowed to discharge them. But there will be extenuating circumstances, you can be sure.

For example, in May, a camper shot and killed a bear in self-defense in Denali National Park. Maybe it is a coincidence that in the first month of the first summer that guns have been allowed, a bear needed to be shot in a park that gets tens of thousands of visitors each year and to the best of my knowledge has never had a fatal bear attack. What I do know is that someone is going to shoot a Brooks River bear, probably very soon. The inevitable way-too-close encounters are not for everyone. Twenty years ago, if I had been the kind of guy who was good with a gun, I would have shot Diver coming down that cutbank toward me looking for all the world like the giant predator he was. There has never been a bear attack of any kind in Brooks Camp in spite of the thousands of visitors there too. But I have a feeling there will be one as soon as there are enough people packing guns there.

About mid-week in my recent trip to Brooks Camp, my innate oblivi-ousness once again put me in harm's way. Five of us set out to fish for pike in an old beaver pond maybe a hundred yards inland from the beach on Naknek Lake, about a mile from the camp. Halfway there we spotted a huge male bear walking toward us along the big lake's edge. We cut inland and bushwhacked through the alders and willows to the beaver pond, the big bear forgotten as soon as we started catching pike. I had drifted away from the others and was by myself, standing in hip-deep water by the huge beaver dam that had created the lake in the first place. There I cast a fly out into the deeper water where I hoped the biggest pike lurked. Casting a fly is one of the few truly pleasurable things a man my age can do repeatedly, for hours on end, with-out either hurting or embarrassing himself. Needless to say, I was not paying attention to anything around me.

Once again it was Deb who called out, "Rich! Bear!"

Maybe thirty feet away, a short cast with a fly rod, the enormous bear sidled across the top of the beaver dam. This was no juvenile delinquent cub or world-weary single mom sow. This was a trophy-sized male bear. There is a reason taxidermists mount bears on small mounds to make them look taller and scarier. It works. Looking upward at the animal there on top of the beaver house, perhaps six feet above my eye level, it looked like a Pleistocene monster: *Arctodus simus*, the nearly two-thousand-pound mega-carnivore of prehistory. It was a jaw-dropping moment, and I just stood there watching it walk past, until Deb barked, "Rich! Come on." I snapped out of my reverie and waded away from the big bear and back toward the company of my fellow meat snacks. There is safety in numbers, primarily because the odds improve that someone is paying attention. It is never I.

My wife has admitted that in the first few years of our relationship she credulously believed that when I drove right past the Safeway Store where we shopped several times a week, when I left the water running in the sink until it overflowed, when I went out to pick up a pizza and some beer and came home without the pizza, I might have been lost in profound thoughts. Somewhere along the line in our more than thirty years of marriage, it dawned on her that I may not be thinking at all. My mother used the old-fashioned saying that I "had my head in the clouds." My wife would locate my head somewhere much closer to the ground and decidedly less ethereal.

Either way, I'll keep going back to Brooks Camp, unarmed and oblivious as ever, to wander among the fabulous bears, happily fishing, and stumbling over their huge furry hulks until one of them knocks my head clean off.

Postscript, August 5, 2015:

Coincidentally, while taking a break from revising this particular essay (written five or six years ago) for inclusion in this book, my wife and I were in Upper Skilak Lake campground here on the Kenai Peninsula two days ago when a young woman had to be medevacked out by helicopter after being mauled by a brown bear.

The attack had occurred miles away from us, on the other side of the big lake. The young woman had been jogging with a friend on a trail near a lodge over there when they ran into the bear. The bear grabbed one woman, and the other one ran for help. Rescuers found the victim, bitten and scratched, but upright and walking down the trail after the bear left her on the ground. They brought her across the lake by boat to the campground where we were staying, because there was just enough room to land the chopper on the road into the camp. But we did not know any of that when the helicopter landed, and the medics began tending to an athletic young woman covered in blood.

For privacy reasons, I suppose, the medics wouldn't give us any information, so all we heard was that there'd been a mauling, and we assumed that since the victim was right there in camp, the bear was too. After she was flown off, gossip and hearsay and ill-informed chatter over the course of the evening only heightened the ominous sense of approaching tooth and claws. Who

A brown bear catching salmon.

knew how close that bear was? Or why it had attacked? We've camped among bears for decades, and this was the first time we'd seen a victim of a mauling.

There are no electric fences around the campsites at Skilak Lake, and as my wife and I got into our sleeping bags in the fading summer light, I think it's fair to say we both wished we were safely ensconced in one of the several gigantic motor coaches in nearby sites instead of in our Big Agnes tent.

Still, it was a warm clear night, and we left the rain cover off the top of the tent in order to see the summer stars materialized in the darkening sky. And, of course, to keep one eye out for anything big coming our way.

In this morning's *Alaska Dispatch News*, the young woman was reported to be in "good" condition but still in the hospital. The bear, it said, had attacked in self-defense; the women had simply run up on top of it before it could get out of their way (which is what almost all bears do when approached by humans), and the animal lashed out in response.

It made me think of all the times I've blundered into them, and, simply put, have been undeservedly fortunate. Will I be a little more careful next summer out in Katmai, more vigilant, more responsible?

The big money is not on me.

CHAPTER 24

EASTERN STEELHEAD

BY JERRY HAMZA

What have I become
My sweetest friend
Everyone I know goes away in the end
And you could have it all
My empire of dirt.
—*Trent Reznor, Nine Inch Nails, from the song "Hurt"*

An eastern steelhead. You can fish for them all year, but fall is the best time.

I have some West Coast friends who occasionally ask me to donate money to help in their battle to preserve their steelhead fishery. I give what I can. I understand the genuine distress they feel over the decline of one of the greatest fisheries on the planet. The steelhead trout is a creature whose mythology is well deserved. The most common description is a rainbow trout on steroids. That really doesn't come close to getting there. Genetically, the description is close. To put that in perspective, we share fifty percent of our DNA with a banana, sixty percent with a fruit fly, seventy five percent with a mouse, eighty percent with a cow, and more than ninety eight percent with a chimp. Small amounts make big differences. So much so that the people who are in the middle of these conservation battles want different strains recognized and protected. The fish have evolved differently in each drainage, meaning steelhead have a slightly different character from fishery to fishery. Like sisters from the same parents. Some have asked if I can sum up what makes a steelhead a steelhead? It is simply a rainbow trout that took an anadromous turn. It was this genetic left turn that also required the fish to get tough to hack it in big water. Very tough.

Occasionally, I get invited out to the West Coast and partake in traditional fly fishing for steelhead. There are some places located on British Columbia's Skeena watershed I absolutely adore. Regrettably over the years, I have noticed the decline of steelhead in some of the more traditional rivers. I know the debate rages over causes and cures. I live on the other side of the continent. My ability to help is limited to the $20 I can stick in an envelope. I love the fish but geography can be a great barrier. Sometimes there can be other barriers, as well—the walls we erect in our hearts and minds. These same people who invite me to fish with them and help them ball right up at the mention of Great Lakes steelhead.

The Great Lakes steelhead program has a long and interesting history. In 1876, Michigan began planting Campbell Creek and McCloud River strains from California and fish from the Klamath River in Oregon. Recent creel studies have shown that the Michigan steelie has become wild and evolved into its own animal. The Great Lakes have had steelhead and biologists have managed them for 120 years. In my neck of the woods in New York State, mainly the Washington steelhead were stocked here. Usually six to twelve pounds of bad, bad, bad temper. There are other strains but the only real impact is when they may sneak into your favorite stream. The experts explain that the juvenile fish imprint on the unique odor of the watershed. This is mostly true. I believe any little tributary with a gravel bottom and a similar smell will capture steelhead runs. I more than believe it; I fish it. (The other great characteristic of steelhead is they can be ravenous and eagerly take flies, while Pacific salmon stocked in the Great Lakes won't because they're spawning.)

I do fish the better-known streams in Western New York and the Great Lakes, and the fishing is wonderful. Steelhead fishing usually starts in September with the fish following the salmon (also stocked in the Great Lakes). Our Great Lakes do a fine job of mimicking the great salmon food cycle in the Pacific Northwest. The tributaries of Lake Ontario never cease to amaze me: in August you could swing a cat and see neither fish nor fowl; by early October you could catch three kinds of salmon and three kinds of trout all better than 10 pounds on the same day. I have not done that but I have come close. (Atlantic salmon are very rare here.) Though the major tributaries are wonderful and provide room to cast, my favorite water will not appear in any brochure or on a Web site. It won't appear in this story, either. It really cannot. It is a small creek that, for some reason, steelhead like.

At its widest spot my creek is perhaps twenty yards, most of it is much smaller. There are really four pools, which I have poetically named Pool One, Two, Three, and Five. Four was a mistake and had to be dropped. It seems my creek, at one point, must have smelled like one of the stocked tributaries. Some steelhead found their way there. Some still do but a fair number are now born there. The New York State Department of Conservation clips a fin of the fish it stocks. About half the fish I catch are without clipped fins. You can tell a bit about the fish from the clip—sometimes even the hatchery it came from. Those without a clipped fin are either missed fish or are wild. It is estimated that thirty percent of the steelhead in Lake Ontario are now wild fish. I like the idea that I am fishing a wild-steelhead stream.

I call my friend Joe from Oregon. He will remain "Joe from Oregon," which may protect his identity some. Joe is one of the most hardcore West Coast steelhead guys (who often call themselves Metalheads). He encouraged me to use a Spey rod for the first time. I tell him about my little stream. I tell him because in the past my invitations to fish Eastern steelhead have been met with anger and disdain—mostly because it was a stocked fishery and he feels the experience is a mockery. I thought that the invitation to fish my little stream with its wild fish would be the ticket. As small as it is, I have had ten-fish days there. I wondered how long it's been since Joe had seen a ten-fish day? The last time I fished with him, we caught two fish over three days. I did notice this was considered good and it was part of the new paradigm on some of the Western steelhead rivers. I didn't mind. Fishing with an old friend is one of life's simple joys.

So I laid it on thick about my stream. I gave Joe the used-car salesman treatment. I told him about all the wild fish. The pretty little stream. How it has a Pool Five when there are only four. That we would have it all to ourselves. I thought I was making some headway with him. Then he just blurted out "Look man, I am never coming East for steelhead. I will for whitetail or brown trout but fucking steelhead have no business there!" I sensed I may have gone too far.

I have other friends out West who have similar feelings. There is a big difference between Eastern and Western fly fishermen. It is a cultural thing with roots running deeply into geography and history. Whenever I fish the West, I always feel like a stranger in a strange land. I love it. It always feels new and brash and craggy. When I watch a Western guy cast a fly line, it is so pretty. It almost makes me want to cry. I can usually tell where a guy is from by the way he casts.

I sit and think about my conversation with Joe for a while. I know he is pissed at me, but we are friends and I also know in a couple days we will be okay again. Grumpy old men have a code. I am in my library reading *Winesburg, Ohio*. When I read I often have music on in the background. Johnny Cash comes on. I love Johnny Cash. I was lucky to get to know him a little when I was in the entertainment business. This song is "Hurt." If you have not heard it, you need to. The video was voted the best music video of all time.

I remember getting a call when it came out. "Hey, Johnny made a music video. I'll send it to you. You have to look at it now." Okay, it sounded urgent, so I looked at it. I was stunned by its overwhelming power. I knew the song. It was written by a man named Trent Reznor. It was about the anguish in his young life. The song had suicidal overtones when Nine Inch Nails recorded it. It was probably Reznor's best song. Now Johnny Cash infused it with a hard life's worth of experience. Made a video to the soundtrack that chronicled his life—and in ways, every life—to the point of overwhelming. It is what artists are good at. What about Trent? These were very personal feelings. How did he feel about his opus being commandeered? He said: "I pop the video in, and wow . . . Tears welling, silence, goose-bumps . . . Wow. [I felt like] I just lost my girlfriend, because that song isn't mine anymore. . . ." I wondered if it was like that for Joe about steelhead. If he felt like he lost his girlfriend.

I think I have a feel for the way some of my friends feel. I hope in the end they realize these fish are really their "children." I can see a scenario in the future in which some of these Great Lakes fish are sent home to California and Oregon and Washington and British Columbia to help rebuild the decimated stocks there. In my heart, I would like to see both East and West fisheries thrive. I am a fisherman and the more places I can whip water, the better I like it. I have stopped bugging Joe. He has promised to come out for some fall brown trout. He may accidentally hook a steelhead. It happens all the time. That will be in the hands of the fishing gods and that is where I will leave it.

I love steelhead fishing as much as any other kind. For a dry-fly guy like me, that means a lot. A ten-pound-plus steelhead hooked in a small stream is fishing's version of a cage match. The setting is usually very quiet. I like fishing in solitude and steelhead are conducive to that. You can catch them all year but the fishing is really seasonal. The fish start coming upstream in waves in September with the weather, all through the winter. I fish for them in every month of the winter. I have one rule. I won't break ice off eyes—mine or any on the rod with which I'm fishing.

There was a day this past October. I love bow hunting in October. If I can get in a tree stand with the foliage on fire and that crisp punky smell of the morning, it is everything. This particular morning had that snap in the air. Just a touch of frost on the grass. Not the killing frost, not yet. It was pre-rut and the young bucks were randy as hell. Chasing does all over creation not knowing it was hopeless. There was a buzz in the air. The earth was electrified. Nature was plugged in and wired for sound. Sitting in the tree stand, I could feel the juice emanating right out of the ground. I could feel it resonate in my chest. It was all happening and I was tuned in and I knew it.

Instinctively, I could feel her coming. I grabbed my bow. Sure enough, the big doe floated through the opening toward my stand. It was over seconds later. It was perfect predation.

It wasn't even eight-thirty a.m. when I had the doe hanging from a tree. The cool fall air eased into my lungs. I thought about going to work. I thought about going fishing. I do not often mix hunting and fishing days. I know there are places that advertise cast-and-blast packages but I think they are better sports for separate days. I am not sure why. It is like going from beer to liquor. It can be done, but I just don't. Well, not often. The thought of hitting the office on this day just felt wrong. Blue sky, no wind, cool, and the electricity was still pouring into me. The internal debate was short. I gathered up my gear and headed to my stream.

When you open my steelhead fly book you might see a sea of orange with a splash of pink here or chartreuse there. Egg patterns are all I fish. I can tell you that not all eggs are what they are cracked up to be. I have become somewhat of an expert on egg patterns. I have some favorites. I did for a long time resist the use of synthetic materials, but that barrier eventually came tumbling down.

I sneak into the Oak Orchard (New York) fly shop and buy a credit-card-limit of some fine epoxy eggs. I still fish the natural materials when I decide to put bamboo in peril. A steelhead on a bamboo rod is Russian roulette for the wood-like fly rod. (Okay—bamboo is actually in the grass family, not wood.) When I have that traditional itch I tend to go traditional right down to the fly. Some friends tease me and suggest that I should invest in silk line. I don't have the heart to tell them I secretly did. In case you are contemplating it, drying silk line is slightly less fun than a colonoscopy.

I finally get to Pool One. I like this pool a lot. There are times when you can see the fish stacked up. Big visible fish can cut both ways. If they are active, it is the ultimate thrill in fly fishing. Watching a ten-pound-plus fish take a fly is bliss. On the other hand, having them ignore repeated presentations can be maddening. Worst of all is doing something doltish and spooking them out of the pool. This is the first of the four pools. There are some pockets between in which a blunder will spook out twenty-five percent of the day's chances.

I can see the fish; there are a couple of big hens in the pool. I make a couple of inadequate casts and on each a fish follows for a short time. They are not aggressive but seem to be workable. I decide to work the tail of the pool. If I hook one, I can lead it to the bottom of the pool and maybe not spook the rest. If you are a steelhead fisherman, you are probably already laughing. If you are not, that's like saying "Maybe if I light this stick of dynamite in the backyard no one will notice." You certainly have a better shot than if you light it in the front yard, so you try.

After a half hour of more careful casting than the first few I made, the line stops. I pull back on a solid object. This fish, without any coaxing, does exactly what I want it to do. It swims methodically down and out of the bottom of the pool without disturbing the other fish. I remember thinking "Damned cordial!" Then it kept moving down. I tried to turn it. It kept moving down. I was into my backing and the fish was pulling hard as hell. This fish didn't jump. All steelhead jump. I keep following the fish down. After a while, the stream begins to deepen. I know what that means and I look up. There she is—Lake Ontario. I followed the fish a little more than an eighth of a mile to the lake. When I say "followed" perhaps you have romantic images of the priest scene in the movie *The Quiet Man* or the wonderful scene of Paul Maclean holding the rod over his head rolling over rapids in *A River Runs Through It*. This was more "*Three Stooges* bank-dick chase scene" with all the slapstick elements. The stream does not have neat trails and in spots the shoreline is as slick as snot.

With the lake in sight, it seemed prudent to pick a bank and work my way to the shore of the lake. I managed this with some dexterity. I actually gained some line on the fish. As I reached the shore at the side of my little stream, I had gained back all the backing. I had steady pressure on the fish. I decided to add a bit more pressure, to tire it out. The additional pressure induced additional will on the fish's behalf. The fish started moving out with determination. I added more pressure and the fish responded with more determination. This was a cause-and-effect relationship that I knew would have a very short shelf life. I looked down as my backing dwindled. This fish was not turning. I was fishing a stout 7-weight with an 0X tippet. This fish was not turning. My backing was gone. I pointed the rod directly at the fish, which produced that high-tensile tone of good mono stretching to its limit. Then the crack. That was it. I never saw the fish. It never jumped.

I have sat around talking about what it could have been. The New York record steelhead is just over thirty-one pounds. I don't think it was a steelie. It would have showed itself. Some say if they get too big they can't jump. The New York record brown trout is just over thirty-three pounds. I never caught one on that stream, but why not? The record king salmon was almost fifty pounds at that time, with much bigger ones netted. Sturgeon grow into the hundreds of pounds. Why not the Loch Ness Monster? Lake Ontario is massive. It is 193 miles long and fifty-three miles wide. Only your imagination limits what can swim in there. I have had several mind-blowing experiences on the lake. This one was a pretty good one. If he had gone upstream? He would have run out of water in a hurry. I probably wouldn't have landed him but I might have seen him. Maybe it's better that I didn't.

I go back to the pool. Why quit fishing over something like that? Besides, the trembling in my hands might impart just the right action to the fly.

A King salmon caught on the Niagara River. Photo Credit: Jay Cassell.

Mending my line a little closer, hands a quivering mess—if you have ever lost (or for that matter landed) a giant fish, you know what I mean.

On the mend, the egg pattern gets a strike and I strike back. It seemed a bit light and I caught flashes of yellow and green. I was thinking this is so odd. I pulled the striped fish from the water. It was a large yellow perch, the kind we call "jack perch." There have been times in my life I have hunted these down. Yellow perch are delicious—cousin to the walleye and every bit as tasty. This guy was three quarters of a pound. I started laughing to myself. I never expected that. I sent the egg pattern along a similar drift and it got hit again. Another jack perch. I was still grinning from the first. My mind was wondering if I could catch a mess of them, enough for a fish fry?

It's funny how an event can trigger memories from deep in the corners of our minds. Thinking about the perch made me remember my grandfather. He was where my fishing began. He passed it to my father when I was very young and started giving it to me. He never fly fished, that would have been too much folly. He was a child of the Great Depression fishing to procure food (although fun had a purpose). Catch-and-release of anything edible was unthinkable. His whole generation shared a kind of frugal no-nonsense atti-tude. Add Catholicism and the meaningful place that fish held at dinner on Fridays during lent, and the fish were never getting off the dinner plate. Being a consummate fish killer and eater, he had a favorite: the yellow perch. If he could have his way, small yellow perch were the best. They would be gutted, scaled, deep-fried, and eaten, bones and all. A little lemon and Tabasco sauce *s'il vous plait.*

I watched the fat yellow perch swim off. I sat there for a moment in the essence of my grandfather's persona. We hold a type of limited immortality that lasts until the final remnant of someone's memory of us dissipates forever. I decided to leave that pool and come back at the end of the day. To come back and catch a perch dinner for Abe. Fillets, that is—not bones and all, that still sounds bad.

The next pool was smaller and deeper. The water flowed directly onto a big boulder. The water deflected around the boulder into the pool and eddied. The best strategy would be to cast above and let the fly drift down to the pool. On the third cast, the fly stopped, and I pulled back. The reel exploded and the steelhead tail-walked across the pool. Minutes later, I released a beautiful seven-pound steelie. A few cast later the line tightened again. This was a peculiar fight. Strong and digging. I lifted and the fish resisted. It was like trying to pull up a garbage-can lid. Several minutes later, the stubborn fish finally gave up. It was a channel catfish. I started to look around. I was wondering if there was a hidden camera somewhere. What the hell was going on? The best I could tell was that the electricity I was feeling was flowing through everything. I had never caught a channel cat in that area, and I never, ever caught one on a fly rod. I could probably try for the rest of my life to catch one on a fly on purpose and *not* do it. The day was becoming surreal. I enjoy it when we seem to become a character in a backdrop.

Here I was in this place all alone. I could always imagine a fishing show similar to Charles Kuralt's *On the Road*. The camera pans in on this picturesque little stream. The shot swings around and you see this distinguished looking middle-aged fly fisherman laying out a beautiful cast. The noise of the place is amplified for the viewers. The babble of the stream, the honking of the migrating geese, the glorious twitter of the songbirds. The camera pulls back to capture it all. There it is, the money shot. The fisherman sets up on a nice strike. He fights the fish valiantly. Then he pulls out a beautiful . . . channel cat. That might be a tough script to sell.

I did appreciate the turning kaleidoscope of the day. At my age, I have found that surprises are usually bad. When the phone rings and you are fifty and someone on the other end says, *Guess what?* You're usually thinking "Oh, fuck." On a day on which I can have several surprises in a row and have them turn out harmless and pleasant, I am pleased.

I fished the rest of the pools and caught two nicer steelhead. One was a ten-pound fish. A day when you kill a beautiful deer and catch-and-release a ten-pound steelhead is really something. I keep days like this in my hip pocket. I trot them out on the bad days to remind myself that I do have it good.

I started to think about my West Coast friend Joe again. And then the Johnny Cash song. I wondered to myself, was this my empire of dirt?

Trent Reznor wrote the words as an angry young man and the despair is obvious. Empire of dirt to him was a disdainful description of a bad place in life. It was powerful and poignant in the way youth knows. When Johnny Cash recorded it, he transformed "empire of dirt" into life's accumulation of possessions. That in the end it means nothing. We leave with what we came with.

I think my empire of dirt is the moment of grandeur I can coax from nature. That the memories I make each day afield are my empire. It changed the way I hear the song, forever.

CHAPTER 25

ZONE OF HABITABILITY

BY W. D. WETHERELL

A small trout stream flowing through a meadow in Glacier National Park, Montana.

T hat's the way the world works now I guess. A Jew born in Morocco becomes a Montana fishing guide. A Vietnamese woman I know finds work as a cowboy. One of my colleagues in the astronomy department was born in Cameroon to Bolivian parents. My fiancé grew up in New Zealand, majored in modern dance at Oklahoma State, and now runs a solar startup in Billings. People shuffle around geographies and destinies like never before.

"Yes, I understand all that," I told Rich when he surprised me with the trip. "Still, a Jew born in Casablanca is not someone you meet every day, particularly on a trout stream."

Rich, who was getting his backpack ready for his own weekend, smirked his cutest Dennis the Menace smirk.

"They claim he's the best fly fishing guide in Montana, only—"

"Only?"

"That's what they say about him. 'He's the best fishing guide in Montana, only—' You'll have to fill in the blank when you get home."

People were surprised, Rich and I racing off on separate trips a week before the wedding. But he likes rock climbing, I like trout fishing, and it seemed the perfect way to celebrate. We weren't spending money on bachelor parties or showers or anything traditional, and once we married, we told each other, we'd have fifty years to do things together.

I left the apartment at three in the morning, hit Livingston just as the sun was edging up over Emigrant Peak, grabbed some tea at a trucker's cafe, and was at the put-in by seven. A truck was already parked there, with an empty boat trailer on back, and the man who climbed down looked, from the groggy way he stumbled, as if he had slept there all night.

"Jonathan Chu," I said, sticking out my hand.

"Eli," he mumbled. "Eli, Eli, Eli."

Was he scolding himself? That's what it sounded like. The cold made the syllables snap like a whip.

"Nice to meet you, Eli. I'm really looking forward to fishing with you today."

"Are you?"

He stared at and around me now, not in a curious way, but like he was evaluating the larger world of which I was a minor, incidental part. He was a big man, with shoulders round from years of rowing drift boats, and I put his age at forty-nine. He didn't wear guide clothes, not the nylon and fleece that's become their uniform, but faded gray work pants and matching shirt, making him look like he worked in a garage.

His face, what I could see of it in the mist, had large expressive features, though not the kind that had anything particularly cheerful to express. His nose was the saddest I ever saw on a man, though I can't tell you how I read that other than the way its weight dragged down his forehead, left it wrinkled. His complexion was pure leather, distressed leather, with dry white patches on his cheeks that looked like they needed to be oiled. Even so, he was tanner and craggier than any guide I'd ever encountered, as if he drew upon a weathering, a tempering, a lot more thorough than anything you could get just in Montana.

"So you want to fish, is that it?"

I held up my rod case. "Raring to go."

He shook his head, scowled with a fierceness that almost made me flinch.

"My boy busted parole last night. Busted it all to hell. And now?" He spat toward the river. "Goddam caddis aren't hatching."

The second part seemed to sadden him more than the first. He waved his hand dismissively toward the bank, which seemed to mean I was supposed to climb in the drift boat.

"She's a beauty," I said, sliding myself down.

"Yaws."

"I sit up here?"

"Suit yourself. We're not going to catch shit."

He pulled on his waders—waders like my grandfather wore, of heavy brown rubber—then put his shoulder against the thwart and shoved us out. Immediately the current had us, taking us in hand with a vigorous side-to-side shake just to demonstrate who was in charge. The few guides I'd gone out with rowed like gondoliers, standing up at the oars, peering hopefully downstream, but Eli's posture was more like Chiron on the river Styx, grim and huddled, his mouth just above the oars as if contemplating biting in.

"What fly should I tie on?" I asked, once I had my rod strung up.

"Know what piles are?"

"How about an Adams?"

"Know what they're like when they bleed?"

I tied on an Adams. At first I was blindly casting into fog, but when we rounded the first bend the sun exploded in a sudden burst that blew it all apart. Glorious! Mountains to the east, mountains to the west, snow already sugaring up the summits, catching the sunlight and making it stick. The gullies, on the nearer ridges, shone cherry red, as if they'd just been polished and hadn't yet dried. Both banks, past their cottonwooded crests, were mostly pastureland, and there was already enough of a breeze that the grass waved and tossed in its top-heavy autumn way.

"And what a great smell!" I said, breathing it in. "Sage, right? And I think there's pine mixed in, too."

Eli, to humor me, sniffed.

"Oil shale," he said sourly. "We'll smell it all day. Pick your nose later and it'll be black."

"Isn't that hundreds of miles away?"

"Cast over there."

A back eddy dug into the right bank, nothing wider than a barrel, but I managed to put my fly right on its rim. A trout came up immediately, a big cutthroat hybrid, and I had it to the net before it realized it was even hooked.

How's that? I said, not out loud, but by glancing back at him. You're always trying to impress a guide when you first go out.

"Wife number three? Served me papers last week. Locked me out. Shtupped my best friend."

He seemed to be explaining this more to the trout than to me. And yet he was extraordinarily gentle with it, taking the hook from its lip like it was a baby with a boo-boo, then swimming it back and forth beside the boat waiting for it to regain its strength before letting go. Then and later, that's

Catch and release in a Montana river.

when he seemed most Semitic to me. He treated trout like they were his wealth, his livelihood, his camels.

"That's too bad," I said. "Your best pal? That's hard."

"VA screwed up my prescription. Hand me that rod."

Twice as fast as I could, his hands smoothly weaving, he tied on a dropper rig, worked out some line in two smooth shakes, then handed the rod back with one of his lesser frowns.

"Chinese shit. Watch it bust."

Was that meant to be personal? Nope—not even close. It had been clear from the first second that he could care less about me. I was just a guy he took fishing, like a thousand others, though maybe, just maybe, I cast better than most. But compared to the other possible attitudes he could adopt toward me, indifference was fine.

We had been paralleling a brush-covered island until now, and where it ended the water became faster and harder to read. Anyone who's fished from a drift boat knows they're remarkably stable when aligned with the current, but tippy when they go broadside. Playing the next fish, with both of us on the same side, there was only an inch or two of freeboard left before we swamped. Eli seemed used to this, but I decided to stay safely in my seat after that. Capsizing would do nothing for his mood.

And it was windy, now that the sun was high. It was behind us from the south and warming the air quickly.

"What a day!" I said again, just because I couldn't help it.

Eli squinted at the sky. "Rain later. Probably a twister."

The obvious trout water was along the banks where grasshoppers might plunk in, but he knew where the sunken ledges were in the middle and on either side of these lay fish. What's more, every new ledge required a different fly—he was always grabbing my line in mid-cast to tie on a new one—and, though at first I thought this was unnecessarily fussy, everything he tried seemed to result in an immediate hit. I'd decided on the drive down that a dozen fish would make for a good day, but I had those already—real cutts now, not hybrids, and that pinkish-red slash below their lips would flash through the water a breathless second before they hit.

"Kid sister's on food stamps and now they've cut them. So who pays for diapers? Eli pays for diapers, that's who pays for diapers."

I fought a small one, netted it myself.

"This whole side of the county, nothing but crystal meth. Like talking to zombies, cause that's what they are. Why'd we bother stealing it from the Blackfeet in the first place?"

Coffee from his thermos, a stop to pee, then a long stretch underneath some willows with four fish in a row. Me trying again.

"Aren't those caddis cases under the water there? Maybe we'll see a hatch after all?"

"That's where my mortgage is. Underwater."

Until now all my trout were on dries, but the next one took the nymph and Eli had to spin the boat around a few times before I could get the right angle on it.

"Mining companies own this state. Governor's in their pocket. I had one of their bosses out here, liquored himself up and confessed. Montana mafia."

That was four—four sentences. Always before he stopped at three.

"Yes, I agree with you there, Eli. That's why I voted for the other guy."

I was staring down at the scum line toward a rise, but my back could feel his eyebrows arc.

"You voted? You fucking voted?"

He did something unexpected with that—he laughed. He laughed loud and he laughed long and it was the worst laugh I ever heard, with a deep grinding edge to it that pulverized any response you might come up with even before you came up with it and ground it into hopeless naivety.

"He voted!" he said, this time toward the mountains. He did that more and more as the morning went on. Addressed his comments to the Absarokas, not to me.

So I stopped trying to be sympathetic, tried blocking him out instead— and for a while it worked. The September sun was so warm I stripped down to my t-shirt and that made casting easier. With the preparations for the wedding, I hadn't fished more than two or three times all summer, and the muscle memory of casting, the elusive rhythm, was slow in coming back—but then it came back big-time, and all my happiness seemed centered in my shoulder, elbow, and wrist. I was clumsy at carpentry as a kid, terrible at sports, and a fly rod is the only tool I've ever learned to wield properly, fly casting the only athletic skill I've mastered. It's how I prove my manhood, though what I mean by that is difficult to explain.

But it paid off. I was reaching fish I knew most of his clients couldn't touch. One of them was nineteen inches long, deep bodied, vibrant with health and beauty.

Eli lifted it from the net, stared at it for what I decided was far too long.

"You can see it in their eyes. Whirling disease. Chase their tails to get rid of the parasite and exhaustion finishes them off. He doesn't have it yet, but he will soon."

Jesus Christ! I felt like saying. Maybe I did say it, too, or at least whispered it under my breath. Bitching I could tolerate, a guy having a bad day, but what got to me was his tone, the way his deep voice turned everything into a pronouncement on mankind and nature and fate. And he made it seem wise, that was the worst part. Only a respected elder, someone who had meditated long and hard on life's condition, could make his voice that grim, that certain, and everything young in me wanted to throw it back in his face.

"That's a gorgeous spot up there," I said, making my voice go deliberately high and girly-girly just to vex him. "Good spot for lunch in that shade."

"Rattlers. They fuck there. Lunch spot's further down."

He pushed us toward shore, dropped the oars, unstrapped the cooler behind his seat, lobbed over a sack and some sodas.

There was a wide pool perfect for wading, and I took three good fish from the tail in between bites of lunch. Eli sat on a dead stump watching, making no secret of the flask resting on his knee. He held it up, but I shook my head.

"You make an awesome bologna sandwich," I said.

He couldn't be charmed, not that easily.

"Enough sodium to kill you."

"My dad used to make them, but not as good as yours."

"Never had a dad," he said, like it was a great stroke of luck.

"Good donuts, too."

"Killed my brother."

There was room on the stump, but I went over to the shade and stretched out where I wouldn't have to listen to him. The bank was so high and steep I could roll on my stomach and stare straight down into the water. It was different than anything we'd drifted over so far. The bottom was sand pebbled with flat blue rocks, and with the sun filtering through the effect was gentle, almost tropical, so for a moment I was tempted to strip naked for a swim. Trout, small ones, were tipping up to suck down midges whenever they crossed the sandy patches, but for once I had no desire to catch them, so beautiful and bird-like were their graceful levitations toward the top.

I'd heard that on a busy day in summer over a hundred drift boats would float this stretch of river, but we hadn't seen anyone else today and it wasn't likely we would now. The only sign of man were contrails left by invisible jets, like ivory furrows tilled between clouds. So far from any cities I wondered where they were bound.

I knew what Eli would say, if I asked him. Bombers off to deliver their cargos on people who probably deserved it. He had curled up for a nap, using a rock as his pillow. He talked in his sleep or bubbled or muttered—something made his lips move vigorously enough to tickle his nose and get him snorting. I listened, curious, but all I could make out was a raspy kind of *V* sound. Vile, I finally decided. In his sleep he was muttering the word vile.

He came awake, went over to squat on his haunches by the river, staring down toward its surface as if it were the only mirror he could trust. But no, it wasn't his face he was studying. He dipped his hands in, squinted at what they brought up, nodded, flung the water back through his fingers like blood from his wrists.

"Blue-winged olives," he said. "Coated in pesticide. Trout spit them out."

He dug the anchor from the sand, shoved the boat back into the current, so for a moment I thought he was leaving without me. I climbed back into the bow, but not before blurting out something that was partly due to happiness, partly due to wanting to bust his chops. Don't like the way the world is heading, Eli? Well, try this on for size.

"I'm really fortunate to fit this trip in before the wedding. Richard is no fisher person. He wonders why anyone would deliberately torment a trout just for fun, and he doesn't actually approve of all this. But know what? It doesn't matter. We're soul mates. Except for astronomy, my life was zero before I met him. I love him very much."

There was no change in his expression, none that I could see. When your mouth is permanently fixed in a scowl, there's not much further it can drop. He reached into his fly box, squinted, tossed a fluffy one over.

"Tie this one," he grunted—his default answer for everything.

The wind swung around to the north in the afternoon and hardened. Navigating the boat became trickier, and I had to make sure I stay centered so we wouldn't tip. I was still taking trout along the banks, but casting turned treacherous, and I worried I'd stick one in Eli's nose. He stood it for as long as he could, then grabbed my rod.

"Like this."

He threw a mend in the line while he cast, mid-air, a trick I can't do myself, and got the fly to land exactly where he wanted it despite the wind. It took a lot of skill, sensitivity, and timing, and yet, like with his rowing, he did it abruptly, almost brutally, as if it wasn't a skill he thought much of. And I wondered about that, even more than I wondered about his pessimism. How someone could be so good at something, something difficult, and not give the slightest damn.

The river widened the further downstream we floated, with spring creeks coming in from both east and west. With the increased flow, he had to devote more attention to rowing, and yet the challenge seemed to get him mumbling even faster than before. At first it was about his Iraq vet cousin who had just become homeless, then it switched to a pal who had joined a militia and ambushed a cop, and then he was complaining about the price of the hookers in Bozeman bars.

He sat a foot behind me in the boat—at no point was his mouth further than twelve inches from my ear. By late afternoon, as fatigue kicked in, I began seeing things his way, despite all my efforts. An abandoned pioneer cabin on the bank didn't seem romantic and wistful like it would normally, but a symbol of defeat and decay. The cumulus, so blue on their undersides, now darkened into storm clouds and took on an ominous stacking. The trout, when I caught them, seemed emaciated, sick with whirling disease or about to be sick, and when I missed a good rise near a deadfall I felt ready to cry.

But there was an odd thing, to put against that. It was past five now, and most guides would have been thinking about what was waiting for them at home, but Eli seemed in no hurry—seemed, in fact, to be deliberately drawing out the day as long as possible. We'd drift past a good stretch of water, take a fish or two, then, instead of continuing with the float, he would turn around in his seat and row us upstream as fast as he could, so we could make another pass, then a third, then a fourth. He wanted more trout, that's the only explanation I could come up with. With forty fish to the boat already, he still wanted more.

"People pretend to care, but they don't. Care about themselves. Start by remembering that, you can't go far wrong."

I put on my rain jacket, pulled the hood up, but the fabric was too thin to block him out.

"Follow the money if you want to know how things operate. Follow the money and if that don't work follow the cocks."

I started humming—Prince, though I couldn't remember all the words, went dah-dah-dahhing instead.

"I would have killed for her. Damn near did once. And what did I get in return once we married? Two hundred pounds of lard."

I wanted to put my rod down, cover my ears with my hands. And I did put it down—but only because we were entering a bad stretch of rapids now, and the drift boat was bucking so much I had to hold on. In our eight miles of river, this was the only dangerous spot, with abrupt granite ledges and a current stiff with turbulence.

And yet even this wasn't enough to shut him up. I tried concentrating on squinting into the spray exploding over the bow into my face. For a moment it worked, his voice became part of the current, something I couldn't read or decipher but merely had to ride. But then, in a calm spot between ledges, I heard him all too clearly, all too well.

"Love, right? Marriage, right? You get to smell their shit and listen to them piss, that's all marriage is my friend."

It was the tipping point, in every sense of the phrase. I stood up as if to jump overboard, then suddenly shifted my weight to the left, the worst possible thing I could do given our circumstances. Eli yanked hard on the oar and threw himself sideways, but too late. The gunwale dipped, righted itself, then dipped again, allowing the river to flood into the boat. Even then it didn't seem we would be swamped, but the bow smashed a rock, and, floating broadside now, the current had us at its mercy and threw us both out.

You hear about waders dragging people under, but mine tightened on my chest and gave me enough buoyancy, so I didn't sink very deep. I was underwater for probably no more than twenty seconds, just enough to feel a great cleansing wash of exhilaration, as if I'd been scrubbed in a cold champagne bath. There was fear mixed in, most definitely there was fear, but I had always been a good swimmer, and I knew it was just a question of calmly riding the rapids out. The confidence allowed me to enjoy it, in a strange kind of way. The bubbles especially. I had just enough lucidity, as they popped against my face, to understand that this is what a trout must experience, rising from the bottom to a floating fly. Sure, a hook was waiting in the end, but in the meantime, what a joyous and hopeful ride it must be!

That was for the first few seconds. I tried standing up, and though my boots scraped bottom the current tumbled me over again and it was another fifty yards before I gained purchase. Somewhere in all this I re-membered Eli, had time to wonder if he could swim as well as I could—or could he even swim at all? Just as I got up, I saw him, or at least the limp gray wad the current made of him. He didn't seem to be trying very hard to stand up.

But this was an illusion, his passivity. Floating past me, about to disappear downriver, something brown shot out from the sodden ball of fabric, and my hand, lunging instinctively, met his hand and grabbed. We both grabbed—me to save him, him to be saved. I yanked and shoved until I had him upstream of me and the current could only bring him against my hips, not sweep him away. Staggering, my arms under his shoulders, I pulled him into the shallows and we both collapsed.

Late forties I had guessed for his age, but his time underwater seemed to have turned the stubble on his chin white, and his hair was matted like wet cat fur down over his nose. His eyes were closed, but he was breathing normally now, and the only thing I could find wrong with him was a jagged red slash across the lobe of one ear.

"What happened there?"

He reached and touched it, though even as I asked I realized it was scar tissue that had been there a long time.

"Arab kids. Bigger than me. Faster too."

We stumbled the rest of the way to the bank, pulled our waders down, dumped out the river. Eli looked like a man who had just had his world view confirmed in spades—but I couldn't take it seriously anymore. Caught in the rapids, offered his ticket out, he had grabbed my hand, grabbed hard.

"Look," I said, pointing downstream.

The driftboat had come to a stop on the edge of a sandbar. It lay low and heavy in the water, and, feeling guilty, I volunteered to go bail. When I got back, Eli was squatting on his heels beside a driftwood fire he'd started with his lighter. It was almost dark now. When I followed the sparks skyward one of them didn't cool out like the others but became fixed in the direction of Emigrant Peak.

"Jupiter," I said, pointing higher. Then, before he could ruin it, I said exactly what I thought.

"So, here's what we've discovered, using all those expensive satellites and telescopes. A lot of stars aren't solitary after all, but lie at the center of solar systems very similar to ours. They have planets—some are the size of earth. We've identified dozens of these, but eventually we'll find thousands, millions. Some of them, if they have this, will certainly know life."

I reached, dipped my hand in the river, let the water flow down my wrist.

"And they have to be just the right distance from their sun. Too close and they fry. Too far and they freeze. We're calling what lies in between the *Zone of Habitability*."

At first I didn't think he heard me, so intently did he stare at the flames.

"A planet like this one?" he finally said, screwing up an eye. "Same exact thing?"

"Sure. Maybe. Why not."

"Another earth?"

He pursed his lips with that, snapped his head down to spit into the fire. "*Ibn el sharmoota!*"

I looked it up on my phone later. It means what you think.

CHAPTER 26

A CAMP ON THE NEVERSINK

BY JAY CASSELL

A camp on the Neversink. Photo Credit: Jay Cassell.

James waded slowly into the fast water below Denton Falls, eyeing the pool carefully. When he found a spot where he could stand without slipping, he pulled line off his flyreel and began his backcast. In less time that it takes to say 'Neversink Skater,' he had snagged his Adams in a branch right behind him. Muttering, he looked over at me, angrily, "I give up," he said. "I can't stand flyfishing."

I wasn't surprised at his reaction. For a kid who was brought up fishing plastic worms and spinnerbaits for bass, trying to switch over to flyfishing is tough. The fact that he was a teenager with zero patience didn't help. But he thought it over, changed his mind, and pretty soon was back at it, trying to cast into the trout pools just below the falls.

Up above the white water, we heard James' buddy, Dave, whooping and hollering. "Got another one," he yelled. "This place is amazing." I could see a dark, gloomy cloud beginning to form over James' head. With a shrug, I turned and started hiking downstream. Rounding the bend, I spied a trout rising to caddisflies in the middle of a long pool. I forgot about the boys, and immersed myself in my own fishing.

The boys had worked for their reward of fishing the river. We were at our hunting and fishing camp, "The Over The Hill Gang," located about a mile from the Neversink Gorge, on land owned by Benjamin Wechsler. Wechsler, who has owned a huge chunk of property, including the Neversink Gorge, since 1968, is one of those rare individuals who actually gets it, who knows how to manage private property correctly. His land is just a "small," couple-thousand-acre parcel in the 100,000 acres of Catskill wilderness that sprawls from the Bashakill Wildlife Refuge to the east, to the Mongaup River Valley to the west. Through his good graces, our camp has survived, first on the east side of the Neversink, and now at its current location on a ridgetop to the west, on the Denton Falls Road.

I had brought the boys up for the club's annual summer work weekend. The deal was that they could fish at the end of the day, so long as they pitched in and helped with the work. And they had, sweeping out the cabin, picking up pieces of wood, twigs and branches from a recent windstorm, stacking firewood . . . anything they could do.

While the boys were hard at it, the rest of us busied ourselves with the chores that must be done to keep a sporting club functioning. Dan Gibson, his 21-year-old son Keith, and I unhitched the splitter from my truck and started splitting the logs we had piled up earlier in the summer. Kevin Kenney, the 40-year-old son of the camp's founder, Jerry, was down the road about a quarter mile, chain sawing a black cherry that had come down in a late-spring windstorm. Last hunting season was an especially cold one, with temperatures consistently below 20 Fahrenheit. We came close to running out of wood for our two woodstoves—one in the kitchen, the other in the bunkroom—so we were making doubly certain that we had enough for the upcoming season.

While all this was going on, Vin Sparano was out behind the cabin, installing a new floor in the outhouse. Every couple of years, the local porcupine population decides it's time to feast on our outhouse, and then we have to rebuild it. It's an ongoing battle, with us staying about one step ahead of the always-hungry porkies. Rod Cochran, out in front, was replacing rotted planks on the front deck, while Matt had grabbed a bucket of paint and was touching up the cabin's trim.

When Ken Surerus and his son, Raymond, showed up, they pitched in with the firewood, stacking the logs that Dan, Keith, and I had been splitting.

By the end of the day, the old camp—it was built in the 1950s—was in pretty good shape. A new American flag was up on the roof, all of the weeds and brush around the building had been cut back, and the inside had been swept clean. By summer's end, we'd all be back again, sighting in our rifles and doing last-minute chores such as getting the propane tank filled and stocking up the kitchen with food for hunting season. Eventually, the roof will have to be replaced. It leaks like crazy in the bunkroom, and we're getting tired of putting new blue tarps on it every year. And the eclectic mixture of tarpaper and multi-colored shingles on the exterior is starting to fall off. But the repairs will be made, because they're important. It's good work.

Author Rick Bass, who wrote "The Deer Pasture," once said this about his hunting camp: "For a place we visit only one week out of the year, we worry about it far too much."

That's the way the guys in my camp feel. We think about that place a lot. We do go there more than one week a year, of course; there's turkey season in May, trout and smallmouth fishing in the Neversink from mid-April to the end of September, plus deer season in November—but we'd all go there more often if we could. It's tough to explain, but a good sporting camp becomes a part of you. The years go by, and members come and go, but you come to realize that part of you is always in camp, cooking up venison stew in the kitchen, debating guns and loads or flies and leaders with your colleagues, or playing poker until the wee hours of the morning. I don't see even most of the guys during the year except at camp, but that doesn't matter. When I do see them, we just pick up where we left off last time. The camp has a life of its own, with a pulse that keeps beating from year to year, generation to generation. So you bring the youngsters along and teach them about the woods, you take them down to the river and teach them flycasting, and you show them the types of pools and riffles where the brown trout like to lie. (James, by the way, did not catch a thing that day, but he did later in the season!) And when they get old enough, you let them into the camp as full members, sharing in the work, in the fun, in the good times and, when they happen, the tough times too.

The Neversink River.

Work weekend—it's the beginning of another cycle of seasons. Before you know it, it'll be opening day of deer season and I'll be in my treestand overlooking the Neversink. Then, in May, I'll be out the woods well before dawn, hoping to find a gobbler. At noon, I'll come back to camp, change out of my hunting clothes and put on my flyvest and waders, and hike down to the river to see if the Hendricksons are hatching in the pools below Denton Falls. And life will be as good as it possibly can be.